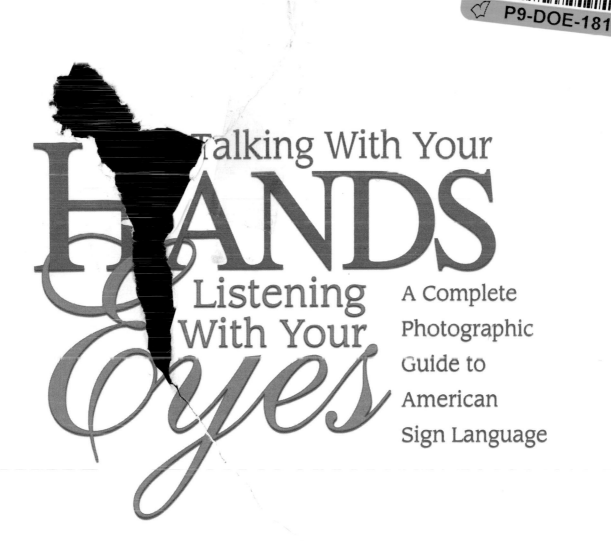

Talking With Your HANDS
Listening With Your Eyes

A Complete
Photographic
Guide to
American
Sign Language

GABRIEL GRAYSON

SQUAREONE
PUBLISHERS

Cover Designer: Phaedra Mastrocola, Oscar Maldonado
In-House Editor: Joanne Abrams
Project Editor: Peggy Hahn
Interior Designer: Phaedra Mastrocola
Typesetter: Gary A. Rosenberg

Square One Publishers
115 Herricks Road
Garden City Park, NY 11040
(516) 535–2010
www.squareonepublishers.com

Permission Credits

The photo on page 59 was reprinted courtesy of the American Foundation for the Blind.
Used with permission of the American Foundation for the Blind, Helen Keller Archives.

The photo on page 72 was reprinted with permission, copyright © Rubberball Productions, Orem, Utah.

The photo on page 104 was reprinted courtesy of the Library of Congress, Prints and Photographs Division [reproduction number, e.g., LC-USZ62-110212]

The photo on page 108 was reprinted courtesy of Research in Motion (R.I.M.).

The photo on page 224 was reprinted courtesy of Exley Foto, Inc.

The photo on page 244 was reprinted courtesy of the National Baseball Hall of Fame Library, Cooperstown, NY.

Library of Congress Cataloging-in-Publication Data
Grayson, Gabriel.
    Talking with your hands, listening with your eyes : a complete
photographic guide to American Sign Language / Gabriel Grayson.
        p. cm.
Includes index.
    ISBN 0-7570-0007-X
    1. American Sign Language. 2. Deaf—Means of communication—United
States. 3. Deaf—United States—Social conditions. I. Title.
    HV2474 .G73 2003
    419—dc21
                                                    2002001125

Printed in Canada

10   9   8   7   6   5

contents

To my Mother and Dad, Dorothy and Gabriel,
who taught me to enjoy a more abundant life inspired by love
and guided by knowledge; to touch people's lives in a positive, optimistic way;
to help people see that they have choices and that they are not alone;
and to be ambitious only for life itself—
to shape, explore, embellish, praise, and grow to understand it.
You showed me that life is an adventure—not a guided tour,
to be grateful for God-given blessings, and to live as truthfully as I can,
and you have provided me with the good fortune of being an American.
All that I am or ever will be I owe to your unconditional love,
guidance, and trust in me.

And to Mary Ann, my beloved and beautiful sister and co-discoverer
in childhood of "The Big Three Rules for a Really Cool Life":
Have fun! Do good! Be happy!
You are a lady of enormous generosity and patience.
Thank you for a lifetime of your love, encouragement, and cheerfulness—
in spite of my shameless freeloading of a thousand
of your delicious home-cooked dinners.

acknowledgments

During the years of research, writing, and photographic production for *Talking With Your Hands, Listening With Your Eyes,* I was blessed with the generosity, kindness, and cooperation of many people who were unfailingly helpful in the birth of this book.

In the early 1970s, Dr. Martin Sternberg, a colleague of mine at the Deafness Research and Training Center of New York University, endeavored to put together a comprehensive dictionary of sign language. The many years of intensive research leading up to the publication of his master work were the source of some good-natured teasing among his friends, mostly along the lines of "Will Martin ever finish his book before he meets Saint Peter, who may or may not be fluent in sign language?" I'm pleased to report that Dr. Sternberg, the father of sign language dictionaries, finally did publish his magnum opus, and that it has even blossomed into a best-selling CD. While I chuckled along with everyone else at the time, it's only now, with the completion of *Talking With Your Hands, Listening With Your Eyes,* that I can fully understand the obstacles he sometimes faced in publishing such a complex work, which seemed to keep his book's publication date always in the uncertain future. I am indebted to Dr. Sternberg not only for the excellent suggestions he made when reviewing my manuscript, but also for his example of determination and perseverance in the creation of such a demanding work.

"Writing may make an exact man," as Francis Bacon observed, but I find it also makes a grumpy, impatient man—especially when the weather's perfect outside and being confined indoors, tapping out an endless stream of tiny letters, seems very close to being a maximum-security prisoner watching the months mature into years. At those times, I depended on my family, friends, and colleagues to help pull me through. Indeed, *Talking With Your Hands, Listening With Your Eyes* was really a collaborative undertaking that involved a whole host of people to whom I am greatly and gratefully indebted.

My deepest gratitude goes to Square One's Publisher, Rudy Shur, whose professional guidance, encouragement, humor, and constancy along the journey to publication tempt me to fax the Vatican to declare him the first Jewish guy from Long Island to be considered for canonization. Thank you, brother Rudy—you are a real mensch. Your attention, insight, and friendship have uniquely touched and inspired my life.

Next, I salute Rudy's fellow professionals at Square One, an impressive team with whom I have enjoyed working: Executive Editor Joanne Abrams, Art Director Phaedra Mastrocola, Photo Retoucher Oscar Maldonado, and Typesetter Gary Rosenberg. A special thank-you goes to Project Editor Peggy Hahn, whose writing contributions have greatly improved the text. I am glad and grateful to have been directed by this talented editorial team.

I'm also deeply grateful to one of my most beloved intellectual homes, New School University in New York City. When I walked through that revolving door at 66 West 12th Street in the fall of 1976 and met several members of the administration who instantly became friends, I knew immediately that I had discovered my truest "alma mater." I'm still in love with this major Manhattan energy center where—after all these happy years—the grownups on the eighth floor permit me to teach in complete academic freedom and joyfully share some of my favorite subjects with lots of enthusiastic people in a stimulating atmosphere of education, entertainment, and inspiration.

My heartfelt thanks and affection go to the late president of the New School, Dr. Jack Everett; Assistant Dean Wallis Osterholtz (along with Muhammad Ali, Wally is "The Greatest"); Dean Emeritus Allen Austill, who gave me the green light to begin my original sign language series and the subsequent various courses, special lectures, and faculty roundtable projects; and the late psychology chair Dr. Lester Singer, who first welcomed me aboard as a member of the New School faculty.

I extend my warmest love to my very dear friend and colleague, foreign language chair Dr. Linda M.A. Rodrigues, who has enthusiastically supported and nurtured the expansion of our sign language curricula and deaf teaching staff at the university. Her charismatic light shines radiantly on our department of sixty faculty members from thirty countries, described by Dr. Dale Lange, director of the Center for Advanced Research on Language Acquisition, as "a national treasure for the teaching and learning of foreign languages."

And to my noticeably brilliant New School faculty confreres who have encouraged my diverse interests over the years, my deepest love, respect, trust, and admiration. Your friendship is among the greatest blessings of my life. This includes the attention, insight, and camaraderie of my "Gang of Four," with whom I have succinctly solved most of the problems of the world in the coffee bar in between classes: anthropologist/philosopher Dr. Harold Blau, psychiatrist/artist Dr. Gerard Sunnen, futurist/normative planner FM-2030, and Victorian scholar/author Dr. Arthur Liebman.

The New School has been supportive of this project not only by encouraging the development of innovative language courses and programs, but also by graciously extending a generous faculty development grant, which contributed greatly to the completion of the photographs in this book.

New School University encompasses eight sister divisions, including the renowned Parsons School of Design. My gratitude to the chair of the Parsons photography department, Michelle Bogre, for her support of the goals of this book, for lending us her students and studios, and for providing the expertise and the venue needed to complete this project. Her lively intelligence, sharp perceptions, and alacrity got the project "jump started" smoothly.

I'd also like to extend my appreciation to Bob Finucane of the Eastman Kodak Corporation, who made possible the state-of-the-art digital camera that was used to produce most of the wonderful photographs in this book. When I first had the idea for this project, the photographic digital technology was not yet perfected to produce a book of this scope and quality. But time turned my dream into a reality.

Approximately 2,500 photographs were created for this book in three sessions at the Parsons studios in New York City. The first shoot included a gifted threesome of young photographers led by Michelle Weisblatt and assisted by William Scalia and George Frangias. The second round, supervised by department head Jim Ramer, included lead photographer Clara Shin assisted by Kerri Shore. The final session also featured the wonderfully perceptive Ms. Shin, as well as Ron Purdy. Master food caterer Carol Durst and make-up artist Shannon O'Neil contributed positively to the daily studio atmosphere. Thank you all for your fresh talented eyes and your unflagging care, diligence, and cheerfulness.

It was a stroke of good fortune to have available for this project three lovely fellow teachers and models: Orchid Sassouni, Alaina Mitchell, and Monique Holt. Their charisma and signing expertise contributed marvelously to the lively photographs in this book. The "I Love You" sign pops up in my mind whenever I think of this trio of beautiful and generous women.

I am honored by the faith, support, and guidance of my "Philadelphia Learning Connection" school partners, City Councilman-at-Large W. Thacher "Mr. Philadelphia" Longstreth and former CBS News analyst and Presbyterian minister Donald Barnhouse. Your steadfast friendship and inspiration have always been a rich and enriching experience, contributing enormously to the growth of my political and spiritual consciousness.

May I express my heartfelt thanks and abiding affection to these lovely, intelligent women, whom I find it difficult to honor in a new way with words. They are appreciated, loved, and valued in my heart—beyond telling—for their enduring nurturing and inspiration: Beate Hemmenn, Sandra Powers, Claudia Babcock, Sybil Henderson, Rose Smith, Dian Kaplan, Dru Ann McGhee, Shari Siegal, Joanna Brock, Mary Gilbert, Donna Drewes, Karina Calabro, Karen Davis, Madelyne Messe, and Rose Newman.

To my dear friend and teacher, Reverend Anthony Russo, C.Ss.R., coordinator of the Deaf Apostolate for the Archdiocese of Philadelphia, I offer my brotherly love—not simply for reviewing this manuscript, but also for your lifelong friendship. I am humbled and inspired by your amazing grace, goodness, and holiness. And to Immaculate Heart of Mary Sister Kathleen Schipani, administrator of the Archdiocesan Department for Pastoral Care for persons with disabilities, a lovely, vivacious, and sophisticated lady—yes, nuns can be cool—thank you for your lifelong commitment to the Philadelphia deaf community. My gratitude also goes to an unforgettable man who gave me the freedom to express my creativity as a boy, and has lived with me in spirit during the writing of this book: the founder of the Venerable Bede Church in Holland, Pennsylvania, the late Reverend James Patrick Martin, priest, magician, and scholar.

Many happy memories surround my thoughts and admiration of two friends and colleagues. I thank the gentle Margaret Borgstrand, who in the mid-fifties became the first recognized interpreter for the deaf in the New York City judicial system, single-handedly establishing sign language interpretation as a profession in the civil and criminal courts of the five boroughs. And I thank another giant figure in our field, Lou Fant, prominent West Coast author, teacher, interpreter, and actor, who collaborated with me as my Los Angeles consultant during the shooting of the Emmy-nominated ABC network After-School special *Mom and Dad Can't Hear Me*.

I offer a simple, loving thank-you to my dear friends Captain and Mrs. Jefferson David Parker of McLean, Virginia, who graciously provided me with a home away from home during my research visits to Washington, D.C., to gather material for this book. All the members of the Parker family are in my thoughts often and in my heart always.

A smiling thanks to Gail Miller, president of Capezio Dance Theater shops, whose heroic last-minute efforts over a holiday weekend produced custom-made leotards for our four signing models.

Finally, I extend my warmest and deepest appreciation to the deaf men and women who were my sign language teachers as I grew up in Philadelphia, and who shared their wisdom with me as I chose the signs for this book. Thank you for your many kindnesses.

And, as the original Tiny Tim observed, "God bless us, everyone."

ORCHID

Orchid Sassouni was born in Tehran, Iran, and escaped with her family to Long Island, New York when the Islamic revolution started in 1979. She graduated from Gallaudet University with a degree in Art History and Museum Studies, and is the first and only deaf person to become a gallery lecturer at the Metropolitan Museum of Art in New York City.

 Pursuing advanced photography courses at the Parsons School of Design, Ms. Sassouni studied with internationally known photographer Annie Leibovitz, and enjoys taking photographs of deaf and hard-of-hearing individuals. "I became fascinated with their pride, their energy, their most important tools in communication, their thoughts, and their consciousness of the world outside."

ALAINA

Alaina Mitchell grew up in Riverside, California, the only deaf member of her family. She received a Bachelor of Arts degree in Communication Arts at Gallaudet University in Washington, DC, and a Master of Arts degree in Rehabilitation at New York University.

 Ms. Mitchell is a Vocational Rehabilitation Counselor for the Deaf and Hard of Hearing in the Manhattan Office of the New York State Educational Services for Individuals with Disabilities.

 A former Miss District of Columbia for the DC area chapter of Black Deaf Advocates, Ms. Mitchell is very involved with the Deaf community in the metro area, including Big Brother/Big Sister programs and American Sign Language instruction.

the models

GABRIEL

A native Philadelphian, Gabriel Grayson is chair of the Sign Language Department of New School University in New York City, founder and director of the New School Faculty Round Table, principal dactylologist of the New York City Judicial System, Chief Sign Language Docent of the American Museum of Natural History, and dean-appointed Sign Language Interpreter of the Cathedral of Saint John the Divine.

Designer of the International Catholic Deaf Association's Fiftieth Anniversary Memorial at San Alphonso Retreat House in Long Branch, New Jersey, Professor Grayson has served as Sign Language Interpreter, advocate for the deaf, and expert court witness in thousands of venues.

MONIQUE

Monique Holt, a deaf Asian actress, holds a Bachelor of Fine Arts from the Tisch School of the Arts at New York University. She has played Katharine in *Taming of the Shrew*, Puck in *A Midsummer Night's Dream*, Ophelia in *Hamlet*, Maria in *Twelfth Night*, and Cordelia in *King Lear*.

Working on her Shakespeare Project, she creatively translated and solved many of the semantic problems of interpreting the original text into sign language. As part of this project, she created the play "Women of Shakespeare" in American Shakespearean Sign Language.

Ms. Holt is a member of the New York American Federation of Television and Radio Artists, the Screen Actors Guild, and the Actors Equity Association.

preface

Welcome to the world of silent music and visual poetry that is the beautiful and expressive art of sign language!

In my twenty-five years of teaching at New School University in New York City, I have witnessed what can only be described as an explosion in the popularity of sign language. Today, my classes are often overflowing with students from all walks of life who have decided to take a leap of faith from the spoken word to signed communication. Some beginners come to the first class with only a casual curiosity. They tell me that they've seen people signing and they want to learn how to do it themselves. Other students have friends or relatives with hearing loss, and are determined to finally commit the time and energy to study sign language. Still others come because they want to work in some capacity in the deaf community, or to expand the scope of their businesses to include deaf customers. And, almost every semester, a few undergraduates attend class because they think that the course looks like "a piece of cake" in the New School bulletin—an effortless way to add some quick credits toward an undergraduate degree. (Of course, these students experience cosmic epiphanies ten minutes into the first workshop lecture, "Sign Language Is Not for Dummies.")

Eventually, almost all of my students tell me that they've become absorbed in the grace and beauty of this totally visual language. People who have studied oral languages are fascinated by the linguistic complexity of a language of signs, and experience great satisfaction when they begin to communicate with their hands, face, and body. They become intrigued by the rich history of sign language and the scope of deaf culture. Even those novice "finger flickers" who expected nothing more than a few undergraduate credits say that they've developed a heightened awareness of the world of the deaf.

I suspect you will also be surprised to discover that sign language is not quite what you expected—that it is, in fact, so much more than you expected. Learning sign language will increase your ability to concentrate, influence your cultural literacy, and even tickle your funny bone! The study of sign language is a transformative journey that is as rewarding as it is challenging. Nonverbal communication is an intense activity that demands total attention, both expressively and receptively.

The idea for *Talking With Your Hands, Listening With Your Eyes* blossomed from my experience teaching beginning signers and observing firsthand (no pun intended) what they liked and disliked about learning sign language. No matter what subject I'm talking about in the classroom, my philosophy has always been that novelty and a fresh, unconventional approach are the keys to helping my students fully understand and appreciate the ideas that I'm presenting. Of course, signing movement and expression are best learned from interaction with a skilled instructor—but since I can't be where you are to personally demonstrate how to form the various signs, I've tried to make this book as clear and user-friendly as possible. My goal has always been to convey the sense of fun, excitement, and creativity that's part of learning the multidimensional art of signing.

This book is all about making it easier to understand, duplicate, and remember the vocabulary of sign language. Each sign is accompanied by one or more photographs of a professional, lifelong signer demonstrating the correct sign formation. Photos are more visually appealing than simple line drawings, and they can also show facial expression, which is integral to effective signing. You'll also find a written description that gives step-by-step instructions for forming the sign, and a helpful "Visualize" tip that connects the sign with its meaning for easier memorization and recall. At the bottom of each pair of facing pages, Helping Hands clarify the key hand-shapes used to sign the terms on that two-page spread. Plus, the book is peppered with informative insets about deaf history and culture.

My wish is that you wholeheartedly enjoy learning this visual language that has continued to fascinate me over a lifetime, and that you will be motivated to pursue your studies long after you've mastered the last sign on the last page of this book. I hope that, as you learn and grow in this subject, you will gain a greater awareness, understanding, and appreciation for deaf people and their culture. Now, get ready to surrender your senses to a visually rich and expressive language in which you "talk" with your hands and "listen" with your eyes.

how to use this book

Talking With Your Hands, Listening With Your Eyes is an introduction to both the beautiful and expressive art of signing and the rich culture of the deaf community. This book is not meant to be an exhaustive dictionary of all the signs used in American Sign Language. Rather, it includes a broad vocabulary of hundreds of basic signs that will enable you to understand and communicate common ideas and concepts.

American Sign Language is not English, but is instead a unique language that's separate and distinct from English—an issue that will be explored in depth in Chapter 1. For our purposes here, it's important to mention that some English words do not have sign equivalents, so a particular sign might not exist for the exact word you have in mind. One simple solution is to look for that sign under a similar word. Because signs are generally used to represent ideas and concepts rather than words, one sign may convey a number of ideas that will suit your needs. But if you can't find a sign to express an exact thought, you can always spell out the word or phrase one letter at a time using the manual alphabet. This is known as fingerspelling, and it's used frequently among all signers, deaf and hearing alike. You'll find everything you need to know about fingerspelling starting on page 11.

The format of this book was carefully determined with the beginning sign language student in mind. Chapter 1 starts with a look at the structure of sign language and its variations, and then provides instructional information about the essential elements of sign language, including handshape, sign location, and movement. The remaining sixteen chapters contain over nine hundred signs that represent nearly two thousand words and phrases. These signs have been grouped according to topic, which is helpful for two reasons. First, it's easy and convenient to find specific signs—just look at the contents page for the appropriate subject heading. Second, many related signs use similar hand-shapes and movements so they're easier to learn and remember.

For each sign, you will find one or more photographs showing the correct sign formation. You will also find a written description that gives instructions for forming the sign in terms of handshape, position in relation to the body, and hand movement. Finally, the "Visualize" tip at the end of each entry connects the sign with its meaning, providing a quick hint that will aid you in recalling the sign in the future.

The best way to learn each sign is to carefully study both the photograph(s) and the written description. First, look at the picture(s) to get a sense of how the sign is formed. What handshapes are used? Where are the hands located? Don't forget to notice the signer's facial expression. Expression and body language are important aspects of signing. If you get into the habit of incorporating these important elements, your signing skills will be all the better. Next, turn your attention to the written description and read the entire entry. Then follow the step-by-step instructions, checking yourself against the signer in the photograph to make sure you're forming the sign correctly. And if you need guidance in forming any of the handshapes, simply refer to the Helping Hands that run along the bottom of each pair of facing pages.

All of the photographs in this book show what the signs look like to an observer. In other words, you will view the signs as you would if someone were signing to you. In some of the photographs, the signer is shown at a slight angle. This was done in cases where the hand-shape or movement would not have been clear from a front view of the signer. All photos show right-handed signers, and the instructions are written for people who are right-handed. If you're left-handed, it's easy enough to reverse the signs. Just look at each photo as if it were your mirror image.

If you're learning sign language on your own, it's totally up to you to decide the order in which you want to learn the signs. However, it's best to learn the manual alphabet before studying the signs themselves. Remember, fingerspelling is a very effective way to express words for which signs do not exist, and fingerspelled words can also substitute for signs you simply can't recall.

Once you're ready to learn individual signs, you have several options. You can start with the first chapter of signs, and proceed in order to the end of the book, or you can skip from chapter to chapter, learning all of the signs contained in each. Of course, you can also skip around in the book, learning only those signs that you want or need to know. Some beginners choose to start with signs that clearly represent their meanings because they find that these signs are easier to remember.

Be aware that although the majority of the signs in this book are used in American Sign Language, in a few cases, I have, instead, included the sign that is most commonly used by deaf people today. In each of these instances, I have indicated this with the phrase "Common usage sign." Also keep in mind that regional differences occur even in the use of standard ASL. In most areas, for instance, the sign for friendship is performed as shown on page 65. In some areas, however, although the first part of the sign—the hooking of the fingers—is completed as shown, the action is not then reversed as it is in standard ASL. Once you become proficient in the use of ASL, though, regional differences will be less confusing.

In my introductory classes, I try to teach sign language in the way my students think and speak as hearing people. I find that this gives them a sense of success early on, which helps to build confidence. Those students who decide to continue their studies in American Sign Language courses taught by deaf native signers have little difficulty making the transition to the unique grammar and syntax of ASL. Overall, the order in which you learn the signs is not as important as taking the time to learn each sign correctly. Then practice, practice, practice—and you'll be signing naturally before you know it!

introduction

According to a National Center for Health Statistics estimate, 28 million Americans—almost 10 percent of the population—have a hearing loss of some degree. Of these 28 million people, about 2 million are classified as deaf; that is, they can't hear speech or everyday sounds, even with the use of a hearing aid. And of these 2 million, about 10 percent were born without the ability to hear; the other 90 percent lost their hearing later in life.

American Sign Language (ASL) is the natural language of approximately 500,000 deaf people in the United States and Canada. A "natural" language, in linguistic terms, is one that's learned as a first language in childhood. Not all deaf people learn ASL as their first language. Some use it as a second language, while others use very little ASL, if any. On the other hand, many hearing people are fluent signers, and more hearing people are registering every day to learn ASL in high school and college classes. In recent years, sign language has experienced such a tremendous increase in popularity that an estimated 13 million people can sign with some level of proficiency. This makes ASL the third most commonly used language in the United States!

The most widespread misconception about American Sign Language is the belief that it's a signed version of English. In fact, ASL is not English at all. Instead, it's a distinct language with its own grammar and syntax. Yet it's as capable as English or any other spoken language of communicating complex and abstract ideas. For deaf people who use ASL, their common language is more than a means of communication. It's also a source of great pride and cultural unity.

American Sign Language—known commonly as ASL—is the "natural" language of 500,000 North Americans. This means that hundreds of thousands of people learned ASL before they learned any other language.

the history of sign language

To truly understand the deaf experience in today's America, we need to look to the past. Historically, as a minority group, deaf people have faced great adversity in

1

attaining their basic civil rights. In ancient times, Aristotle and other philosophers claimed that people could learn only by hearing spoken words. As a result, the accepted belief among many cultures was that deaf people did not have the capacity to learn, and so were not entitled to any rights under the law. The deaf were forced into inferior social positions or labeled "non-persons" by law. Most of the time, deaf people were not permitted to marry or to own property. In some cultures, they were even assigned to the care of a guardian.

Aristotle's words went unchallenged until the 1500s. Then, as the Renaissance spread through Europe, new ideas emerged about the intellectual potential of the deaf. The revival of learning and experimentation characteristic of the times inspired a few pioneering scholars in different countries to make the first serious attempts to educate the deaf. Their separate successes changed beliefs about deafness that had endured for nearly 2,000 years, and helped pave the way for the development of a standard language of signs. But many years would pass before sign language was widely accepted as a means of communication and education for the deaf.

THE DEVELOPMENT OF DEAF EDUCATION

An Italian physician named Geronimo Cardano was one of the first known scholars to recognize that hearing is not essential to the learning process. In the 1500s, he announced that deaf people could be educated through the written word. Believing that "the mute can hear by reading and speak by writing," Cardano tried using a code of symbols to teach his own deaf son. At about the same time in Spain, Pedro Ponce de Leon, a Benedictine monk, showed much success in educating the deaf sons of Spanish noble families. He taught the boys how to read, write, and even speak so that they would be permitted to inherit their family's property.

The earlier successes of Cardano and Ponce de Leon inspired Juan Pablo de Bonet, also a Spanish monk, to use his own variation of proven methods in teaching the deaf. Bonet used not just reading, writing, and speechreading as tools for education, but also a manual alphabet, in which a series of handshapes represented the various speech sounds. In 1620, Bonet published the first book on instructional methods for teaching deaf people, which included his manual alphabet.

Despite the successes of Bonet and his predecessors, organized education for the deaf was virtually nonexistent until the 1750s. At that time, Abbé Charles Michel de L'Epée, a French priest, established the first religious and social assocation for the deaf in Paris. As the story goes, Abbé de L'Epée met two deaf sisters one day while he was visiting a poor section of Paris. When the girls' mother asked him to give her daughters religious instruction, L'Epée was inspired to help the two girls and other children like them. This chance meeting sparked his lifelong commitment to deaf education.

In 1771, Abbé de L'Epée founded the first free public school for deaf children, the Institut National des Jeune Sourds-Muets (National Institute for Deaf-Mutes). Students from all over the country came to the school, bringing with them the different sign systems used in their own homes. L'Epée learned his students' signs, and then used the signs to teach them the French language. Gradually, a standard language of signs emerged. As more schools were established, many more students

A physician, mathematician, astrologer, and psychiatrist, Geronimo Cardano made significant discoveries in all of the disciplines in which he was involved. Basing his beliefs on personal observation, Cardano was one of the first scholars to recognize that deaf individuals can be educated through the written word.

learned the language—now called Old French Sign Language   and brought it back to their own communities. In this way, L'Epée's language of signs gained popularity throughout France.

In all, Abbé de L'Epée established twenty-one schools for the deaf. To further promote the use of sign language in teaching deaf children, he published *The Instruction of Deaf and Mute Persons Using Methodological Signs,* in which he wrote: "The natural language of the deaf is the language of sign . . . they have no other language as long as they have no other instructors." He also published the first dictionary of standard French signs. Today, L'Epée is called "The Father of Sign Language and Deaf Education" because of his many contributions to the deaf community.

While Abbé de L'Epée advocated the use of sign language in deaf education, proponents of a method called oralism were also making progress with deaf students. Oralism, or the oral method, uses a system of speech and speechreading instead of signs and fingerspelling. One of the most successful promoters of oralism was Samuel Heinicke, a German educator. Heinicke taught his students speech by having them feel the vibrations of his throat as he spoke. Although his teaching methods were different from L'Epée's, Heinicke's contributions were no less important in proving that deaf people are as capable of intelligent thought and communication as hearing people.

Oralism emphasizes the use of lipreading and speech rather than sign language. Proponents of oralism believe that deaf people need to lipread and speak in order to fully function in society.

AMERICAN SIGN LANGUAGE IS BORN

There isn't much information available about the use of sign language among America's deaf population before 1815. We do know that about 2,000 deaf people were living in America in the early 1800s. Although there was no standard language of signs at this time, different signing systems developed independently within small deaf communities. Many of these early signs—now called Old American Sign Language—are related to our modern American Sign Language.

The clearly known history of ASL can be traced back to 1814, when Dr. Thomas Hopkins Gallaudet, a minister living in Hartford, Connecticut, met his neighbor's nine-year-old deaf daughter, Alice Cogswell. Gallaudet recognized that Alice was highly intelligent, even though she couldn't hear or speak, and became interested in teaching her to communicate. Although he had some success in teaching Alice how to spell and read, Gallaudet didn't know of any effective methods for educating deaf children. So with the help of Alice's father, Mason Fitch Cogswell, Gallaudet gathered support from the community, and by 1815 had raised enough money to travel to Europe, where he could study proven methods in deaf education.

In London, Gallaudet met Abbé Roche Ambroise Sicard, the successor to Abbé de L'Epée as the head of the National Institute for Deaf-Mutes in Paris. Abbé Sicard was visiting London to lecture on his theories of deaf education and to demonstrate his successful teaching methods. With him were two highly accomplished deaf teachers at the National Institute, Jean Massieu and Laurent Clerc, who had once been Sicard's students. Amazed by all that he saw and learned in London, Gallaudet accepted an invitation from Sicard to visit the Paris school.

During his two months at the National Institute, Gallaudet attended daily classes with Sicard, Massieu, and Clerc to study their methods of teaching. He also

The first permanent school for the deaf was founded in Hartford, Connecticut in 1817. Originally called the American Asylum for Deaf-Mutes, that school is now known as the American School for the Deaf.

Laurent Clerc, a deaf Frenchman, was the first teacher of sign language in America's first school for the deaf. Thus, American Sign Language—the system that gradually evolved from these early efforts—has more in common with French Sign Language than it has with British Sign Language.

took private signing lessons from Clerc, who had been teaching at the school since his graduation in 1806. Clerc was regarded as one of Sicard's best teachers, and Gallaudet knew that his help would be invaluable in establishing a school for the deaf in America. When Gallaudet was ready to return home, he invited Clerc to join him. Eager to help promote deaf education in America, Clerc agreed to make the journey.

In 1817, Gallaudet and Clerc welcomed seven students to the American Asylum for Deaf-Mutes (now the American School for the Deaf) in Hartford, Connecticut. Their school was the first free public school for the deaf in America, and Alice Cogswell was the first student to enroll. With Gallaudet as principal, and Clerc as head teacher, the school quickly grew in size, and a large number of deaf people from across America were brought together for the first time. As in L'Epée's National Institute, students of the Hartford school brought with them the different signs used within their own communities. Gradually, these signs blended with the French signs that Clerc taught in the classroom, and the result was the standard language of signs that we know as American Sign Language. Perhaps two-thirds of today's sign language has evolved from the French sign language.

Gallaudet retired from his job as principal of the Hartford school in 1830. Clerc continued to teach at the school until the late 1850s. Many of Clerc's students and trained teachers—deaf and hearing—founded other schools around the nation or taught in them, using Clerc's teaching methods. By 1863, there were twenty-two schools for the deaf operating in the United States.

HOPE FOR HIGHER EDUCATION

After Thomas Hopkins Gallaudet's death in 1851, two of his sons continued his pioneering work in deaf education. Thomas Gallaudet opened Saint Ann's Church for Deaf-Mutes in New York City in 1852. His younger brother, Edward Miner Gallaudet, accepted a teaching position at the Hartford school. Edward's dream was to one day establish a college for the deaf, although a lack of funds made the achievement of his dream seem impossible. But the outlook changed in 1857 when Edward received a letter from Amos Kendall, a wealthy philanthropist from Washington. Kendall had donated several acres of Kendall Green, his own estate in Washington, D.C., to establish a residential school he called the Columbia Institution for the Deaf and Dumb and the Blind. On the recommendation of a friend, he wrote to Edward to offer him a position as the school's superintendent. Edward accepted the job, but he was not ready to give up his hope of founding a college for the deaf.

With Amos Kendall's help, Edward presented his idea before Congress. In 1864, Congress passed legislation, signed by President Abraham Lincoln, allowing the Columbia Institution to confer college degrees. The school's college division became the National Deaf-Mute College, which opened in June of 1864 with eight students. In 1869, the first three graduates of the college received their diplomas. Sadly, Kendall died just a few short months after sharing in the triumph of this first commencement. The remaining eighty-one acres of his estate were eventually sold to the Columbia Institution for $85,000. More than two decades later, in 1891, the first training center for teachers of the deaf associated with a United States college was established at the school.

At the request of the alumni association, the National Deaf-Mute College was renamed Gallaudet College in 1893 in honor of Dr. Thomas Hopkins Gallaudet. The school's name was changed again to Gallaudet University in 1986. Today, Gallaudet University is known as the first and only liberal arts university for the deaf in the world.

SIGN LANGUAGE SURPASSES THE SPOKEN WORD

Today, sign language is accepted as a natural method of communication and education for the deaf, but this wasn't always the case. Even as sign language became widely used among deaf and hearing people, proponents of oralism insisted that the deaf should learn spoken language in order to fully participate in the hearing world. In 1867, the Institution for the Improved Instruction of Deaf-Mutes in New York and the Clarke Institution for Deaf-Mutes in Northampton, Massachusetts, began pioneering techniques for teaching by oral means alone. Methods of teaching speech, listening, and speechreading became common in schools across the country.

Alexander Graham Bell was one of the most ardent supporters of oralism. Bell regarded sign language as a foreign language, and believed that deaf people needed to lipread and speak English in order to function in society. In 1872, Bell opened a school in Boston to train teachers of the deaf to use the oral method. Several years later, in 1890, he founded the American Association to Promote the Teaching of Speech to the Deaf, Inc., which is now called the Alexander Graham Bell Association for the Deaf.

The debate over the value of signed communication versus spoken languge intensified during the last two decades of the 1800s. In 1880, the International Congress on the Education of the Deaf convened in Milan, Italy, to address the issue, with leading educators from around the world in attendance. Proponents of oralism triumphed when the Congress passed a resolution affirming "the incontestable superiority of speech over sign for integrating the deaf-mute into society and for giving him better command of the language." The results were dramatic and far-reaching. In the ten years following the conference, the use of sign language in education declined dramatically. Strong arguments in favor of oralism resulted in the decision to add lipreading and speech to the curriculum in many schools for the deaf. Some supporters of oral communication suggested eliminating sign language entirely. By 1920, 80 percent of deaf students were taught in oral education programs. The numbers of deaf teachers dropped drastically from 40 percent of the profession in the 1860s to 15 percent.

Despite the controversy surrounding manual education versus oralism, sign language continued to be widely used outside of the classroom. In the United States, the National Association of the Deaf (NAD) was founded and gained support in reaction to the Milan resolution. Arguing that oral communication alone was inadequate for many deaf people, the NAD was instrumental in keeping sign language and manual education alive.

Finally, in 1960, a hearing Gallaudet College professor named William Stokoe published a breakthrough monograph that "legitimized" sign language once and for all. In *Sign Language Structure*, Stokoe presented his thesis that American Sign

Despite the support of oralism by such notables as Alexander Graham Bell, and despite the American government's early claim that speech is superior to sign, sign language, once developed, was used widely in the United States.

For many years, American educators considered signing to be a poor substitute for speech. That attitude was changed by William C. Stokoe, the Gallaudet professor who proved scientifically that American Sign Language is a fully developed language.

The educational philosophy called Total Communication encourages the development of many different communication skills, including sign language, writing, mime, speech, lipreading, gestures, and facial expressions.

Language is a unique language, separate and distinct from English—not a simple translation or "mimicry" of English. His research proved that ASL is a natural language with its own grammar and syntax, as capable as spoken languages of communicating abstract ideas and complex information. As a result of Stokoe's research and advocacy, American Sign Language was finally recognized as an important national language. Stokoe went on to co-author the *Dictionary of American Sign Language* in 1965, and to establish the Linguistics Research Laboratory at Gallaudet in 1970, which he ran until 1984.

Supporters of sign language received more welcome news in 1964, when Congress issued the Babbidge Report on oral deaf education. The report stated that oral education was a "dismal failure," finally and effectively dismissing the Milan resolution after almost a century. Many deaf and hearing people alike viewed the report as a long-overdue acknowledgment of the superiority of sign language in deaf education.

Interestingly, a movement that began in 1970 did not attempt to establish the superiority of either signed or oral education, but rather to blend several different methods. The result was Total Communication, a philosophy that became the foundation for a new approach to deaf education. Total Communication allows deaf people the right to any information through all possible means, including sign language, fingerspelling, pantomime, speech, lipreading, writing, computers, pictures, gestures, facial expressions, reading, and hearing aid devices.

By 1975, Public Law 94-142 passed, requiring handicapped children in the United States to be provided with free and appropriate education and allowing many to be mainstreamed into regular public schools, where they receive special instruction but interact with the general public school population.

the deaf community

Not all deaf people use American Sign Language. But those who do share a common language bond that unites them as part of the deaf community. In addition to using the same language, members of the deaf community are linked by similar beliefs and attitudes about themselves and the world around them. Some deaf people choose not to view themselves as disabled. Instead, they describe themselves as sharing a common cultural experience, and take pride in their rich heritage. This strong sense of identity is nurtured by others in the deaf community, and is passed down through generations.

Because the shared language of ASL is the common bond among the members of the deaf community, people who do not use this language are not considered part of this group. However, hearing individuals who use ASL can take part in the social and cultural life of the deaf community. For instance, the hearing children of deaf parents acquire ASL naturally in childhood. They grow up using ASL to communicate with their parents and others around them who use the language.

As a minority group in a hearing world, deaf people have faced restrictions and adversity. However, joining together in the struggle to advance deaf causes has helped them to define their culture. As we have already discussed, the acknowledgment in the late 1960s that sign language is appropriate in deaf education was

What Causes Deafness?

The main cause of deafness in children seems to be heredity. Most of the time, the trait is not passed directly from one generation to the next. In fact, a great majority of children who are born deaf actually have hearing parents. However, deafness at birth is not always hereditary, but may be attributed to complications during the mother's pregnancy. For instance, in the 1960s, a large number of babies were born deaf because their mothers contracted rubella, or German measles, during pregancy.

Causes of hearing loss in children and adults can also include certain illnesses, such as meningitis, or prolonged high fever; the use of certain medications; and head injury. About half of the cases of hearing loss in adults are due to either continual exposure to loud noise—including loud music—or the aging process. Approximately 30 percent of all people 65 and older have some trouble hearing.

Hearing losses that are caused by disease or obstructions in the outer ear can sometimes be corrected or lessened with surgery or a hearing aid. For people who have a malformation or deterioration of the cochlea in the inner ear, cochlear implant surgery is sometimes successful, although this procedure is still somewhat controversial. (See the inset on page 303.)

a triumph for members of the deaf community. Renewed support for signing in education meant that many deaf students and their teachers were able to use their native language in the classroom for the first time.

Another triumph for deaf rights was the Deaf President Now (DPN) movement at Gallaudet University. DPN was set in motion in March of 1988, when the University's Board of Trustees named a hearing candidate, Elisabeth A. Zinser, as Gallaudet's seventh president. Students, faculty, and alumni of Gallaudet were stunned that a hearing candidate was chosen over two qualified deaf finalists, and demanded that a deaf president replace Zinser. In a movement that made national headlines, the protestors shut down the entire campus. After a week of protests and pressure, Zinser resigned and I. King Jordan—a long-time faculty member at Gallaudet—was appointed as the university's first deaf president.

DPN was remarkable in more than its immediate success. The movement unified deaf and hard-of-hearing people of different ages and backgrounds in a collective struggle to be heard. Their ultimate triumph was a reminder that they don't have to accept society's limitations.

True proficiency in sign language goes beyond building an extensive sign vocabulary. The best approach to gaining a genuine appreciation of the language and its complexities is to understand signing in the context of deaf culture. Practice your skills with people who use sign language in day-to-day life, and soon you will begin to notice many of the subtle nuances that make the language so beautiful and unique.

In 1988, students at Gallaudet University rose in protest when yet another hearing president was hired. The result was not only the appointment of the university's first deaf president, but also an increased awareness of the roadblocks faced by qualified deaf and hard-of hearing people everywhere.

The Telecommunications Relay Service

In 1990, Title IV of the Americans with Disabilities Act mandated the establishment of the Telecommunications Relay Service (TRS), giving hard-of-hearing and deaf individuals, as well as people with speech disabilities, unprecedented access to communication with standard telephone users. TRS enables people who have difficulty hearing or speaking to talk to people who use a standard voice telephone through the aid of a trained communication assistant (CA). Essentially, the CA acts as a go-between for both parties by transmitting the content of the conversation back and forth, thus making possible real-time communication.

The two most common types of relay calls are voice carry over (VCO) and hearing carry over (HCO). Voice carry over is useful for people who can speak clearly but have difficulty hearing. The hard-of-hearing or deaf person's voice is "carried over" to the voice telephone user. During a VCO call, the CA relays the conversation by speaking the words typed by the TTY (text telephone) user aloud to the standard telephone user, and typing the words spoken by the standard telephone user to the TTY user. (For more information about text telephones, see page 116.) People who can hear well but have difficulty speaking clearly can make hearing carry over calls. HCO callers also use a TTY to type what they want to say to the CA, who then reads the words to the voice telephone user. With three-way calling, the HCO caller is able to hear the spoken words of the person to whom he or she is speaking.

In order to best meet the communications needs of the individuals they serve, CAs are required to be proficient in typing and to have good spelling and grammar skills. Additionally, CAs must be able to effectively interpret typewritten American Sign Language (ASL), and need a strong knowledge of the culture and etiquette of hard-of-hearing and deaf individuals. The CA's sole responsibility during a TRS call is to enable conversation between the parties involved—he or she otherwise remains as unobtrusive as possible. All relay calls are confidential and, as with regular voice telephone systems, TRS is available twenty-four hours a day, seven days a week.

Until recently, individuals who wished to make relay calls were required to use local TRS numbers in different states. As of October 2001, however, a nationwide system became available to allow TRS users to connect to relay services anywhere in the United States. Today, anyone can access TRS simply by dialing 711. This not only makes connecting to a relay service faster, but is also convenient for travelers, who now don't have to look up local TRS numbers when they're visiting other states. Calls to the TRS center are toll free; however, the TRS user is billed once the call is put through, just as calls are billed between voice telephone users on a standard network. Billing rates are the same for TRS calls as for standard voice-to-voice calls.

People who have never received a relay call before may at first be confused and may even hang up. When you receive a TRS call, the communication assistant will first ask you if you have received a relay call before. Then you will be free to proceed with your conversation!

the basics

B y now you're probably tempted to jump right in and start signing. But there's more to sign language than meets the eye. This chapter will help you get started on the right track with an overview of some fundamental aspects of sign language that all beginners should know. We'll start with a look at the structure of the language and its variations, and then move on to essential elements such as hand shape and position, sign location, and movement. Finally, we'll review some signing "etiquette" tips that will give you the confidence to sign naturally in almost any situation.

what is sign language?

Sign language is a visual means of communication that uses handshapes and gestures to represent ideas or concepts. It's actually a very broad term used to describe a number of visual languages that use the same basic signs but have different rules of grammar and syntax. At one end of the spectrum is *American Sign Language*, also known as ASL or Ameslan, which is a unique language with its own grammar and syntax that's not related to English. The other extreme is *Manually Coded English*, which uses the signs of ASL to represent all aspects of the English language. The balance between these extremes is *Pidgin Sign English*. Like the manually coded systems, Pidgin Sign English uses ASL signs in the word order of the English language; however, not all words are signed, so it's not an exact representation of English.

AMERICAN SIGN LANGUAGE

American Sign Language is the sign system used by an estimated 500,000 deaf people in the United States and Canada. It is not English, nor is it derived from the English

There is no universal sign language. Any country or region with a substantial population of deaf people is likely to have developed one or more types of sign language. American Sign Language, as its name suggests, is a product of North America.

One of the most common misconceptions about American Sign Language is that it is a manual form of the English language. In reality, ASL is a separate language with its own rules of syntax and grammar.

language. Instead, it's a distinct and recognizable language that has been developed over hundreds of years by deaf people as a means of communicating with one another.

In American Sign Language, signs are generally used to represent ideas and concepts rather than words. Because one sign may signify a number of ideas, appropriate facial expression and body language are essential in order to convey the full meaning of the sign. Deaf people depend as much on reading these non-manual characteristics of ASL as they do on reading each other's hands. Speech is not used, but there may be some lip movement. Fingerspelling is used mainly to indicate people and places.

Signs can be arranged in various word orders to form sentences in ASL. For example, the sentence "I am happy" may be signed as "I happy I," "I happy," or "Happy I." Definite and indefinite articles (*a, an,* and *the*) are not signed. (For more information on articles, see page 18.) Furthermore, there is no distinction between the different grammatical forms for nouns, adjectives, and adverbs. For instance, "happy," "happiness," and "happily" are all signed exactly alike, so the appropriate meaning must be determined from the context.

Not all deaf people use American Sign Language. But those who do share a common language bond that unites them as members in the deaf community, a group of people who—in addition to using the same language—are linked by similar beliefs, attitudes, and experiences. Hearing individuals who use ASL can also share in the rich social and cultural life of the deaf community. In recent years, thousands of hearing people have learned ASL as a second language. ASL is now offered as part of the curriculum in schools and colleges nationwide, and may sometimes satisfy a foreign language degree requirement.

MANUALLY CODED ENGLISH SYSTEMS

Manually Coded English, which is also known as *Manual English,* is a general term for any system that uses signs, fingerspelling, and speech to represent the English language exactly. Two of the more common systems are *Signing Exact English* and *Signed English.* Unlike American Sign Language, which uses one sign to represent a number of English words, these systems specifically indicate an English word by combining the fingerspelled handshape with the basic movement of the ASL sign. Manual English systems indicate changes in the forms of words by adding markers such as prefixes, suffixes, plural endings, and tenses, rather than relying on context to give the intended form. Definite and indefinite articles are also incorporated.

Unlike ASL, Manually Coded English is not considered a separate and distinct language. Instead, it uses signs, fingerspelling, and speech to exactly represent the English language.

Manually Coded English is just what its name suggests—a code. It is not recognized as a unique and distinct language, as is American Sign Language. Because Manual English systems require each sign to represent an English word rather than an entire idea or concept, opponents argue that these systems distort the meaning of the ASL signs. However, many educators and parents support the use of these systems in educational settings as a way of better teaching deaf children the English language.

PIDGIN SIGN ENGLISH

A *pidgin language* results when some of the characteristics of two separate languages are combined to produce a third common language. Pidgins can serve as a communication link between two groups that are hampered by a language barrier. *Pidgin Sign English* (PSE) combines the signs, facial expressions, and body language of American Sign Language with the word order of the English language to help deaf people and hearing people communicate more easily with each other.

You'll probably agree that it's easier to learn the vocabulary of an unfamiliar language than to learn entirely new rules of grammar and syntax. American Sign Language is no exception. PSE enables hearing people to use the sign vocabulary of ASL in the familiar word order of English, which facilitates learning and communication. As with Manual English, signs are used to represent the meanings of English words in PSE. However, markers such as prefixes, suffixes, plural endings, and tenses are not signed, nor are definite and indefinite articles.

Although Pidgin Sign English is an acceptable and widely used method of communication, it's not a true language, so there are no hard-and-fast rules of grammar and syntax. It's more or less up to you to decide how closely you want to follow English word order. And, as you'll see in the next section, the people with whom you sign will also influence your decision to sign more like English or more like ASL.

The signs in this book may be used in English word order or in the non-English order of ASL—or in any word order that falls between the two. As a beginning signer, you'll probably find it easier to use your sign vocabulary according to the grammar and syntax of the English language. Deaf people are usually patient when hearing people make an effort to use their sign language skills, even if those skills are limited. Many deaf people will try to help out by signing in English word order, as well. However, as your skills improve, you should become more aware of the sign language systems preferred by the deaf people with whom you sign, and try to adjust your signing style accordingly.

No matter what sign language system you decide to use, it's important to remember that sign language is a continuum, so one type of signing is no better than another. Above all, your goal should always be the same—clear communication.

the importance of fingerspelling

As you learn to communicate using sign language, you need to master the skill of *fingerspelling,* in which words are spelled out by hand one letter at a time. Fingerspelling is used with sign language to indicate names, places, or ideas for which there are no officially recognized signs. Fingerspelled words can also substitute for signs that have not yet been learned.

The foundation of fingerspelling is the *manual alphabet*—twenty-six handshapes that stand for the twenty-six letters of the English alphabet. (See pages 12 to 13.) You'll notice that many of the handshapes resemble the written letters they represent. This makes it easy to learn and memorize the entire alphabet in a few hours. However, as with any other skill, proficiency takes time and practice. Ideally, you

Pidgin Sign English, which combines the signs of ASL with the word order of the English language, is not a true language. However, it is the means by which the majority of hearing parents, teachers, doctors, speech therapists, counselors, psychologists, and employers communicate with the deaf people with whom they live and work.

THE ALPHABET

The following manual alphabet is, quite simply, the American alphabet produced through twenty-six hand positions. When studying the alphabet, you will note that a number of handshapes—those for *C, O,* and *L,* for instance—resemble the written letters they represent. And in a few cases—*J* and *Z*—the hand is moved to trace the shape of the letter in the air. This makes the alphabet relatively easy to master, although proficiency at fingerspelling takes practice. (For tips on fingerspelling, see page 14.)

The manual alphabet is used to communicate names, places, and ideas for which there are no signs. Thus, it is an important complement to American Sign Language.

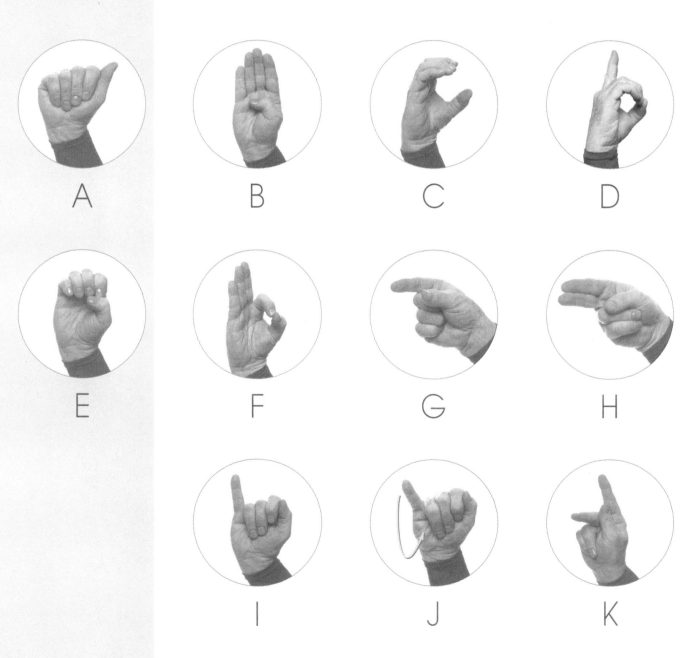

THE ALPHABET

L

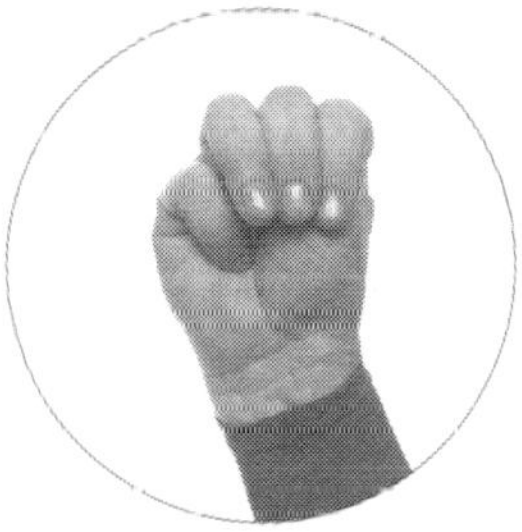

M

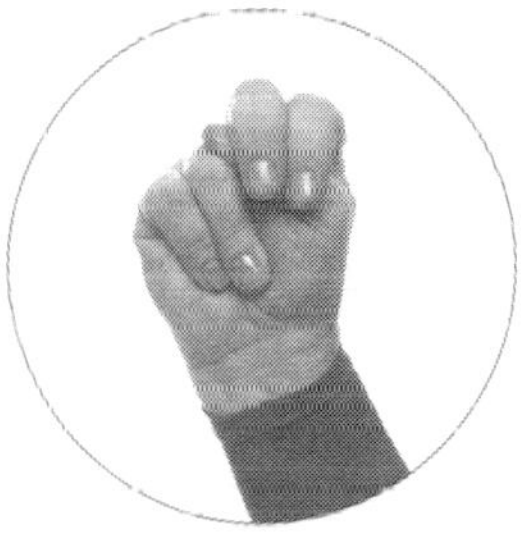

N

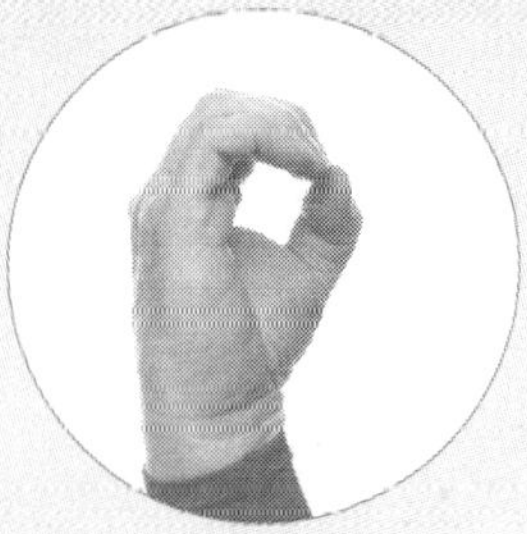

O

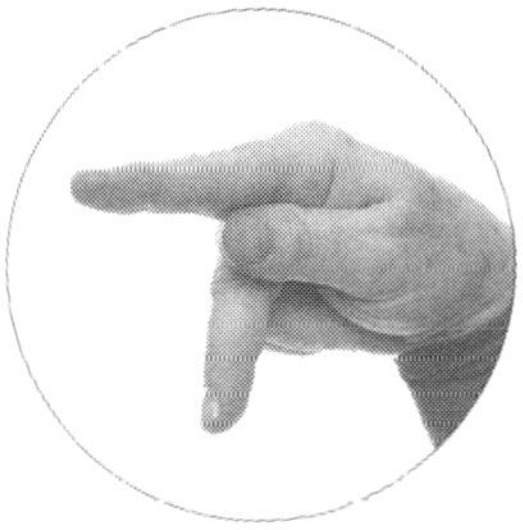

P

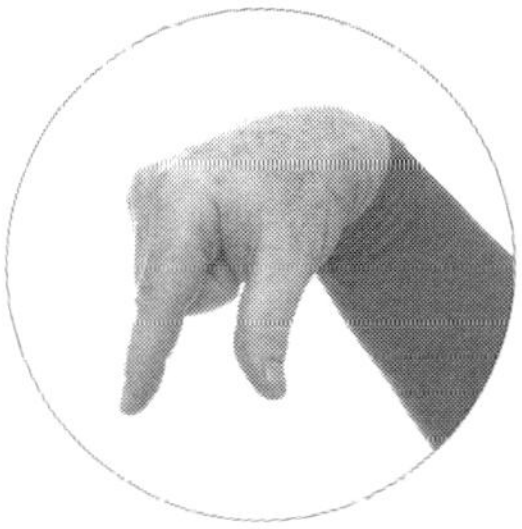

Q

R

S

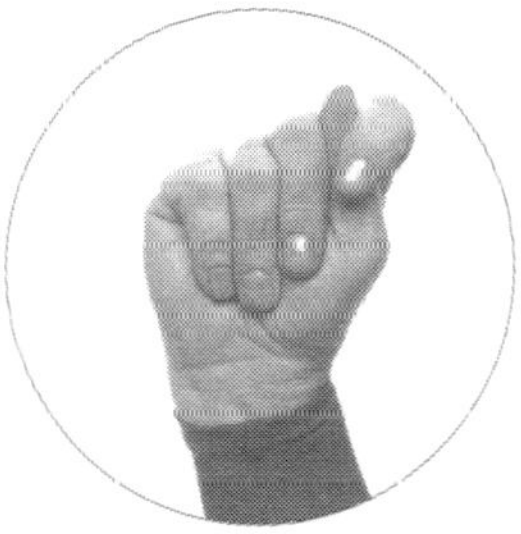

T

U

V

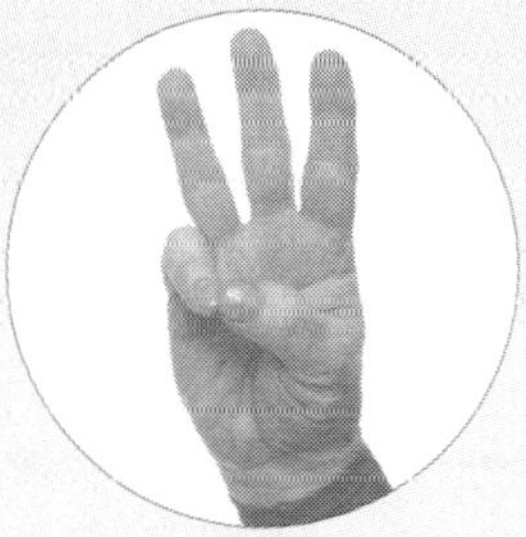

W

X

Y

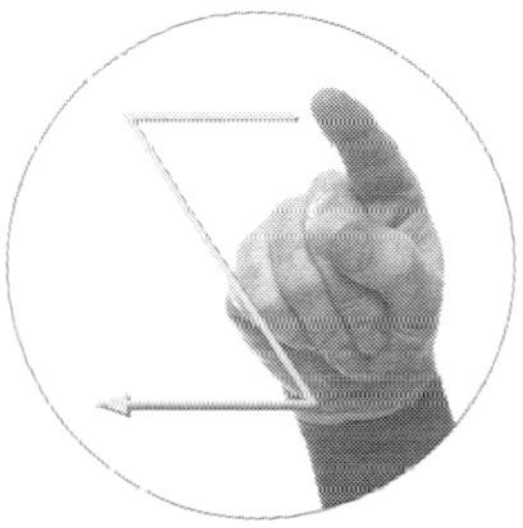

Z

Signing with One Hand Only

When only one hand is used to form a particular sign, keep the other hand in a relaxed position—usually resting comfortably on your lower torso—so that it is ready to instantly get involved in subsequent two-handed signs. (See the photo above.) Note, though, that in this book, the photos of one-handed signs show the inactive hand held *behind* the body. This was done to clarify that the resting hand is not involved in that sign.

A mastery of the manual alphabet is essential to the mastery of American Sign Language. The manual alphabet is used not only in the making of ASL signs, but also to indicate names, places, and ideas for which there are no officially recognized signs.

should practice with a partner, so that you can become comfortable using the manual alphabet, as well as reading fingerspelling. The following guidelines will help you get started:

- Hold your hand upright in a comfortable position in front of your shoulder, with the palm facing forward at a slight angle. If you want to incorporate lip movement—an important aspect of fingerspelling with some deaf people—hold your hand close enough to your mouth that your lips can be read along with the fingerspelling.

- Maintain a smooth rhythm as you combine individual handshapes to spell words. At this point, your goal is articulation, not speed. Speed will come naturally with practice. Avoid the tendency to spell easy words more quickly than difficult ones. Instead, spell the words at a comfortable rate, allowing a slight pause between words. Do not drop the hand between words.

- Speak or mouth each word as you begin to fingerspell it, rather than pronouncing each letter individually. When reading fingerspelling, try to read the words in syllables so you'll grasp the words more quickly. If you do not understand the word being spelled, ask your partner to repeat it at the same speed. Slowing the rate of fingerspelling will only encourage you to read words letter by letter.

- To spell words with double letters, open the hand slightly before repeating the letter. For words with double open letters such as *C* and *L*, simply hold the handshape and move your hand to the right with a very slight bounce.

- In order to distinguish an abbreviation from other words, you'll need to capitalize each letter of the abbreviation. You can do this by moving your hand in a small clockwise circle as you sign each letter.

Obviously, it's neither comfortable nor convenient to fingerspell every word of every conversation. But the value of fingerspelling as a complement to sign language cannot be overstated. A firm grasp of the manual alphabet is especially important when you're new to sign language, before you have built up an extensive vocabulary of signs. In time, as you learn more signs, you'll find that you need to rely less and less on fingerspelling to communicate.

signing 101

In the English language, we see each word for what it is because of the precise arrangement of its letters. But what makes a sign unique? Just as an English word is made up of letters, each sign is composed of several elements that must be combined in a very precise way for that sign to be understood. Two obvious components of signs are handshape and movement. Equally important—although not as readily apparent—are palm orientation and sign location. And, of course, facial expression and body language must be incorporated for more effective signing.

As you begin to understand how all of the elements of ASL interact, you'll gain a greater appreciation for the expressive capability of the language. Often, one sign is the equivalent of several English words, making the English language seem rather "wordy" by comparison!

THE DOMINANT HAND

As you look at the photos throughout this book, you'll notice that many signs are formed using only one hand, while the other hand remains motionless. When this is the case, the *dominant hand* moves while the other hand is held still. *Invite* (page 90) and *beautiful* (page 325) are just two examples of signs that require the movement of only one hand. If you are right-handed, your right hand is dominant; if you are left-handed, of course, your left hand is dominant. If you are equally comfortable using either your right or left hand, you should decide early on which hand will be your dominant hand. Try signing first with one hand and then with the other to determine which feels most natural.

The photos included in this book show right-handed signers. However, if you're uncomfortable signing with your right hand, you can certainly sign with your left hand. Just keep in mind that this will reverse the signs to your audience.

In the photos in this book, the right hand is the dominant one. In other words, it is used for every sign that involves the movement of only one hand. If you find it uncomfortable to use your right hand as your dominant hand, simply sign with your left hand.

THE BASIC HANDSHAPES

Before you begin to learn the vocabulary of sign language, there are a few basic handshapes you should know. Practice forming the handshapes shown below. You'll find they're invaluable in forming the signs described in this book.

open hand
Hold the hand flat, with fingers spread apart.

flat hand
Hold the hand flat, with fingers and thumb touching.

curved hand
Curve the hand, with fingers and thumb touching.

bent hand
Bend the hand at the knuckles, with fingers and thumb touching and held straight.

clawed hand
Curve the hand and separate the fingers.

and hand
Hold the hand so that all fingertips are touching.

one hand
Hold up the index finger with the palm facing forward.

THE SIGNING AREA

The *signing area* is a space in front of the body that extends from the top of the head down to the waist and from shoulder to shoulder. Most signs are formed within this area so the audience can follow the signing motion, making the signs easier to understand. Of course, the size of signs should be adjusted according to the size of the audience. For example, when you're signing for one person or for a small group, your signs should not extend beyond the signing area. However, when you're signing for a larger group, you should increase the size of your signs appropriately. Keep in mind that as you increase the size of your signs, you should also decrease the rate at which you sign, so your signs will still be easy to read.

SYMMETRY

Just as there are signs that require the movement of only one hand, there are also signs that require the movement of both hands. These signs are symmetrical—they use the identical handshape and type of movement for both hands. The location of the hands is also the same. For example, both hands may be held in front of the chest, at the waist, near the temples, and so forth. *Dessert* (page 138), for instance, uses both D hands held in front of the chest.

DIRECTION

In some cases, the direction of a sign's movement is as significant as the handshape itself. For example, a sign can have one meaning when it's moved in one direction, and an opposite meaning when it's moved in the other direction. This is best illustrated by opposites such as *in* and *out* (pages 262 and 263), *up* and *down* (pages 266 and 264), and *open* and *close* (pages 96 and 79). In other instances, the direction of the sign provides important information about the subject and object of a sentence. *Give* (page 87) can be moved away from you to indicate that you are giving an object to someone else, but moved toward you to show that someone is giving an object to you. This is also true for signs such as *tell* (page 32) and *send* (page 100), among others.

A word should be said about movements that you're directed to make in a clockwise or counterclockwise direction. Always keep in mind that in signing, the words "clockwise" and "counterclockwise"—as well as "right" and "left"—refer to the action as seen from the perspective of the person who's signing, rather than the person who's reading the sign. For an example, look at the term "think" on page 103. Although the "Movement" section prescribes a counterclockwise action, the arrow on the photo is actually moving clockwise because it shows the model from the perspective of the person who's reading the sign. In other words, the photo shows a mirror image of the signer's action.

PRESENT, PAST, AND FUTURE TENSE

In the English language, the spelling of words changes to show present, past, or future tense. This is not so in American Sign Language. Instead, ASL uses the body as

Whenever the "Movement" text in this book directs you to move your hand in a clockwise direction or to the left or right, keep in mind that this refers to the perspective of the signer, rather than that of the person who's reading the sign. So if the text tells you to move your hand to the right, be sure to move it to *your* right rather than the right of the person who's facing you.

a point of reference to indicate tense, with the space directly in front of the body representing the present. Thus, signs such as *today* (page 184) and *now* (page 182), which indicate present time, are formed in front of the body. Accordingly, *tomorrow* (page 184), *someday* (page 179), and other signs that refer to the future are formed in a forward motion away from the body. And along these lines, signs referring to the past, including *yesterday* (page 186), move backward from the body.

INTENSITY AND DEGREE

In the English language, the intensity or degree of actions, feelings, and colors is often expressed by adding words. For some descriptive qualities, a stronger word may even be substituted to provide emphasis. In ASL, the same effect is achieved by varying the speed or intensity with which a sign is made, or by incorporating facial expression. Consider the following examples: The sign for *walk* (page 105) can be made quickly or slowly, depending on the intended meaning. *Light blue* (page 351) is signed with a very slight turning motion from the wrist, while *bright red* (page 353) is shown by adding emphasis as the hand is pulled down across the lips. *Smart* (page 331) becomes *brilliant* and *pretty* (page 325) becomes *beautiful* when the signs are exaggerated.

In American Sign Language, additional signs are not needed to indicate the intensity of a signed action or description. Instead, the intensity of the sign itself is varied. For instance, you can turn *pretty* into *beautiful* simply by making a larger, more emphatic circle around your face. (See the photos on page 325.)

While adding this new dimension to your signing will no doubt improve your communication skills, remember that your goal is still to make your signs as clear as possible. The intensity or forcefulness with which you make a sign should never be so extreme that the sign is unreadable.

ICONIC SIGNS

When a sign's shape or movement resembles the concept it represents, the sign is said to be *iconic*. Often, signs that are very iconic can be recognized even by people who are not familiar with sign language. Many signs for animals clearly portray their meanings. For instance, the sign for *elephant* (page 193) is reminiscent of an elephant's trunk. Sports signs are often iconic, as well. *Baseball* (page 244) mimics swinging a bat, *swimming* (page 248) simulates the breaststroke, and so forth.

Some signs appear to be arbitrary at first glance. However, when the roots of these signs are revealed, their iconicity becomes apparent. The sign for *home* (page 113), for example, is shown by placing the hand first on the lips, then on the cheek, to suggest the place where one eats and sleeps. Understanding the root of a sign will usually make the sign easier to remember.

INITIALIZED SIGNS

An *initialized* sign is formed with the fingerspelled handshape of the first letter of the word it represents. You'll encounter several of these signs as your ASL vocabulary begins to grow. The initial handshape can be a very helpful clue to the exact meaning of a sign that represents several similar ideas. For example, the sign for *doctor* (page 225) is formed with the initial *D*; the sign for *nurse* (page 228) is formed with the initial *N*. Although the basic concept of these two signs is the same, it's easy to distinguish between the two because they are initialized.

THE *PERSON* ENDING

A person's occupation or nationality is shown by adding the *person* ending after a noun or verb sign. For example, the person ending can be signed after *teach* (page 220) to indicate *teacher* and after *America* (page 275) to form *American*. To add this ending, point both flat hands forward in front of the chest with the palms facing each other; then move both hands down at the same time. (See the photos at left.) The movement is used to indicate the body of the person involved in the previous sign.

GENDER

The location of signs helps to indicate gender in ASL. Most male signs are formed on or near the forehead, and most female signs are formed on or near the cheek or chin. For example, the sign for *father* (page 65) is shown by touching the thumbtip to the forehead, while *mother* (page 67) is signed by touching the thumbtip to the chin.

The Person Ending

POSSESSIVES AND PLURALS

It's not necessary to sign possessives and plurals in American Sign Language, since this information is usually understood within context. However, you may feel more comfortable including these markers in signed conversation, especially if you're signing in exact English. To indicate a possessive, form the *S* handshape after you sign or fingerspell the word, then twist the hand so the palm faces in toward the body. To indicate plurals, you have a few different options. Probably the most common way to make a sign plural is to repeat the sign several times on either side of the body. Repeating the sign for *cat* (page 191), for instance, would mean *many cats.* You can also add a sign indicating number or quantity after the noun sign. For example, *car* (page 269) plus *many* (page 164) equals *many cars.* Another alternative is to form the sign, then point your index finger at a number of locations. Signing *house* (page 113) and then pointing in different directions would signify many houses.

NEGATIVES

Negatives are sometimes indicated in ASL by signing *not* before the intended word. (See the photos at left.) For some signs, this is the equivalent of adding the negative prefixes *un-, im-, in-,* and *dis-* to negate words in the English language. Therefore, *not* plus *happy* (page 358) becomes *unhappy.* An alternative is to shake the head back and forth while signing the word. For instance, signing *believe* (page 75) and shaking the head "no" makes the sign *don't believe.*

Some signs become negative by twisting the hand(s) forward or downward from the wrist(s). *Don't know* is indicated by signing *know* (page 92) and then twisting the hand so the palm faces forward. *Don't want* is shown by signing *want* (page 106) and then twisting both hands so the palms face down.

Signing a Negative

A, AN, AND *THE*—THE MISSING ARTICLES

Generally, the articles *a, an,* and *the* are omitted when adults use American Sign

Language. This omission is made because these words are both cumbersome and time-consuming to use, and because they can be left out of conversation without causing confusion. However, articles are used as teaching tools when deaf students learn English. When it is desirable to include these words, simply sign them as follows. To sign *a*, move the right A hand slightly to the right. To sign *an*, fingerspell. To sign *the*, begin with a T hand that is positioned with the palm facing left, and rotate the wrist until the palm is facing forward.

PUNCTUATION

Like articles, just discussed, punctuation marks—commas, periods, apostrophes, colons, exclamation points, and question marks—are rarely used in American Sign Language. In most cases, their use not only is unnecessary, but also is disruptive to the flow of conversation. If, however, you decide that a mark of punctuation is required to clarify what you're signing, simply trace the shape of the appropriate punctuation mark in the air with the index finger of your right ONE hand as if you were drawing on a blackboard.

INCORPORATING NUMBERS

In sign language, years, money amounts, addresses, and phone numbers are signed much as they are spoken in English. For example, the year 1864 is signed *eighteen* and then *six four*. Similarly, an uneven amount of money, such as $19.95, would be expressed as *nineteen dollar nine five cents*. For addresses, such as 16 First Street, each number is signed separately—*one six*—and the street name is either signed or fingerspelled. The digits of the phone number 555–4321 are also signed individually, allowing a slight pause where the dash is located.

All number signs can be found on pages 149 to 158.

REPEATING SIGNS

On page 18, you learned that repeating a sign several times can make that sign plural. Repetition can add other dimensions to ASL, as well. For example, to show a continuous action, the sign is formed with a repeated, slow circular movement. To show a recurrent action, on the other hand, the sign is repeated in several quick movements. Therefore, while *look* (page 93) signed several times with a slow motion means that you gazed steadily at something, the same sign repeated with a quick motion means that you glanced at something numerous times.

signing etiquette

Like most beginning signers, you'll probably be eager to show anyone and everyone what you've learned. But what can you do to get the conversation rolling—and then how can you keep it going? If you really want to look like you know your stuff, take a few minutes to read the following hints before you get started.

In American Sign Language, marks of punctuation are generally not used. Instead, facial expression, pauses, and gesture intensity are employed to indicate question marks, periods, exclamation points, and the like. However, if you feel that a mark of punctuation is needed, simply trace its shape in the air with the index finger of your ONE hand.

STARTING A CONVERSATION

Before you start a conversation with a deaf person, make sure to get his or her visual attention. Make eye contact, tap the person's shoulder, or touch the person's arm. Then maintain eye contact throughout the conversation.

In the hearing world, we're accustomed to calling out a name, snapping our fingers, or clapping our hands to get someone's attention. But we must remember that not everyone will respond to sound. Deaf people rely on visual cues or touch. One way to get a deaf person's attention is to try to make eye contact. It's also very common to tap the person's shoulder or arm. Once you are engaged in signed conversation, it's very important to maintain eye contact. If you look away, the person to whom you're talking might think that's the end of the conversation.

A word of caution: Just as standing too close to people having a private spoken conversation might be construed as eavesdropping, watching two people having a private signed conversation is also considered to be inappropriate.

STATEMENTS AND QUESTIONS

In spoken conversation, we use inflections and tone of voice to mark the end of a sentence, or to make the distinction between a statement and a question. Since this is not an option in sign language, signers must rely on other cues. A slight pause between two sentences is usually sufficient to indicate the end of one sentence and the beginning of the next. However, a change in body posture and facial expression is required to show that you are asking a question, rather than making a statement. Lean forward with a quizzical facial expression as you ask your question, and hold the last sign slightly longer than you would if you were making a statement. (For information on use of punctuation marks, see page 19.)

NAME SIGNS

In signed conversation, a person's proper name is usually fingerspelled when he or she is first introduced or mentioned. Then it becomes more convenient to use a *name sign*. A person's name sign is created by combining the first letter of the name with a gesture showing a physical or personality characteristic that makes that person unique. (Remember to be polite!) For example, my name sign is an initialized *G* for Gabriel swung from ear to ear under the chin to indicate my beard (see the photos at left).

VARIATIONS IN SIGNS

As with any spoken language, American Sign Language is subject to local and regional variations, or dialects. More often than not, these differences crop up as new signs are added to the ASL vocabulary. Sometimes, several signs for the same idea or concept are developed independently of each other by different communities. Some signs are assimilated into the language of the national deaf community; others are used only by certain groups in smaller communities. In fact, individual families may even have a few signs or variations of signs that are used only among family members.

As a beginning signer, you may be confused the first few times you encounter signs that are made differently from the way you learned them. Remember that

Signing "Gabriel"

these variations are not right or wrong—they're just different ways of expressing the same idea. Try to be aware of variations in signs when you're traveling. For example, you might want to ask deaf members of a community about the sign for a popular store in their neighborhood. If you keep an open mind, you shouldn't have any trouble adjusting to variations in signs, and it's likely that you'll even come to embrace them.

CLOTHING

Since your clothing acts as a backdrop against which your signs are read, it's a good idea to wear a solid color that contrasts with your skin color when you're signing. That way, your signs will be easy to read, so your audience will be more comfortable. Interpreters, lecturers, and teachers need to be especially mindful of this, since their signs must be read for longer stretches of time.

ready, set, sign!

Now that you're armed with the basics, it's time to embark on your exciting adventure in sign language. Certainly, learning to sign can be challenging. But your studies should also be stimulating and—above all else—fun. Remember to go at your own pace so you can take the time to truly enjoy expressing yourself in this unique and natural way.

Enough said. Turn the page and let's get started!

Like any living language, American Sign Language is constantly changing and evolving. New signs are always being added to keep pace with our changing society. Sometimes, several signs for the same concept are developed independently by different communities, resulting in regional variations of the language.

Readings About Deaf Culture

Deaf culture, kept alive by generations of American Sign Language (ASL) users, is rich with its own unique customs, legends, poetry, and celebrations. In fact, this culture is so complex and diverse that it's now recognized by anthropologists and many others who are intrigued by different modes of communication. After all, studying the language and customs of deaf people not only helps us to understand their way of life, but also gives us fresh insight into our own culture.

Want to learn more about the fascinating culture of ASL users? There's no shortage of excellent books available. To help you in your studies, I've provided a brief list of books that are well worth reading.

❏ *At Home Among Strangers: Exploring the Deaf Community in the United States* by Jerome Schein (Washington, D.C.: Gallaudet University Press, 1989).

Schein provides a comprehensive look at the deaf community—with discussions of deaf culture, family life, education, activism, and economics—and offers insights into why and how the deaf community grew and flourished.

❏ *Deaf Heritage: A Narrative History of Deaf America* by Jack Gannon. (Silver Spring, MD: National Association of the Deaf, 1981).

Here is a detailed history of nearly every aspect of deaf culture in America, from education and the arts, to the debate over signing versus the oral method of communication.

❏ *Deaf History Unveiled: Interpretations From the New Scholarship* edited by John Vickrey Van Cleve (Washington, D.C.: Gallaudet University Press, 2000).

This collection includes fourteen essays on the deaf experience in the Western hemisphere from the sixteenth century to the present day. The book discusses such topics as early deaf education, patterns of suppression, the deaf experience in Europe, and the cultural impact of cochlear implants.

❑ *Deaf in America: Voices From a Culture* by Tom Humphries and Carol Padden (Cambridge, MA: Harvard University Press, 1988).

A terrific introduction to deaf culture, *Deaf in America* covers a broad range of topics, from poetry and folklore to what it means to be part of the deaf community.

❑ *Deaf President Now! The 1988 Revolution at Gallaudet University* by John B. Christiansen and Sharon N. Barnartt (Washington, D.C., Gallaudet University Press, 1995).

This is the incredible story of the 1988 Gallaudet uprising, when students and other advocates protested the appointment of another hearing president to the university. Interviews with student leaders and other key figures are included.

❑ *Never the Twain Shall Meet: Bell, Gallaudet, and the Communications Debate* by Richard Winefield (Washington, D.C.: Gallaudet University Press, 1996).

The author explores the controversy over speech versus sign language in educating deaf children, focusing on the nineteenth century, when the debate was at its height, and looks at how both viewpoints continue to influence deaf education.

❑ *No Walls of Stone: An Anthology of Literature by Deaf and Hard of Hearing Writers* edited by Jill Jepson (Washington, D.C.: Gallaudet University Press, 1997).

This groundbreaking collection of poetry, essays, short stories, and drama by twenty-three hard-of-hearing and deaf writers offers extraordinary accounts of the deaf experience.

❑ *A Phone of Our Own: The Deaf Insurrection Against Ma Bell* by Harry G. Lang (Washington, D.C.: Gallaudet University Press, 2000).

Lang tells the story of how three men from very different walks of life collaborated to develop the TTY, and relates their ensuing battle with big business to make their invention available to deaf people.

❑ *Pictures in the Air* by Stephen C. Baldwin (Washington, D.C.: Gallaudet University Press, 1993).

Baldwin reflects on the people who were instrumental in helping the National Theatre of the Deaf evolve into an internationally acclaimed touring troupe, and tells of the advocates who promoted public consciousness of sign language as both an expressive medium and a fascinating new art form.

❑ *The Story of My Life* by Helen Keller (New York, NY: Bantam Doubleday Dell Publishing Group, 1991).

Helen Keller tells her remarkable and inspirational life story in her own words, from her early years in lonely isolation; to her first meaningful communication with her teacher, Annie Sullivan; and on through her many amazing accomplishments, including a successful writing career.

conversing— common & polite phrases

L ooking to bridge the communication gap? You can use the signs in this chapter to get the conversation started! Whether you want to *talk* to a good friend, *ask* for a favor, *discuss* the meaning of life, *demand* a raise, say you're *sorry,* or wish a friend *good luck,* these signs will help you communicate clearly and correctly.

POLITE PHRASES

excuse me • excuse • exempt

HANDSHAPES: Right CURVED hand and left FLAT hand

POSITION: In front of the chest

MOVEMENT: Brush the fingertips of the right CURVED hand over the upturned palm of the left FLAT hand from the heel of the hand to the fingertips a few times.

VISUALIZE: Wiping away mistakes in order to get a fresh start.

SEE HELPING HANDS ON NEXT PAGE.

goodbye

HANDSHAPE: Right OPEN hand

POSITION: In front of the right shoulder

MOVEMENT: Hold up the right OPEN hand in front of the right shoulder with the palm facing forward. Bend and straighten the fingers a few times.

VISUALIZE: Waving goodbye to someone.

good luck

HANDSHAPE: Right A hand with thumb extended

POSITION: In front of the right shoulder

MOVEMENT: Hold the right A hand in front of the right shoulder with the palm facing left; then push the hand forward quickly.

VISUALIZE: Giving someone the "thumbs-up" gesture to wish good luck.

good morning

HANDSHAPE: Right and left FLAT hands

POSITIONS: **1.** Starts on lips **2.** In front of chest

MOVEMENT: **1.** Hold fingertips of right FLAT hand near lips with palm facing in. Then touch back of right hand to upturned palm of left FLAT hand. (The sign for *good*.) **2.** Point right FLAT hand forward with palm facing up. Place little finger side of left FLAT hand in crook of right bent elbow; then bring right hand up toward body, ending with palm facing in. (The sign for *morning*.)

VISUALIZE: Combining the signs for *good* and *morning*.

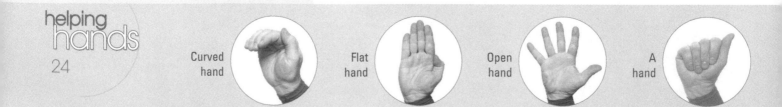

Curved hand   Flat hand   Open hand   A hand

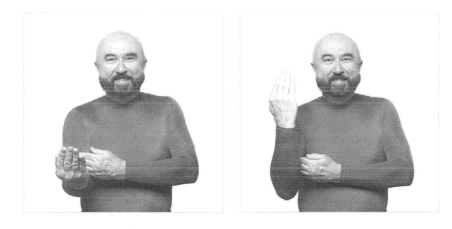

hi • hello

HANDSHAPE: Right B hand

POSITION: Starts on the right temple

MOVEMENT: Touch the index finger side of the right B hand to the right temple with the palm facing left; then move the hand out to the right.

VISUALIZE: Greeting someone by saluting.

Baby Talk

Research has shown that deaf babies of deaf parents "babble" with their hands, much in the way that hearing babies babble with their voices. While hearing babies babble by repeating a few key noises—such as "dadada" or "bababa"—deaf babies repeat specific gestures over and over in a deliberate fashion.

Dr. Laura Ann Petitto, a psychologist at McGill University in Montreal, and her graduate student, Paula F. Marentette, observed five infants at ages ten, twelve, and fourteen months, when language skills are beginning to develop. Two of the babies were deaf children of deaf parents who used American Sign Language to communicate; the other three babies were hearing children of hearing parents who spoke English. Petitto and Marentette video taped and analyzed hundreds of hours worth of the infants' hand gestures, and then compared the patterns of hand gestures between the two groups.

The researchers found that, while the hearing infants made many different hand motions, the gestures never became repetitive—in other words, there was no pattern to them. However, the deaf infants made deliberate hand motions and repeated them over and over again in a systematic way. Presumably, the deaf babies had picked up certain key elements of sign language from watching their parents sign at home, just as hearing babies pick up certain syllables from listening to their parents speak.

B
hand

how (are) you?

HANDSHAPES: 1. Right and left CURVED hands
2. Right ONE hand

POSITION: In front of the chest

MOVEMENT: 1. Hold the CURVED hands together
with knuckles touching and fingertips pointing
down; then twist hands forward from wrists,
ending with the palms facing up and the
shoulders slightly raised. (The sign for *how.*)
2. Point index finger of right ONE hand toward
person being addressed. When referring to
more than one person, move hand from right
to left in sweeping motion. (The sign for
you.) It's not necessary to sign *are*.

VISUALIZE: Combining the signs for *how* and *you.*

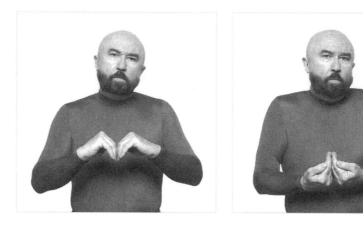

I love you

HANDSHAPE: Right OPEN hand

POSITION: In front of the right shoulder

MOVEMENT: Hold up the right OPEN hand
with the palm facing forward, and touch the
middle and ring fingertips to the palm, so
the thumb, index, and little fingers remain
pointing up.

VISUALIZE: Combining the manual alphabet
letters *I, L,* and *Y* suggests the phrase.

Curved hand   One hand   Open hand

(I'm) fine

HANDSHAPE: Right OPEN hand

POSITION: Starts on the chest

MOVEMENT: Touch the thumbtip of the right OPEN hand to the chest with the fingers pointing up, and wiggle the fingers. (This is the sign for *fine* only; *I am* is understood.)

VISUALIZE: Happy feelings springing forth from the heart.

(I'm) sorry

HANDSHAPE: Right S hand

POSITION: In front of the chest

MOVEMENT: With the palm facing in, rub the right S hand in a few circles on the chest over the heart. (This is the sign for *sorry* only; *I am* is understood.)

VISUALIZE: Rubbing the S hand over your heart suggests feelings of sorrow.

my name (is). . .

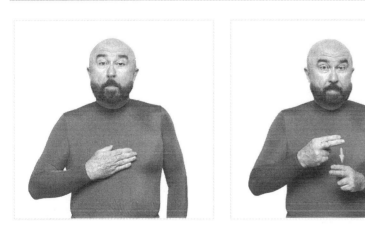

HANDSHAPES: **1.** Right FLAT hand **2.** Right and left H hands

POSITIONS: **1.** On the chest **2.** In front of the chest

MOVEMENT: **1.** Touch the palm of the right FLAT hand to the center of the chest. (This is the sign for *my*.) **2.** Tap the middle finger of the right H hand against the index finger of the left H hand. (This is the sign for *name*.)

VISUALIZE: Combining the signs for *my* and *name*.

S hand

Flat hand

H hand

27

please • pleasure • enjoy • willing

HANDSHAPE: Right FLAT hand

POSITION: On the chest

MOVEMENT: Rub the right FLAT hand in a circle on the chest over the heart.

VISUALIZE: Rubbing the hand over your heart suggests warm, positive feelings.

thank you • thanks

HANDSHAPE: Right FLAT hand

POSITION: Starts on the lips

MOVEMENT: Touch the fingertips of the right FLAT hand to the lips with the palm facing in; then move the hand forward and downward, ending with the palm facing up. This sign can also be expressed by sweeping the right FLAT hand in toward the body.

VISUALIZE: Blowing a kiss in gratitude.

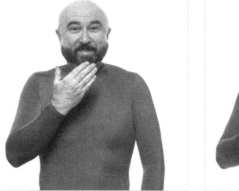

you're welcome

HANDSHAPE: Right FLAT hand

POSITION: Starts in front of the chest

MOVEMENT: Hold the right FLAT hand forward and to the right, with the palm facing left. Then move the hand in a sweeping motion toward the stomach, ending with the palm facing up.

VISUALIZE: Come on in; you're always welcome here.

Flat hand

COMMON WORDS & PHRASES

because

HANDSHAPES: Right ONE hand changing to A hand

POSITION: Starts on the forehead

MOVEMENT: Touch the index fingertip of the right ONE hand to the forehead. (This resembles the sign for *think*.) Then sweep the hand off the forehead to the right while changing it to the A handshape.

VISUALIZE: Taking a thought from the head to create a reason for something.

can • possible • could • able • ability

HANDSHAPE: Right and left S hands

POSITION: In front of the shoulders

MOVEMENT: Hold the right and left S hands in front of the shoulders with the palms facing down. Then simultaneously move both hands downward in a firm manner.

VISUALIZE: The classic hand positions of a French can-can dancer.

can't • impossible • unable

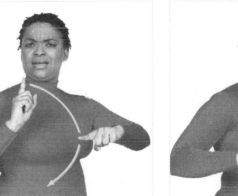

HANDSHAPE: Right and left ONE hands

POSITION: In front of the chest

MOVEMENT: Hold the left ONE hand with the palm facing down and the index finger pointing to the right. Then, in a downward motion, sharply strike the tip of the right index finger against the left index finger.

VISUALIZE: Shame on you; you can't do that.

One hand

A hand

S hand

29

how

HANDSHAPE: Right and left CURVED hands

POSITION: In front of the chest

MOVEMENT: Hold the right and left CURVED hands together with the knuckles touching and the fingertips pointing down; then twist the hands forward from the wrists, ending with the palms facing up and the shoulders slightly raised.

VISUALIZE: Examining a seam to see how two pieces are joined together.

how many?

HANDSHAPES: 1. Right and left CURVED hands **2.** Right and left S hands changing to OPEN hands

POSITION: In front of the chest.

MOVEMENTS: 1. Hold the right and left CURVED hands together with the knuckles touching and the fingertips pointing down; then twist the hands forward from the wrists, ending with the palms facing up and the shoulders slightly raised. (This is the sign for *how*.)
2. Hold the right and left S hands forward with the palms facing up. Then sharply flick the fingers and thumbs open a few times. (This is the sign for *many*.)

VISUALIZE: Combining the signs for *how* and *many*.

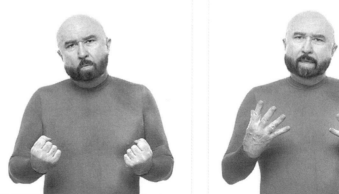

 Curved hand   Open hand

maybe • may • probably • perhaps • possibly

HANDSHAPE:	Right and left FLAT hands
POSITION:	In front of the chest
MOVEMENT:	Point the right and left FLAT hands forward with the palms facing up; then move the hands up and down alternately.
VISUALIZE:	Weighing two possibilities.

me, too

HANDSHAPE:	Right Y hand
POSITION:	In front of the chest
MOVEMENT:	Touch the thumbtip of the right Y hand to the chest with the palm facing left. Move the hand forward off the chest and then touch the thumbtip again to the chest.
VISUALIZE:	Showing that I feel the same way you do.

must • have to • should • need • necessary

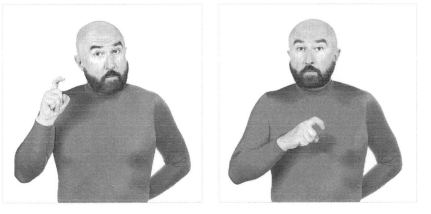

HANDSHAPE:	Right X hand
POSITION:	Starts in front of the right shoulder
MOVEMENT:	Hold the right X hand in front of the right shoulder with the palm facing forward. Then firmly move the hand down several times, each time ending at the center of the chest.
VISUALIZE:	I need to get my hook into this.

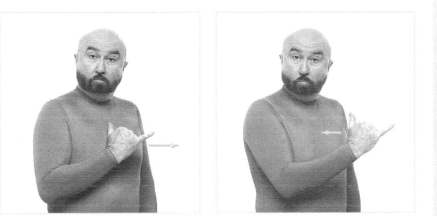

Flat hand   Y hand   X hand

no

HANDSHAPE: Right fist with thumb, index, and middle fingers extended

POSITION: In front of the chest

MOVEMENT: Hold up the right hand in front of the chest and touch the right thumb, index, and middle fingertips together quickly.

VISUALIZE: A quick, pinching movement that cuts off a thought, action, or statement.

not • do not • don't • doesn't • didn't

HANDSHAPE: Right A hand with thumb extended

POSITION: Under the chin

MOVEMENT: Hold the A hand with the palm facing left and the thumb under the chin. Then move the hand sharply forward, away from the body.

VISUALIZE: The chin doesn't stop the thumb from moving forward.

say • speak • mention • tell • remark • speech

HANDSHAPE: Right ONE hand

POSITION: In front of the mouth

MOVEMENT: Point the index finger of the right ONE hand to the left in front of the mouth with the palm facing in. Then move the hand forward and away from the mouth in small circles.

VISUALIZE: Words tumbling out of the mouth. (Depending on the context in which it is used, this sign is identical to the one that is used for "hearing person.")

A hand

One hand

than

HANDSHAPE: Right and left FLAT hands

POSITION: In front of the chest

MOVEMENT: With the palms of the right and left FLAT hands facing down, brush the index finger edge of the right hand against the fingertips of the left hand and continue the downward motion a few inches.

VISUALIZE: Noting the placement of your right hand—first higher than, then lower than your left.

what

HANDSHAPES: Left OPEN hand and right ONE hand

POSITION: In front of the chest

MOVEMENT: Point the left OPEN hand forward with the palm facing right and brush the index fingertip of the right ONE hand down over the left palm.

VISUALIZE: The fingertip of your right hand choosing one of several options from your left hand.

The Missing Articles

In spoken English, conversations are liberally sprinkled with the articles *a, an,* and *the.* A person might, for instance, relate how she "bought *a* pear and *an* apple at *the* store." However, these words are generally omitted when adults use American Sign Language. The omission is made because these words are both cumbersome and time-consuming to use, and because they can easily be left out of conversation without causing confusion. However, articles are used as teaching tools when deaf students learn English. When it is desirable to include these words, simply sign them as follows. To sign *a,* move the right A hand slightly to the right. To sign *an,* fingerspell. To sign *the,* begin with a T hand that is positioned with the palm facing left, and rotate the wrist until the palm is facing forward.

Flat hand   Open hand

what happened?

HANDSHAPES: **1.** Left OPEN hand and right ONE hand **2.** Right and left ONE hands

POSITION: In front of the chest

MOVEMENT: **1.** Point the left OPEN hand forward with the palm facing right and brush the index fingertip of the right ONE hand down over the left palm. (This is the sign for *what*.) **2.** Point the right and left ONE hands forward with the palms facing each other; then pivot both hands forward from the wrists so the palms face downward. (This is the sign for *happen*.)

VISUALIZE: Combining the signs for *what* and *happen*.

what time is it?

HANDSHAPES: Right ONE hand with index finger curved, and left A hand

POSITION: In front of the chest

MOVEMENT: With the palms facing down, tap the curved index finger of the right ONE hand on the wrist of the left A hand a few times. Assume an inquisitive facial expression.

VISUALIZE: A common way to nonverbally ask about the time.

Open hand
One hand
A hand

when

HANDSHAPE: Left and right ONE hands

POSITION: In front of the chest

MOVEMENT: Hold the left ONE hand with the palm facing right and the index finger pointing up. Move the index finger of the right ONE hand in a small clockwise circle around the left index finger; then touch the right index fingertip to the left index fingertip.

VISUALIZE: We're flying around in a circle; when are we going to stop?

where

HANDSHAPE: Right ONE hand

POSITION: In front of the right shoulder

MOVEMENT: Hold up the right ONE hand in front of the right shoulder with the palm facing forward and shake the hand from left to right.

VISUALIZE: Where are we going, this way or that way?

which • whether • either

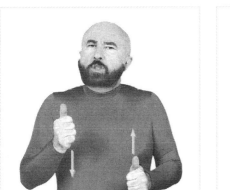 

HANDSHAPE: Right and left A hands

POSITION: In front of the chest

MOVEMENT: Hold the right and left A hands forward with the palms facing each other and move the hands up and down alternately.

VISUALIZE: Comparing two alternatives.

who • whom

HANDSHAPE: Right L hand

POSITION: In front of the mouth

MOVEMENT: Starting with the thumbtip of the right L hand pointing to the chin, move the forefinger up and down a few times. (In common usage, this sign can also be made by using the right index finger to trace a clockwise circular motion around the lips.)

VISUALIZE: A gesture suggesting the question "who was that?"

why

HANDSHAPES: Right CURVED hand changing to Y hand

POSITION: Starts on the forehead

MOVEMENT: Touch the fingertips of the right CURVED hand to the forehead; then draw the hand downward while changing it to the Y handshape.

VISUALIZE: The motion suggests taking a thought from the mind, and the initial Y is the cue for the word.

 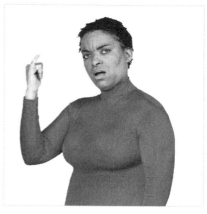

yes

HANDSHAPE: Right S hand

POSITION: In front of the chest

MOVEMENT: Shake the right S hand up and down from the wrist.

VISUALIZE: Using your fist to nod in agreement.

L hand   Curved hand   Y hand   S hand

PREPOSITIONS

above • over

HANDSHAPE: Right and left FLAT hands

POSITION: In front of the chest

MOVEMENT: With the palms facing down, move the right FLAT hand in a counterclockwise circle above the left FLAT hand.

VISUALIZE: A plane circling above an airport.

across • cross • over

HANDSHAPE: Left and right FLAT hands

POSITION: In front of the chest

MOVEMENT: Point the left FLAT hand to the right with the palm facing down; then slide the little finger side of the right FLAT hand forward over the left knuckles.

VISUALIZE: Crossing over a bridge.

at

HANDSHAPES: Left FLAT hand and right BENT hand

POSITION: In front of the chest

MOVEMENT: Hold the left FLAT hand forward at an angle. Then, with the palm facing down, touch the fingertips of the right BENT hand to the back of the left hand. (This sign is often fingerspelled.)

VISUALIZE: The right and left hands meeting at one place.

Flat hand

Bent hand

behind

HANDSHAPE: Right and left A hands

POSITION: In front of the chest

MOVEMENT: Hold the right and left A hands forward with the palms facing each other; then move the right hand back toward the body and behind the left hand.

VISUALIZE: One racer falling behind the other.

below • beneath • under • bottom

HANDSHAPE: Right and left FLAT hands

POSITION: In front of the chest

MOVEMENT: With the palms facing down, move the right FLAT hand in a counter-clockwise circle below the left FLAT hand.

VISUALIZE: A submerged submarine circling beneath a ship.

by • near • close to • adjacent

HANDSHAPE: Right and left CURVED hands

POSITION: In front of the chest

MOVEMENT: Hold the right and left CURVED hands forward, palms facing in, with the left hand farther away from the body than the right. Then move the right hand toward the left palm without touching it.

VISUALIZE: Two objects moving close to each other.

A
hand

Flat
hand

Curved
hand

down

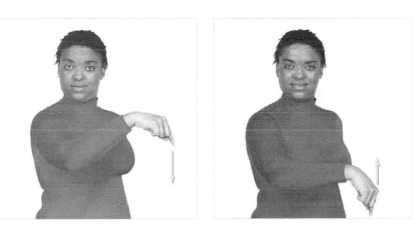

HANDSHAPE: Right ONE hand

POSITION: In front of the chest

MOVEMENT: Point the right ONE hand down with the palm facing in and move it up and down a few times.

VISUALIZE: Pointing straight down.

during · while · in the meantime

HANDSHAPE: Right and left ONE hands

POSITION: In front of the chest

MOVEMENT: Hold the right and left ONE hands in front of the chest with the palms facing in, and the index fingers pointing slightly downward. Then simultaneously move both hands in an upward curve until the index fingertips are pointing directly forward.

VISUALIZE: The parallel movement of the hands suggests two things happening simultaneously.

for

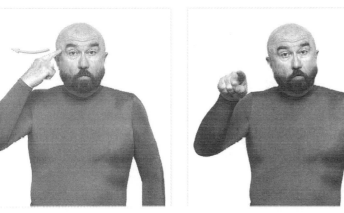

HANDSHAPE: Right ONE hand

POSITION: Starts at the right temple

MOVEMENT: Touch the index fingertip of the right ONE hand to the right temple. Then move the fingertip away from you with a slight dipping motion until the finger is pointing forward.

VISUALIZE: A thought for you, from my head to yours.

One hand

from

HANDSHAPES: Right X hand and left ONE hand

POSITION: In front of the chest

MOVEMENT: Hold up the right X hand and left ONE hand, palms facing in, with the right index finger touching the left index fingertip. Then move the right hand down and back toward the body.

VISUALIZE: Pulling a paper match from a matchbook.

in

HANDSHAPES: Left C hand and right AND hand

POSITION: In front of the chest

MOVEMENT: Hold the left C hand forward with the fingers pointing right. Then place the fingers of the right AND hand in the opening of the left C hand.

VISUALIZE: Making a hole in one.

off

HANDSHAPES: Right FLAT hand and left S hand

POSITION: In front of the chest

MOVEMENT: Hold the right FLAT hand and left S hand forward, palms facing down, with the right hand on the back of the left; then lift the right hand upwards.

VISUALIZE: Peeling off a label.

X
hand

One
hand

C
hand

And
hand

on

HANDSHAPE: Right and left FLAT hands

POSITION: In front of the chest

MOVEMENT: With the palms facing down, place the right FLAT hand on the back of the left FLAT hand.

VISUALIZE: The laying on of hands.

to • toward

HANDSHAPE: Right and left ONE hands

POSITION: In front of the chest

MOVEMENT: Point the left ONE hand up with the palm facing right; then touch the index fingertip of the right ONE hand to the index fingertip of the left hand.

VISUALIZE: The right fingertip moving to meet the left fingertip.

with

HANDSHAPE: Right and left A hands

POSITION: In front of the chest

MOVEMENT: Hold the right and left A hands in front of the chest, with the palms facing each other. Then bring the hands together.

VISUALIZE: Two objects coming in contact with each other.

Flat hand   S hand   A hand

CONJUNCTIONS

and

HANDSHAPES: Right OPEN hand changing to right AND hand

POSITION: In front of the chest

MOVEMENT: Hold the right OPEN hand forward and to the left, with the palm facing in and the fingers pointing to the left. Then move the hand to the right while bringing the thumb and fingertips together into an AND hand.

VISUALIZE: The movement suggests that *and* stretches a sentence by adding another idea.

but • however • although

HANDSHAPE: Right and left ONE hands

POSITION: In front of the chest

MOVEMENT: Cross the index fingers of the right and left ONE hands in front of the chest. Then sharply draw the fingers apart by moving them a short distance in opposite directions.

VISUALIZE: First I'm cross, but then I'm not.

or • either

HANDSHAPES: Right ONE hand and left L hand

POSITION: In front of the chest

MOVEMENT: Hold the left L hand in front of the chest with the index finger pointing forward and the palm facing right. Then bounce the index fingertip of the right ONE hand from the tip of the left thumb to the top of the left index finger, moving it back and forth several times.

VISUALIZE: Choosing one *or* the other.

 Open hand   And hand   One hand   L hand

CONVERSING

advise • advice • counsel • influence

HANDSHAPES: Right AND hand changing to OPEN hand and left FLAT hand

POSITION: In front of the chest

MOVEMENT: With the palms facing down, place the fingertips of the right AND hand on the back of the left FLAT hand; then open the right hand while moving it forward and off of the left hand.

VISUALIZE: Offering a hand in giving advice.

announce • proclaim • declare

HANDSHAPE: Right and left ONE hands

POSITION: Starts on the lips

MOVEMENT: Point the index fingertips of the right and left ONE hands toward the lips with the palms facing in; then twist the hands from the wrists so the palms face forward and swing the hands above the shoulders.

VISUALIZE: Spreading the word far and wide.

answer • reply • respond • react

HANDSHAPE: Right and left ONE hands

POSITION: Starts in front of the mouth

MOVEMENT: Hold up the right and left ONE hands in front of the mouth with the left hand in front of the right; then twist both hands from the wrists so the index fingers are pointing forward.

VISUALIZE: Words directed from the mouth in response to a question.

Flat hand

argue • debate • quarrel • controversy

HANDSHAPE: Right and left ONE hands

POSITION: In front of the chest

MOVEMENT: Point the index fingers of the right and left ONE hands towards each other, with the palms facing in, and vigorously shake them up and down from the wrists. (Note that some people move the right and left fingers up and down alternately, while others move them up and down together.)

VISUALIZE: The two fingers having a shootout with each other.

ask • request

HANDSHAPE: Right and left FLAT hands

POSITION: In front of the chest

MOVEMENT: Hold the right and left FLAT hands together with the palms touching and the fingers pointing forward; then draw the hands upward and in toward the body, ending with the fingers pointing up.

VISUALIZE: Resembles the sign for *pray* to suggest asking for assistance.

call • summon

HANDSHAPES: Right FLAT hand changing to A hand and left OPEN hand

POSITION: In front of the chest

MOVEMENT: With the palms facing down, place the fingers of the right FLAT hand on the back of the left OPEN hand. Then draw the right hand up while changing it to the A handshape.

VISUALIZE: Gently touching a person to get his or her attention.

 One hand   Flat hand   A hand   Open hand

complain • object • protest

HANDSHAPE: Right CLAWED hand

POSITION: In front of the chest

MOVEMENT: Strike the fingertips of the right CLAWED hand against the chest a few times.

VISUALIZE: Indicating that you have something itchy to get off your chest.

demand • require • insist

HANDSHAPES: Left FLAT hand and right ONE hand with index finger curved

POSITION: In front of the chest

MOVEMENT: Point the left FLAT hand forward with the palm facing right. Touch the index fingertip of the right ONE hand to the left palm; then pull both hands back toward the body.

VISUALIZE: Showing a list of your demands.

disagree • contradict • object • contrary to

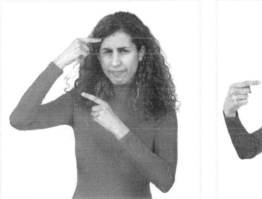 

HANDSHAPE: Right and left ONE hands

POSITIONS: 1. On the forehead 2. In front of the chest

MOVEMENT: 1. Touch the index fingertip of the right ONE hand to the forehead. (This resembles the sign for *think*.) 2. Touch the index fingertips of the right and left ONE hands together with the palms facing in; then pull the hands apart to the sides. (This is the sign for *opposite*.)

VISUALIZE: Thoughts that move in opposite directions.

Clawed hand

discuss

HANDSHAPES: Right ONE hand and left FLAT hand

POSITION: In front of the chest

MOVEMENT: Tap the index finger of the right ONE hand on the upturned palm of the left FLAT hand a few times.

VISUALIZE: Striking the palm to emphasize a point.

fingerspelling • manual alphabet • dactylology

HANDSHAPE: Right OPEN hand

POSITION: In front of the chest

MOVEMENT: With the palm facing down, move the right OPEN hand to the right while wiggling the fingers.

VISUALIZE: The motion suggests fingers roving across a piano keyboard.

inform • notify • information

HANDSHAPES: Right and left AND hands changing to OPEN hands

POSITION: Starts on the forehead

MOVEMENT: Touch the fingertips of the right and left AND hands to the sides of the forehead; then move both hands forward and downward while opening them, ending with the palms facing up.

VISUALIZE: Taking information from the mind and offering it to others.

One hand   Flat hand   Open hand   And hand

interpret • translate • interpreter

HANDSHAPE: Right and left F hands

POSITION: In front of the chest

MOVEMENT: Hold up the right and left F hands, palms facing each other, with the right palm facing out and the left palm facing in. Then reverse the positions of the hands so the right palm faces in and the left palm faces out. To sign *interpreter,* add the *person* ending. (See page 18.)

VISUALIZE: The itsy-bitsy spider spoke two languages.

lipreading • speechreading

HANDSHAPE: Right V hand with index and middle fingers curved

POSITION: In front of the mouth

MOVEMENT: Point the extended fingers of the right V hand toward the mouth and move the hand in a small counterclockwise circle.

VISUALIZE: Forming a sign similar to *read* near the lips suggests lipreading.

listen • hear

HANDSHAPE: Right C hand

POSITION: Next to the right ear

MOVEMENT: Cup the right C hand around the right ear with the palm facing forward; then turn the head slightly to the left.

VISUALIZE: Cupping the hand around the ear to hear better.

F hand

V hand

C hand

misunderstand

HANDSHAPE: Right v hand

POSITION: On the forehead

MOVEMENT: Touch the middle fingertip of the right v hand to the forehead with the palm facing in. Then twist the hand from the wrist so the palm faces forward, and touch the index fingertip to the forehead.

VISUALIZE: An idea being twisted around in the mind.

question • question mark

HANDSHAPE: Right ONE hand

POSITION: In front of the right shoulder

MOVEMENT: Trace the shape of a question mark in the air with the index finger of the right ONE hand. Add the dot under the question mark by pointing the index finger forward.

VISUALIZE: The shape of the sign gives the meaning.

shout • yell • cry out • scream

HANDSHAPE: Right c hand

POSITION: Starts in front of the mouth

MOVEMENT: Point the thumbtip and fingertips of the right c hand toward the corners of the mouth. Then move the hand forward and upward with a wavy motion.

VISUALIZE: The motion suggests that the voice is loud and travels far.

V hand • One hand • C hand

The Pause That Refreshes

During long stretches of continuous signing at a court trial, business conference, convention, or similar setting, the appropriate—although expensive—protocol is to switch back and forth between two interpreters about once every ten minutes. This practice is not only more visually interesting to the deaf people in the audience, but it also ensures that the interpreters remain focused and fully alert while signing. While an extra-long signing session is enough to anesthetize the sensibilities of even the most skilled interpreter, frequent breaks help to keep the interpreter fresh, engaged, and on a roll.

sign • sign language

HANDSHAPES: **1.** Right and left ONE hands **2.** Right and left L hands

POSITION: In front of the chest

MOVEMENT: **1.** Point the index fingers of the right and left ONE hands up, with the palms facing each other. Then circle the hands alternately back toward the body. (This is the sign for *sign*.) **2.** Hold the right and left L hands with the palms facing forward and move the hands simultaneously to the sides with a twisting motion of the wrists.

VISUALIZE: The first motion suggests signing, and the initial L suggests the word "language."

talk • communicate • conversation • dialogue

HANDSHAPE: Right and left ONE hands

POSITION: In front of the mouth

MOVEMENT: Hold up the right and left ONE hands in front of the mouth with the palms facing toward each other; then move the hands alternately back and forth from the lips.

VISUALIZE: Words being exchanged in a conversation.

L
hand

Assisted Listening

Although there's no question that hearing aids can be very helpful for deaf or hard-of-hearing people, there are some situations for which they're not well designed. Hearing aids are most useful in one-on-one interactions, when there's little background noise. However, in environments that are flooded with many different sounds—such as classrooms, lecture halls, and group meetings—hearing aids amplify *everything,* including background noise. And that can be pretty distracting. In these situations, assisted listening devices, or ALDs, may offer a solution.

ALDs are designed to be helpful in specific listening situations, because they amplify only desired sounds. How does this work? The ALD's microphone is placed right at the source of the sound so that it cuts down on background noise. A transmitter sends the sound signal to a receiver; then the receiver transmits the sound to the listener's ear or hearing aid.

There are four different types of ALDs, which differ in the method used to send the sound signal from the microphone to the receiver:

• In a hardwired system, the microphone is attached by a thin cable to the receiver, creating a direct connection between the source of the sound and the listener. This type of ALD is most useful for one-to-one conversation.

• The transmitter in an FM system sends frequency modulated (FM) radio waves through the air to the receiver, which is tuned to the same frequency. FM systems are often used in classrooms, because they can be used for a broader audience than hardwired systems.

• An infrared system uses invisible lightwaves to send signals to individual wireless receivers, similar to the way a remote control works with a television set. The receivers then change the lightwaves into electrical energy and finally into sound. These systems are often used in the home to amplify the television, as well as in movie theaters and public speaking arrangements.

• An audio loop system sends signals from the transmitter through a loop of wire that surrounds a seating area—such as a chair or even an entire room—or that is worn around the neck or at the ear. The loop of wire generates an electromagnetic field that is picked up by individual receivers. This type of system can be used in the home for watching television, as well as in the classroom.

understand • comprehend • perceive

HANDSHAPES: Right s hand changing to ONE hand

POSITION: In front of the forehead

MOVEMENT: Hold the right s hand to the right of the forehead with the palm facing in. Then flick the index finger up to form the ONE handshape.

VISUALIZE: A light bulb being turned on in the mind.

S
hand

One
hand

pronouns, people & relationships

Want to work on your people skills? You can use the signs in this chapter to add the personal touch to all your signed conversations. Soon you'll be ready for almost any social situation—whether you want to meet new *people,* contact an old *friend,* plan a *family* reunion, fuss over a newborn *baby,* or just make *someone* happy.

PRONOUNS

anyone • anybody

HANDSHAPES: 1. Right A hand **2.** Right ONE hand

POSITION: In front of the chest

MOVEMENT: 1. Hold the right A hand forward with the palm facing left; then twist the hand to the right in an arc so the palm faces forward. (This is the sign for *any.*) **2.** Keeping the hand in the same position, point up the right index finger. (This is the sign for *one.*)

VISUALIZE: Combining the signs for *any* and *one.*

SEE HELPING HANDS ON NEXT PAGE.

everyone • everybody

HANDSHAPES: 1. Left and right A hands **2.** Right ONE hand

POSITION: In front of the chest

MOVEMENT: 1. Hold the left A hand in front of the chest with the palm facing right; then slide the knuckles and thumb of the right A hand down on the left thumb a few times. (This is the sign for *each*.) **2.** Hold up the right ONE hand. (This is the sign for *one*.)

VISUALIZE: Combining the signs for *each* and *one*.

he • him

HANDSHAPES: 1. Right hand held as if grasping the brim of a baseball cap **2.** Right ONE hand

POSITIONS: 1. At the forehead **2.** In front of chest

MOVEMENT: 1. Hold the right hand at the forehead as if grasping the brim of a baseball cap; then move the hand forward a few inches while bringing the fingertips and thumbtip together. (This is the sign for *male*. If it's already clear that the person referred to is male, the sign for male is not necessary.) **2.** Point the index finger of the right ONE hand toward the person being discussed.

VISUALIZE: The baseball cap-wearing guy is him.

his • her • hers • their • your • yours

HANDSHAPE: Right FLAT hand

POSITION: In front of the chest

MOVEMENT: Hold the right FLAT hand forward with the palm facing toward the person or persons being discussed. Then move the hand across the front of the body from left to right.

VISUALIZE: Showing a person or thing separate from yourself.

A hand · One hand · Flat hand

my

I

HANDSHAPE: Right I hand

POSITION: On the chest

MOVEMENT: Touch the thumb side of the right I hand to the center of the chest with the palm facing left.

VISUALIZE: Holding the initial I close to the body indicates oneself.

me

HANDSHAPE: Right ONE hand

POSITION: On the chest

MOVEMENT: Touch the index fingertip of the right ONE hand to the center of the chest. (In common usage, this motion is often also used to sign *I*.)

VISUALIZE: Common sign for "me."

my • mine • personal • my own

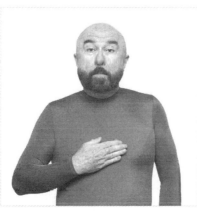

HANDSHAPE: Right FLAT hand

POSITION: On the chest

MOVEMENT: Touch the palm of the right FLAT hand to the center of the chest.

VISUALIZE: Common sign for "mine."

I
hand

myself • self

HANDSHAPE: Right A hand with thumb extended

POSITION: On the chest

MOVEMENT: Touch the thumb side of the right A hand to the center of the chest with the palm facing left.

VISUALIZE: I did it all by myself.

other • another

HANDSHAPE: Right A hand with thumb extended

POSITION: In front of the right side of the chest

MOVEMENT: Hold the right A hand in front of the right side of the chest, with the extended thumb pointing upward. Then pivot the hand from the wrist so that the thumb points to the right.

VISUALIZE: Pointing the thumb toward another person.

our • ours

HANDSHAPE: Right CURVED hand

POSITION: Starts in front of the right shoulder

MOVEMENT: Hold up the right CURVED hand in front of the right shoulder with the palm facing left. Then make a circular motion across the chest to the left shoulder, ending with the palm facing right.

VISUALIZE: All this is ours.

A
hand

Curved
hand

ourselves

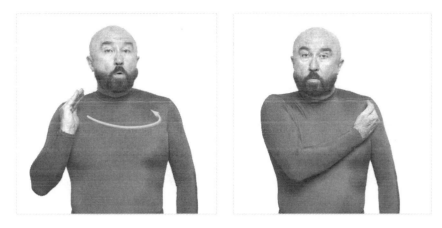

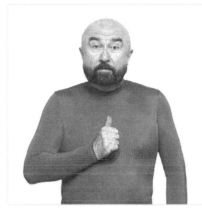

HANDSHAPES: **1.** Right CURVED hand **2.** Right A hand

POSITIONS: **1.** Starts in front of the right shoulder **2.** On the chest

MOVEMENT: **1.** Hold up the right CURVED hand in front of the right shoulder with the palm facing left. Then make a circular motion across the chest to the left shoulder, ending with the palm facing right. (This is the sign for *our*.) **2.** Touch the thumb side of the right A hand to the center of the chest, palm facing left. (This is the sign for *self*.)

VISUALIZE: Combination of the signs for *our* and *self*.

she • her

HANDSHAPES: **1.** Right A hand **2.** Right ONE hand

POSITIONS: **1.** Starts below the right earlobe **2.** In front of the chest

MOVEMENT: **1.** Starting below the right earlobe, trace the thumbtip of the right A hand down along the jawbone to the chin. (This is the sign for *female*. If it's already clear that the person referred to is female, the sign for female is not necessary.) **2.** Point the index finger of the right ONE hand toward the person being discussed.

VISUALIZE: The one with the makeup on the face is her.

One
hand

someone • somebody • something

HANDSHAPE: Right ONE hand

POSITION: In front of the right shoulder

MOVEMENT: Hold up the right ONE hand in front of the right shoulder with the palm facing forward and shake the hand back and forth slightly from left to right.

VISUALIZE: I know something you don't know. . . .

that

HANDSHAPES: Right Y hand and left FLAT hand

POSITION: In front of the chest

MOVEMENT: Place the palm side of the right Y hand on the upturned palm of the left FLAT hand.

VISUALIZE: The *Y* that seals the agreement.

they • them • these • those

HANDSHAPE: Right ONE hand

POSITION: In front of the chest

MOVEMENT: Point the index finger of the right ONE hand in the direction of the people or objects being discussed. Then move the hand to the right.

VISUALIZE: Pointing to the people or objects being discussed.

One hand   Y hand   Flat hand

this

HANDSHAPES: Right ONE hand and left FLAT hand

POSITION: In front of the chest

MOVEMENT: Touch the index fingertip of the right ONE hand to the upturned palm of the left FLAT hand.

VISUALIZE: Making the point that this is it.

we • us

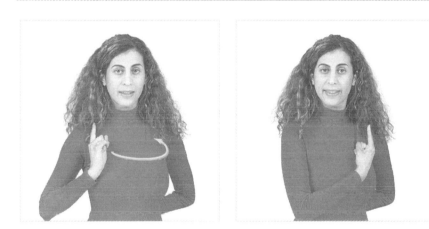

HANDSHAPE: Right ONE hand

POSITION: Starts in front of the right shoulder

MOVEMENT: Touch the index finger of the right ONE hand to the right shoulder. Then move the hand in a forward semicircle across the chest until it touches the left shoulder. This sign can also be made with the W hand, to suggest "we," or the U hand, to suggest "us."

VISUALIZE: A sweeping motion including all of us.

who • whom

HANDSHAPE: Right L hand

POSITION: In front of the mouth

MOVEMENT: Starting with the thumbtip of the right L hand pointing to the chin, move the forefinger up and down a few times.

VISUALIZE: A gesture suggesting the question "Who was that?"

L
hand

57

you

HANDSHAPE: Right ONE hand

POSITION: In front of the chest

MOVEMENT: Point the index finger of the right ONE hand toward the person being addressed. When referring to more than one person, move the hand from right to left in a sweeping motion.

VISUALIZE: The classic "Uncle Sam wants you" pose.

PEOPLE

adult

HANDSHAPE: Right A hand

POSITIONS: **1.** On the right side of the forehead. **2.** On the right side of the chin

MOVEMENT: With the palm facing left, touch the thumbtip of the right A hand first to the right side of the forehead, then to the right side of the chin.

VISUALIZE: Holding the initial A at the male and female sign positions.

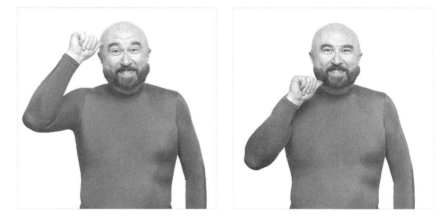

baby • infant

HANDSHAPE: Right and left FLAT hands

POSITION: In front of the chest

MOVEMENT: Cradle the right bent elbow in the upturned palm of the left FLAT hand, with the palm of the right FLAT hand facing up. Then rock the arms back and forth.

VISUALIZE: Rocking a baby in the arms.

One hand · A hand · Flat hand

Helen Keller

Internationally acclaimed author and lecturer Helen Keller was the embodiment of the human virtues of intelligence, courage, and determination. Born in Tuscumbia, Alabama, in 1880, Helen lost both her sight and hearing at just eighteen months of age when she was stricken with meningitis. Although Helen was virtually unable to communicate, her parents believed that she could learn, and would not abandon their search to find a tutor for her. Their hopes were fulfilled when they met Anne Sullivan, a graduate of the Perkin's Institute for the Deaf and Blind in Boston. Anne was partially blind herself, but had learned the manual alphabet in order to talk with a fellow student at the Perkin's Institute.

Anne was able to teach Helen the manual alphabet by touch, pressing each handshape directly into her student's palm. Soon, Helen also learned to read Braille and to write with a special typewriter. She even learned to speak by pressing her fingers against her teacher's throat and imitating the

Helen Keller and Anne Sullivan

vibrations. In 1904, Helen made history as the first deaf and blind person to graduate from college when she received her degree—with honors—from Radcliffe College. She was a published author even before she earned her college degree, with the release of *The Story of My Life* in 1903. She went on to publish many other books, including *The World I Live In* (1908), *Let Us Have Faith* (1940), and *The Open Door* (1957). Throughout most of her life, Helen lectured all over the world, speaking out about issues such as child labor, capital punishment, and war. She became a champion for people with disabilities, providing much-needed inspiration to people who might otherwise have lost hope.

Anne Sullivan was Helen's constant companion until her own death in 1936. Helen Keller died in 1968 at the age of eighty-eight in Westport, Connecticut. The women's lifelong friendship was the basis for playwright William Gibson's celebrated drama *The Miracle Worker.*

boy • male

HANDSHAPE: Right hand held as if grasping the brim of a baseball cap

POSITION: At the forehead

MOVEMENT: Hold the right hand at the forehead as if grasping the brim of a baseball cap; then move the hand forward a few inches while bringing the fingertips and thumbtip together.

VISUALIZE: A man tipping his cap.

child • children

HANDSHAPE: Right CURVED hand

POSITION: Just above the waist

MOVEMENT: With the palm facing down, move the right CURVED hand up and down just above the waist. To indicate more than one child, repeat the motion several times.

VISUALIZE: Patting a child on the head.

girl • female

HANDSHAPE: Right A hand

POSITION: Starts below the right earlobe

MOVEMENT: Starting below the right earlobe, trace the thumbtip of the right A hand down along the jawbone to the chin.

VISUALIZE: The thumb tracing the old-fashioned bonnet strings worn by *Little House on the Prairie* girls.

man

HANDSHAPE: Right OPEN hand

POSITIONS: **1.** On the forehead **2.** On the chest

MOVEMENT: With the palm facing left, touch the thumbtip of the right OPEN hand to the center of the forehead, then to the center of the chest.

VISUALIZE: Combining the signs for *father* and *fine*.

Curved hand

A hand

Open hand

people

HANDSHAPE: Right and left P hands

POSITION: In front of the chest

MOVEMENT: With the palms facing down, move the right and left P hands forward in alternating circles.

VISUALIZE: Two ferris wheels packed with people.

person

 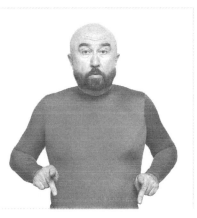

HANDSHAPE: Right and left P hands

POSITION: In front of the chest

MOVEMENT: Hold the right and left P hands in front of the chest, with the index fingers pointing forward. Then move both hands downward simultaneously.

VISUALIZE: The initial P showing the torso of a person.

woman

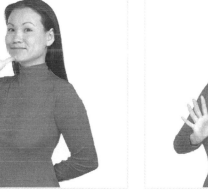 

HANDSHAPE: Right OPEN hand

POSITIONS: **1.** On the right side of the chin **2.** On the chest

MOVEMENT: With the palm facing left, touch the thumbtip of the right OPEN hand to the right side of the chin, then to the center of the chest.

VISUALIZE: Combining the signs for *mother* and *fine*.

P hand

RELATIONSHIPS

aunt

HANDSHAPE: Right A hand

POSITION: Next to the right cheek

MOVEMENT: Hold the right A hand next to the right cheek, palm facing left. Then shake the hand back and forth slightly from the wrist.

VISUALIZE: Holding the initial A near the female sign position suggests *aunt*.

brother

HANDSHAPES: **1.** Right hand held as if grasping brim of baseball cap **2.** Right and left ONE hands

POSITIONS: **1.** At forehead **2.** In front of chest

MOVEMENT: **1.** Hold the right hand as if grasping the brim of a baseball cap; then move the hand forward a few inches while bringing the fingertips and thumbtip together. (The sign for *male*.) **2.** Point the index fingers of the right and left ONE hands forward in front of the chest, palms facing down, and bring the hands together. (The sign for *same*.)

VISUALIZE: Combining the signs for *male* and *same* suggests a male member of the same family.

A
hand

One
hand

cousin

HANDSHAPE: Right C hand

POSITIONS: Next to the right temple (male) or right cheek (female)

MOVEMENT: With the palm facing left, hold the right C hand next to the right temple for a male cousin or the right cheek for a female cousin; shake the hand back and forth slightly from the wrist.

VISUALIZE: Holding the initial C near the male or female sign position suggests a male or female *cousin*.

daughter

HANDSHAPES: **1.** Right A hand **2.** Right CURVED hand

POSITIONS: **1.** Starts below the right earlobe **2.** In front of the chest

MOVEMENT: **1.** Starting below the right earlobe, trace the thumbtip of the right A hand down along the jawbone to the chin. (This is the sign for *female*.) **2.** Cradle the right CURVED hand, palm facing up, in the crook of the left bent elbow.

VISUALIZE: Cradling a female baby—your daughter—in your arms.

divorce

HANDSHAPE: Right and left D hands

POSITION: In front of the chest

MOVEMENT: Hold the right and left D hands together in front of the chest with the palms facing each other and the knuckles touching. Then twist the hands outward and sideways from the wrists so the palms facing forward.

VISUALIZE: Pulling the initial D hands apart suggests the separation of divorce.

C hand   Curved hand   D hand

family

HANDSHAPE: Right and left F hands

POSITION: In front of the chest

MOVEMENT: Hold up the right and left F hands with the thumbtips touching. Then move both hands in an outward circular motion until the little finger sides of the hands are touching.

VISUALIZE: Moving the initial F hands in a circular motion suggests a family circle.

Growing Up With Deaf Parents

Both of my parents were born hearing and became deaf early in their lives. My father lost his hearing as the result of an automobile accident and my mother became deaf after a bout with scarlet fever. They met as young students at the Paul Hamilton Haynes School for the Deaf in Philadelphia, married in their early twenties, and had two hearing children. At the time of my father's death in 1983, they had been together for more than 50 years.

I've often been asked what it was like to grow up as the hearing child of deaf parents. Some people seem to think my childhood was a silent one, without the sounds of language, laughter, radio, television, or any of the other infinite sounds that compose the symphony of life. The reality was quite the opposite. My mother, Dorothy—now in her ninth decade of life—speaks as well as any

The Author's Parents

hearing person, which is often confusing to hearing people when they first meet her. My father, Gabriel, though not as perfectly proficient as my mother, also spoke clearly and distinctly, and his charismatic personality made him a natural as the president of a number of deaf organizations. As a child, he became fluent in Polish because of his immigrant grandparents; I suspect that, as an adult, he amazed some people with his ability to both speak and lipread in Polish.

With my parents, I spoke and signed in English. I didn't use what is now called American Sign Language, but instead signed in a short, pidgin style while also moving my lips. In this way, my parents and I were able to communicate freely and easily with each other, as well as with most of the deaf people who came to our home.

F
hand

father • dad • papa

HANDSHAPE: Right OPEN hand

POSITION: On the center of the forehead

MOVEMENT: With the palm facing left, touch the thumbtip of the right OPEN hand twice to the center of the forehead while wiggling the fingers.

VISUALIZE: Holding the hand at the male sign position suggests the male head of a family.

friend • friendship

HANDSHAPE: Right and left X hands

POSITION: In front of the chest

MOVEMENT: Hook the index finger of the right X hand over the index finger of left X hand; then repeat the action in reverse.

VISUALIZE: Two people linked together in friendship.

grandfather

HANDSHAPE: Right OPEN hand

POSITION: Starts on the center of the forehead

MOVEMENT: Touch the thumbtip of the right OPEN hand to the center of the forehead, palm facing left. (Resembles the sign for *father*.) Then move the hand forward in two small arcs.

VISUALIZE: Moving the sign for *father* away from the forehead suggests a father one generation back.

Open hand

X hand

grandmother

HANDSHAPE: Right OPEN hand

POSITION: Starts on the center of the chin

MOVEMENT: Touch the thumbtip of the right OPEN hand to the center of the chin, palm facing left. Then move the hand forward in two small arcs.

VISUALIZE: Moving the sign for *mother* away from the chin suggests a mother one generation back.

husband

HANDSHAPES: **1.** Right hand held as if grasping the brim of a baseball cap **2.** Right and left CURVED hands

POSITIONS: **1.** At the forehead **2.** In front of the chest

MOVEMENT: **1.** Hold the right hand at the forehead as if gripping the brim of a baseball cap; then move the hand forward a few inches while bringing the fingertips and thumbtip together. (This is the sign for *male*.) **2.** Clasp the right and left CURVED hands together with the right hand on top. (This is the sign for *marry*.)

VISUALIZE: Combining the signs for *male* and *marry* suggests a husband.

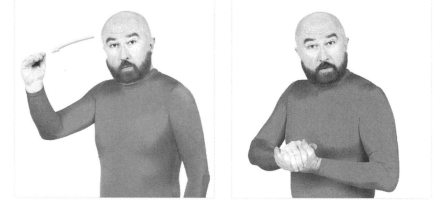

marry • marriage

HANDSHAPE: Right and left CURVED hands

POSITION: In front of the chest

MOVEMENT: Clasp the right and left CURVED hands together with the right hand on top.

VISUALIZE: Two people joining hands in marriage.

Open hand   Curved hand

mother • mom • mama

HANDSHAPE: Right OPEN hand

POSITION: On the center of the chin

MOVEMENT: With the palm facing left, touch the thumbtip of the right OPEN hand twice to the center of the chin while wiggling the fingers slightly.

VISUALIZE: Holding the hand at the female sign position suggests the female head of a family.

name • named • called

HANDSHAPE: Right and left H hands

POSITION: In front of the chest

MOVEMENT: Tap the middle finger of the right H hand against the index finger of the left H hand once or twice.

VISUALIZE: Signing one's name with and "X."

neighbor

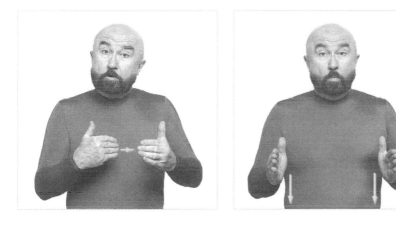

HANDSHAPE: **1.** Right and left CURVED hands **2.** Right and left FLAT hands

POSITION: In front of the chest

MOVEMENT: **1.** Hold the right and left CURVED hands forward, palms facing in. Then move the right hand toward the left hand. (This is the sign for *near*.) **2.** Sign the *person* ending.

VISUALIZE: Signing *near* followed by the *person* ending suggests a person who lives nearby.

H hand

Flat hand

nephew

HANDSHAPE: Right N hand with index and middle fingers extended

POSITION: Next to the right temple

MOVEMENT: Point the extended fingers of the right N hand toward the right temple and shake the hand back and forth slightly from the wrist.

VISUALIZE: Holding the initial N near the male sign position suggests *nephew*.

niece

HANDSHAPE: Right N hand with index and middle fingers extended

POSITION: Next to the right side of the chin

MOVEMENT: Point the extended fingers of the right N hand toward the right side of the chin and shake the hand back and forth slightly from the wrist.

VISUALIZE: Holding the initial N near the female sign position suggests *niece*.

parents

HANDSHAPE: Right P hand

POSITIONS: **1.** On the right temple **2.** On the chin

MOVEMENT: Touch the middle fingertip of the right P hand to the right temple, then to the right side of the chin.

VISUALIZE: Holding the initial P at the male and female sign positions.

N
hand

P
hand

sister

HANDSHAPES: **1.** Right A hand **2.** Right and left ONE hands

POSITIONS: **1.** Starts below the right earlobe **2.** In front of the chest

MOVEMENT: **1.** Starting below the right earlobe, trace the thumbtip of the right A hand down along the jawbone to the chin. (This is the sign for *female*.) **2.** Point the index fingers of the right and left ONE hands forward in front of the chest, palms facing down, and bring the hands together. (This is the sign for *same*.)

VISUALIZE: Combining the signs for *female* and *same* suggests a female member of the same family.

son

HANDSHAPES: **1.** Right hand held as if grasping the brim of a baseball cap **2.** Right CURVED hand

POSITIONS: **1.** At the forehead **2.** In front of the chest

MOVEMENT: **1.** Hold the right hand at the forehead as if grasping the brim of a baseball cap; then move the hand forward a few inches while bringing the fingertips and thumbtip together. (This is the sign for *male*.) **2.** Cradle the right CURVED hand, palm facing up, in the crook of the bent left elbow.

VISUALIZE: Cradling a male baby—your son—in your arms.

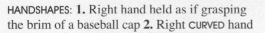

A hand	One hand	Curved hand

sweetheart • lover • courtship • beau

HANDSHAPE: Right and left A hands

POSITION: In front of the chest

MOVEMENT: Hold the right and left A hands together in front of the chest with the palms facing in and the knuckles touching. Then simultaneously straighten and bend both thumbs a couple of times.

VISUALIZE: Two sweethearts nodding affectionately to each other.

uncle

HANDSHAPE: Right U hand

POSITION: Next to the right temple

MOVEMENT: Point the right U hand up next to the right temple, palm facing foward. Then shake the hand back and forth slightly from the wrist.

VISUALIZE: Holding the initial U near the male sign position suggests *uncle*.

wife

HANDSHAPES: **1.** Right A hand **2.** Right and left CURVED hands

POSITIONS: **1.** Starts below the right earlobe **2.** In front of the chest

MOVEMENT: **1.** Starting below the right earlobe, trace the thumbtip of the right A hand down along the jawbone to the chin. (This is the sign for *female*.) **2.** Clasp the right and left CURVED hands together with the right hand on top. (This is the sign for *marry*.)

VISUALIZE: Combining the signs for *female* and *marry* suggests a wife.

A hand   U hand   Curved hand

actions

The words presented in this chapter represent the most common actions—your actions and everybody else's. When you want to *accept* a proposal, *build* a house, *break* a date, *deliver* a newspaper, *applaud* a performer, or *close* a door, this chapter will help you express yourself with accuracy and precision.

accept

HANDSHAPES: Right and left OPEN hands changing to AND hands

POSITION: Starts in front of the chest

MOVEMENT: Point the right and left OPEN hands forward with the palms facing down. Then bring the hands in toward the chest while changing them to the AND handshape and touch the fingertips to the chest.

VISUALIZE: Drawing something towards yourself.

SEE HELPING HANDS ON NEXT PAGE.

When Actions Speak Louder Than Words

Nonverbal communication includes facial expressions, gestures, eye contact, patterns of touch, expressive movements, and any behaviors other than spoken or written communication that create or represent meaning. It's often been said that "actions speak louder than words," and for good reason—nonverbal messages can substitute for, emphasize, or even contradict spoken words. Indeed, nonverbal communication makes it impossible to *not* communicate, because any attempt to obscure or disguise communication is very telling in and of itself.

The importance of nonverbal communication was most prominently studied by the late anthropologist Dr. Ray Birdwhistell of the University of Pennsylvania, who estimated that the average individual actually uses words for only ten to eleven minutes each day, with the standard spoken sentence lasting for around two-and-a-half

Nonverbal communication includes hand gestures and facial expressions.

seconds. According to Birdwhistell, when two people are conversing, less than 35 percent of their communication is verbal, while about 65 percent of the meaning is conveyed by a variety of silent speech signals. Further, Birdwhistell felt that all movements of the body have meaning, and that such movement forms a system of communication that is just as precise as spoken language. While not all experts agree that nonverbal actions have specific language equivalents, studies have shown that up to 90 percent of all communication is nonverbal. And interestingly, 60 percent of that nonverbal communication is expressed, in part, with the hands. This means that during any typical exchange, whether it's an intimate encounter, a casual conversation between friends, an important job interview, or delicate and crucial negotiations, *what* you say often matters far less than *how* you say it.

agree • consent • correspond • coincide

HANDSHAPE: Right and left ONE hands

POSITIONS: **1.** On the forehead **2.** In front of the chest

MOVEMENT: **1.** Touch the index fingertip of the right ONE hand to the forehead while pointing the left ONE hand forward. (This resembles the sign for *think*.) **2.** Move the right hand next to the left, so both are pointing forward with palms facing down. (This is the sign for *same*.)

VISUALIZE: Thinking the same as another person.

Open hand

And hand

One hand

allow • let • permit

HANDSHAPE: Right and left FLAT hands

POSITION: In front of the chest

MOVEMENT: Point the right and left FLAT hands forward with the palms facing each other. Then tilt both hands up until the fingertips point slightly upward and outward. To sign *let*, use L hands; for *permit*, use P hands.

VISUALIZE: Opening the gates to let someone through.

analyze • sort out

HANDSHAPE: Right and left V hands with index and middle fingers curved

POSITION: In front of the chest

MOVEMENT: Point the extended fingers of the right and left V hands toward each other with the palms facing down. Then draw the hands apart to the sides.

VISUALIZE: Peeling back an outer layer to look at what's inside.

appear • rise • show up

HANDSHAPES: Left OPEN hand and right ONE hand

POSITION: In front of the chest

MOVEMENT: Hold the left OPEN hand in front of the chest with the palm facing down. Then poke the index finger of the right ONE hand up between the index and middle fingers of the left hand.

VISUALIZE: Something suddenly popping into view.

Flat hand

V hand

arrive • reach • get to

HANDSHAPE: Right and left CURVED hands

POSITION: In front of the chest

MOVEMENT: Hold the right and left CURVED hands forward, palms facing in, with the right hand about a foot behind the left. Then move the right hand forward until it touches the left palm.

VISUALIZE: The right hand arriving abruptly at the left hand.

attempt • try • effort

HANDSHAPE: Right and left S hands

POSITION: In front of the chest

MOVEMENT: Hold the right and left S hands forward with the palms facing each other. Then push both hands forward. To sign *try,* use T hands; for *effort,* use E hands.

VISUALIZE: Using your fists in an attempt to fight your way through.

behave • behavior

HANDSHAPE: Right and left B hands

POSITION: In front of the chest

MOVEMENT: Hold up the right and left B hands side by side with the palms facing forward. Then swing both hands simultaneously from side to side.

VISUALIZE: Showing your behavior upfront for everyone to see.

Curved
hand

S
hand

B
hand

believe • belief

HANDSHAPES: **1.** Right ONE hand **2.** Right and left CURVED hands

POSITIONS: **1.** On the right side of the forehead **2.** In front of the chest

MOVEMENT: **1.** Touch the index fingertip of the right ONE hand to the forehead. (This resembles the sign for *think*.) **2.** Then clasp the right and left CURVED hands together in front of the chest.

VISUALIZE: Your firm beliefs are worth holding onto.

bother • disturb • interfere

HANDSHAPE: Left and right FLAT hands

POSITION: In front of the chest

MOVEMENT: Hold the left FLAT hand forward with the palm facing in. Bring the little finger side of the right FLAT hand down sharply between the left thumb and index finger several times.

VISUALIZE: The right hand disturbing the left hand.

break • fracture • snap

HANDSHAPE: Right and left s hands

POSITION: In front of the chest

MOVEMENT: Hold the right and left s hands forward, palms facing down, with the index finger sides touching. Then twist the hands outward and apart.

VISUALIZE: Snapping a wooden ruler in half.

One hand

Flat hand

bring • carry • deliver • return

HANDSHAPE: Right and left FLAT hands

POSITION: In front of the chest

MOVEMENT: Hold the right and left FLAT hands forward, palms facing up, with the right hand slightly in front of the left. Then move both hands in toward the body, out toward another person, or to the left or right, depending on where you want to bring the item.

VISUALIZE: A careful waiter carrying a tray.

build • construct • erect

HANDSHAPE: Right and left BENT hands

POSITION: In front of the chest

MOVEMENT: Hold the right and left BENT hands forward, palms facing each other, with the fingers of the right hand above the fingers of the left hand. Then move the hands upward alternately, one above the other.

VISUALIZE: Laying bricks to build a wall.

call • summon

HANDSHAPES: Right FLAT hand changing to A hand and left OPEN hand

POSITION: In front of the chest

MOVEMENT: With the palms facing down, place the fingers of the right FLAT hand on the back of the left OPEN hand. Then draw the right hand up while changing it to the A handshape.

VISUALIZE: Gently touching a person to get his or her attention.

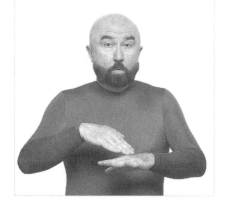

Flat hand

Bent hand

A hand

Open hand

cancel • annul • correct • criticize

HANDSHAPES: Right ONE hand and left FLAT hand

POSITION: In front of the chest

MOVEMENT: Trace an X on the upturned palm of the left FLAT hand with the index fingertip of the right ONE hand.

VISUALIZE: Crossing something out with an "X" to cancel it.

catch • capture • seize • grab • grasp

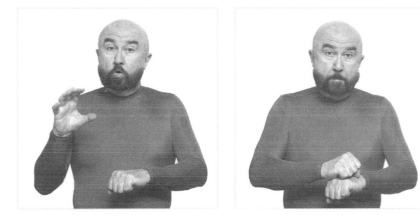

HANDSHAPES: Right CLAWED hand changing to S hand and left S hand

POSITION: In front of the chest

MOVEMENT: With the palms facing down, bring the right CLAWED hand down toward the left S hand while changing the right hand to the S handshape. Let the right hand rest on the back of the left.

VISUALIZE: Catching a sluggish fly in mid-air.

celebrate • rejoice • celebration • triumph • victory

HANDSHAPE: Right and left modified X hands

POSITION: Next to the sides of the head

MOVEMENT: Hold up the right and left modified X hands next to the sides of the head and move both hands in small circular motions.

VISUALIZE: Waving noisemakers at a celebration.

One hand • Clawed hand • S hand • X hand •

change • adjust • adapt • alter

HANDSHAPE: Right and left X hands

POSITION: In front of the chest

MOVEMENT: Hold up the right and left X hands, palms facing each other, with the right palm facing out and the left palm facing in. Then reverse the positions of the hands so the right palm faces in and the left palm faces out.

VISUALIZE: The right hand changing positions with the left.

choose • choice • pick • select

HANDSHAPE: Right OPEN hand and left V hand

POSITION: In front of the chest

MOVEMENT: Use the thumb and index finger of the right OPEN hand to make a picking motion from the extended fingers of the V hand.

VISUALIZE: Picking one particular object from many.

clap • applaud • ovation • praise

HANDSHAPE: Right and left FLAT hands

POSITION: In front of the chest

MOVEMENT: Clap the right and left FLAT hands together several times.

VISUALIZE: The hand motions producing the sound of applause.

X hand   Open hand   V hand   Flat hand

close • shut

HANDSHAPE: Right and left B hands

POSITION: In front of the chest

MOVEMENT: Hold up the right and left B hands side by side with the palms facing forward. Then bring both hands together sharply so the index fingers touch.

VISUALIZE: Two sliding doors coming together.

come

HANDSHAPE: Right and left ONE hands

POSITION: In front of the chest

MOVEMENT: Point the index fingers of the right and left ONE hands toward each other with the palms facing in. Rotate the index fingers in small circles around each other while moving the hands back toward the chest.

VISUALIZE: The hands coming toward the body.

continue • endure • lasting • persevere

HANDSHAPE: Right and left A hands

POSITION: In front of the chest

MOVEMENT: With the palms facing down, touch the thumbtip of the right A hand to the thumbnail of the left A hand and move both hands forward together.

VISUALIZE: A pushing motion suggesting a resolve to continue forward.

B
hand

One
hand

A
hand

control • manage • direct • govern • operate

HANDSHAPE: Right and left modified A hands

POSITION: In front of the chest

MOVEMENT: Hold the right and left modified A hands forward with the thumbtips in the crook of the index fingers and the palms facing each other. Move the hands back and forth a few times.

VISUALIZE: Controlling the reins of a horse-drawn carriage.

cry • sob • weep • tears

HANDSHAPE: Right and left ONE hands

POSITION: Starts just below the eyes

MOVEMENT: Starting just below the eyes, draw the index fingertips of the right and left ONE hands down the cheeks several times.

VISUALIZE: Tears running down the cheeks.

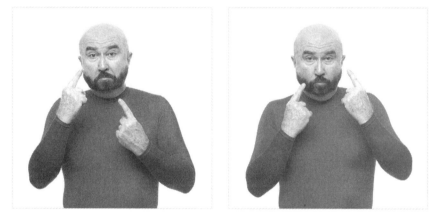

decide • determine • decision • make up one's mind

HANDSHAPES: **1.** Right ONE hand **2.** Right and left F hands

POSITIONS: **1.** On the forehead **2.** Starts in front of the chest

MOVEMENT: **1.** Touch the index fingertip of the right ONE hand to the forehead. **2.** Hold up the right and left F hands in front of the shoulders with the palms facing each other; then drop both hands down in front of the chest.

VISUALIZE: Having thought about something and presenting your decision.

A
hand

One
hand

F
hand

defend • guard • protect

HANDSHAPE: Right and left s hands

POSITION: In front of the chest

MOVEMENT: With the palms facing down, touch the little finger side of the right s hand to the thumb side of the left s hand. Then move the hands forward together.

VISUALIZE: Protecting the body from harm.

develop

HANDSHAPES: Left FLAT hand and right D hand

POSITION: In front of the chest

MOVEMENT: Hold up the left FLAT hand with the palm facing right. Then slide the index finger side of the right D hand up along the left hand from the heel of the hand to the fingertips.

VISUALIZE: A sign suggesting upward growth.

disagree • contradict • object • contrary to

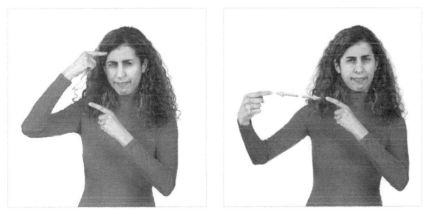

HANDSHAPE: Right and left ONE hands

POSITIONS: 1. On the forehead **2.** In front of the chest

MOVEMENT: 1. Touch the index fingertip of the right ONE hand to the forehead. (This resembles the sign for *think*.) **2.** Touch the index fingertips of the right and left ONE hands together with the palms facing in; then pull the hands apart to the sides. (This is the sign for *opposite*.)

VISUALIZE: Thinking the opposite of another person.

S hand   Flat hand   D hand

disappear • vanish

HANDSHAPES: Left OPEN hand and right ONE hand

POSITION: In front of the chest

MOVEMENT: Hold the left OPEN hand forward with the palm facing down. Place the index finger of the right ONE hand between the left index and middle fingers; then drop the right hand down.

VISUALIZE: Something disappearing from view, Houdini-style.

disappoint • disappointment • disappointed • miss

HANDSHAPE: Right ONE hand

POSITION: On the chin

MOVEMENT: Touch the index fingertip of the right ONE hand to the center of the chin and assume an appropriate facial expression.

VISUALIZE: One who is disappointed might "take it on the chin."

do • action • perform • conduct • deed

HANDSHAPE: Right and left C hands

POSITION: In front of the chest

MOVEMENT: Hold the right and left C hands forward with the palms facing down. Then swing both hands simultaneously from side to side.

VISUALIZE: The motion shows that both hands are busy with some activity.

 Open hand

 One hand

 C hand

don't believe • skeptical

HANDSHAPE: Right V hand

POSITION: In front of the eyes

MOVEMENT: Point the extended fingers of the right V hand toward the eyes; then bend and straighten the V fingers a few times.

VISUALIZE: Showing your skepticism as someone speaks with a forked tongue.

don't care

HANDSHAPES: Right AND hand changing to OPEN hand

POSITION: Starts on the forehead

MOVEMENT: Touch the fingertips of the right AND hand to the forehead; then twist the hand from the wrist so the fingers are pointing forward while changing it to the OPEN handshape.

VISUALIZE: Pulling concerns out of the mind and throwing them away.

don't know • don't recognize • unaware

HANDSHAPE: Right SLIGHTLY CURVED hand

POSITION: Starts on the forehead

MOVEMENT: Tap the fingertips of the right SLIGHTLY CURVED hand against the right side of the forehead. (This is the sign for *know*.) Then twist the hand from the wrist so the palm faces forward.

VISUALIZE: Twisting the hand forward makes the sign for *know* negative.

V hand   And hand   Curved hand

don't want

HANDSHAPE: Right and left CLAWED hands

POSITION: In front of the chest

MOVEMENT: Point the right and left CLAWED hands forward with the palms facing up. Then twist the hands from the wrists so the palms face down.

VISUALIZE: Twisting the hands down makes the sign for *want* negative.

embarrass • shy • bashful

HANDSHAPE: Right and left OPEN hands

POSITION: In front of the face

MOVEMENT: Hold up the right and left OPEN hands in front of the face with the palms facing in and move the hands up and down alternately.

VISUALIZE: Trying to hide the face behind the hands.

encourage • motivate

HANDSHAPE: Right and left FLAT hands

POSITION: In front of the chest

MOVEMENT: Hold the right and left FLAT hands out at the sides of the chest with the palms facing forward and the fingertips pointing out to the sides. Then move the hands forward and toward each other with several short circular motions.

VISUALIZE: Gently urging someone forward with your hands.

Clawed hand

Open hand

Flat hand

enjoy • please • willing • pleasure

HANDSHAPE: Right FLAT hand

POSITION: On the chest

MOVEMENT: Rub the right FLAT hand in a circle on the chest over the heart.

VISUALIZE: Rubbing the hand over the heart suggests a heart-warming experience.

explain • define • describe

HANDSHAPE: Right and left F hands

POSITION: In front of the chest

MOVEMENT: Point the right and left F hands forward with the palms facing each other. Then move the hands alternately away from and toward the body. To sign *define* and *describe*, use D hands.

VISUALIZE: Going back and forth with an idea in an effort to clearly explain it.

fall

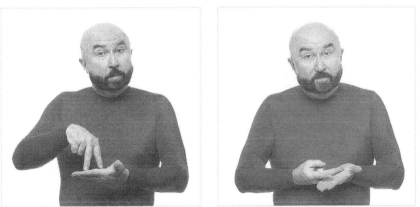

HANDSHAPE: Right V hand and left FLAT hand

POSITION: In front of the chest

MOVEMENT: Place the fingertips of the right V hand on the upturned palm of the left FLAT hand. Then flip the right hand over and place the backs of the V fingers on the left palm.

VISUALIZE: A person falling down on his back.

 F hand V hand

85

find • discover

HANDSHAPES: Right OPEN hand changing to F hand

POSITION: In front of the chest

MOVEMENT: Hold the right OPEN hand forward with the palm facing down. Then raise the hand while changing it to the F handshape.

VISUALIZE: Picking up an object.

finish • complete • all over • done • end

HANDSHAPE: Right and left OPEN hands

POSITION: In front of the chest

MOVEMENT: Point the right and left OPEN hands up in front of the chest with the palms facing in. Then quickly shake them outward a few times.

VISUALIZE: A common gesture for "I wash my hands of the whole thing."

follow • chase • pursue • disciple

HANDSHAPE: Right and left A hands with thumbs extended

POSITION: In front of the chest

MOVEMENT: Hold the right and left A hands forward, palms facing each other, with the right hand slightly behind of the left. Then move both hands forward simultaneously. To sign *disciple,* add the *person* ending.

VISUALIZE: The right hand following the left.

Open hand

F hand

A hand

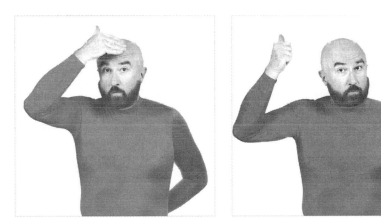

forget • forsake

HANDSHAPES: Right FLAT hand changing to A hand

POSITION: Starts on the forehead

MOVEMENT: Brush the fingertips of the right FLAT hand across the forehead from left to right; then pull the hand off the forehead to the right while changing it to the A handshape.

VISUALIZE: Wiping thoughts from your head.

get • acquire • obtain

HANDSHAPES: Right and left OPEN hands changing to S hands

POSITION: In front of the chest

MOVEMENT: Point the right and left OPEN hands forward with the palms facing each other. Then bring the hands together while closing them into the S handshape, and place the right hand on top of the left.

VISUALIZE: Grabbing something for oneself.

give

HANDSHAPES: Right and left AND hands changing to OPEN hands

POSITION: In front of the chest

MOVEMENT: Hold the right and left AND hands forward with the fingers pointing up. Then move both hands forward while opening them.

VISUALIZE: Giving an object to someone.

Flat hand   S hand   And hand

go

HANDSHAPE: Right and left ONE hands

POSITION: In front of the chest

MOVEMENT: Point the index fingers of the right and left ONE hands toward each other with the palms facing in. Rotate the fingers in small circles around each other while moving the hands forward and away from the chest.

VISUALIZE: Going in circles.

have • has • had • possess

HANDSHAPE: Right and left CURVED hands

POSITION: On the chest

MOVEMENT: Touch the fingertips of the right and left CURVED hands to the chest.

VISUALIZE: Holding personal property close to the body to show possession.

help • aid • assist • boost

HANDSHAPES: Left S hand and right FLAT hand

POSITION: In front of the chest

MOVEMENT: Place the little finger side of the left S hand on the upturned palm of the right FLAT hand and lift both hands together.

VISUALIZE: The right hand provides a boost for the left hand.

One
hand

Curved
hand

S
hand

Flat
hand

hide • conceal

HANDSHAPES: Left BENT hand and right A hand

POSITION: In front of the chest

MOVEMENT: Hold the left BENT hand forward with the palm facing down. Touch the thumbnail of the right S hand to the lips. (This is the sign for *secret*.) Then move the right hand down and under the left hand.

VISUALIZE: Hiding the right hand under the left.

hit

HANDSHAPES: Left ONE hand and right S hand

POSITION: In front of the chest

MOVEMENT: Hold up the left ONE hand with the palm facing in. Then strike the knuckles of the right S hand aggressively against the left index finger.

VISUALIZE: Hitting an object.

hold

HANDSHAPE: Right and left S hands

POSITION: In front of the chest

MOVEMENT: Hold the right and left S hands forward, palms facing in, with the right hand on top of the left. Then move both hands a short distance in toward the body.

VISUALIZE: Holding on to a baseball bat.

Bent hand A hand

89

include · involve

HANDSHAPES: Left c hand and right OPEN hand changing to AND hand

POSITION: In front of the chest

MOVEMENT: Hold the left c hand forward with the fingers pointing to the right. Then, starting with the palm facing up, sweep the right OPEN hand in front of the body from right to left while changing it to the AND handshape. Finally, tuck the fingers of the right AND hand into the left c hand.

VISUALIZE: Including an object with others in a group.

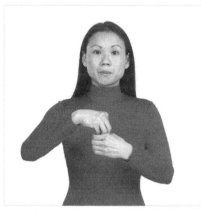

introduce

HANDSHAPE: Right and left FLAT hands

POSITION: Starts near the sides of the chest

MOVEMENT: Hold the right and left FLAT hands near the sides of the chest, palms facing up, with the fingertips pointing toward each other. Then bring the hands together until the fingertips almost touch.

VISUALIZE: Introducing the right hand to the left.

invite · greet · welcome · hire · employ

HANDSHAPE: Right FLAT hand

POSITION: In front of the chest

MOVEMENT: Hold the right FLAT hand forward with the palm facing up. Then swing the hand down and in toward the right side. To sign *hire,* use the H hand.

VISUALIZE: Inviting a friend to come inside and join you; a common gesture of welcome.

 C hand

Open hand

And hand

Flat hand

jump · hop · leap

HANDSHAPES: Right V hand and left FLAT hand

POSITION: In front of the chest

MOVEMENT: Place the fingertips of the right V hand on the upturned palm of the left FLAT hand and imitate a jumping motion.

VISUALIZE: The V fingers show the motion of the legs when jumping.

keep

HANDSHAPE: Right and left K hands

POSITION: In front of the chest

MOVEMENT: Hold the right and left K hands forward with the palms facing in opposite directions. Then tap the little finger side of the right hand a few times on the index finger side of the left hand.

VISUALIZE: The initial K fingertips represent eyes looking around to suggest the phrase "keep an eye out."

kiss

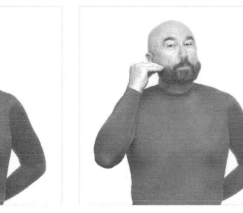

HANDSHAPE: Right AND hand

POSITION: Starts on the lips

MOVEMENT: Touch the fingertips of the right AND hand to the lips, then to the right cheek. (Common usage sign.)

VISUALIZE: A kiss on the lips and then on the cheek.

V hand

K hand

know • recognize • knowledge • intelligence

HANDSHAPE: Right SLIGHTLY CURVED hand

POSITION: On the forehead

MOVEMENT: Tap the fingertips of the right SLIGHTLY CURVED hand against the right side of the forehead a few times.

VISUALIZE: Knowledge being stored in the mind.

laugh • chuckle • giggle • smile

HANDSHAPES: Right and left L hands changing to A hands

POSITION: Starts near the corners of the mouth

MOVEMENT: With the palms facing in, point the index fingers of the right and left L hands toward the corners of the mouth. Then move both hands outward and upward while changing them to the A handshape.

VISUALIZE: The mouth broadening into a smile, and that's A-Okay.

lead • guide • conduct

HANDSHAPES: Left FLAT hand and right AND hand

POSITION: In front of the chest

MOVEMENT: Point the left FLAT hand forward with the palm facing to the right. Grasp the fingertips of the left hand with the thumbtip and fingertips of the right AND hand and pull the left hand forward.

VISUALIZE: One hand pulling the other hand forward.

Curved hand

L hand

A hand

Flat hand

leave • depart • retire • withdraw

HANDSHAPES: Right and left OPEN hands changing to A hands

POSITION: Starts near the left side of the chest

MOVEMENT: With the palms facing down, point the right and left OPEN hands forward near the left side of the chest. Then bring both hands up and toward the center of the chest while changing them to the A handshape.

VISUALIZE: Withdrawing the fingers as the hands retire.

look • look at • gaze • observe • watch

HANDSHAPE: Right V hand

POSITION: In front of the eyes

MOVEMENT: Point the extended fingers of the right V hand at the eyes; then point the fingers in the intended direction.

VISUALIZE: The V fingertips represent my eyes looking at you.

lose

HANDSHAPES: Right and left AND hands changing to OPEN hands

POSITION: In front of the chest

MOVEMENT: Touch the fingertips of the right and left AND hands together with the palms facing up. Then pull the hands apart and drop them down while opening the fingers.

VISUALIZE: Losing something as it drops from your hands.

And hand

Open hand

V hand

make • fashion • fix

HANDSHAPE: Right and left s hands

POSITION: In front of the chest

MOVEMENT: Strike the right s hand, palm facing left, on top of the left s hand, palm facing right. Then twist the hands slightly so the palms face inward. Repeat a few times.

VISUALIZE: Screwing two pieces of pipe together.

mean • intend • purpose

HANDSHAPES: Left FLAT hand and right v hand

POSITION: In front of the chest

MOVEMENT: Point the left FLAT hand forward with the palm facing right. Then, with the palm facing down, touch the fingertips of the right v hand to the left palm. Draw the right hand away from the left palm slightly, rotate it in a clockwise direction, and then touch the v fingertips again to the left palm.

VISUALIZE: Carefully mapping out your moves.

meet • encounter • greet

HANDSHAPE: Right and left ONE hands

POSITION: In front of the chest

MOVEMENT: Hold up the right and left ONE hands with the palms facing each other. Then bring both hands together until the knuckles touch.

VISUALIZE: Two people meeting each other.

S hand

Flat hand

V hand

One hand

miss • guess

HANDSHAPES: Right C hand changing to S hand

POSITION: In front of the forehead

MOVEMENT: Hold up the right C hand in front of the forehead with the fingers pointing to the left. Then move the hand to the left while changing it to the S handshape.

VISUALIZE: Trying to catch something that's moving quickly.

misunderstand

HANDSHAPE: Right V hand

POSITION: On the center of the forehead

MOVEMENT: Touch the middle fingertip of the right V hand to the center of the forehead with the palm facing in. Then twist the hand from the wrist so the palm faces forward, and touch the index fingertip to the forehead.

VISUALIZE: An idea being twisted around in the mind.

offer • present • suggest • propose • submit

 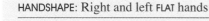

HANDSHAPE: Right and left FLAT hands

POSITION: In front of the chest

MOVEMENT: Point the right and left FLAT hands forward with the palms facing up. Then move both hands upward and forward.

VISUALIZE: Offering an object or idea to someone.

C
hand

open

HANDSHAPE: Right and left FLAT hands

POSITION: In front of the chest

MOVEMENT: Hold the right and left FLAT hands with the palms facing forward and the side of the thumbs touching. Then simultaneously move both hands to the sides while rotating the wrists, so that the hands end up apart with the palms facing each other.

VISUALIZE: Drawing open a pair of doors.

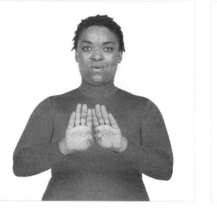 

pay attention • attention

HANDSHAPE: Right and left FLAT hands

POSITION: Near the sides of the face

MOVEMENT: Hold up the right and left FLAT hands near the sides of the face with the palms facing each other. Then move both hands forward.

VISUALIZE: Focusing attention on something directly ahead.

play • recreation

HANDSHAPE: Right and left Y hands

POSITION: In front of the chest

MOVEMENT: Hold the right and left Y hands forward with the palms facing in. Pivot the hands from the wrists a few times.

VISUALIZE: The Y hands playing around with each other.

 Flat hand  Y hand

practice • discipline • training

HANDSHAPES: Left ONE hand and right A hand

POSITION: In front of the chest

MOVEMENT: Point the left ONE hand forward with the palm facing right. Then slide the knuckles of the right A hand back and forth along the left index finger.

VISUALIZE: Polishing up your act.

prevent • block • hinder • obstruct

HANDSHAPE: Left and right FLAT hands

POSITION: In front of the chest

MOVEMENT: Hold up the left FLAT hand with the palm facing right. Then, with the palm facing down, touch the little-finger side of the right FLAT hand to the index finger of the left FLAT hand and move both hands forward together.

VISUALIZE: A typical karate blocking position.

push

HANDSHAPE: Right and left FLAT hands

POSITION: In front of the chest

MOVEMENT: Hold up the right and left FLAT hands with the palms facing forward. Then push both hands forward.

VISUALIZE: Pushing a swinging door open.

One hand

A hand

put • move

HANDSHAPES: Right and left CURVED hands changing to AND hands

POSITION: In front of the chest

MOVEMENT: Hold the right and left CURVED hands forward with the palms facing down. The draw the hands up and over to the right while changing them to the AND handshape.

VISUALIZE: Lifting an object and putting it down in a different place.

read

HANDSHAPES: Left FLAT hand and right V hand

POSITION: In front of the chest

MOVEMENT: Point the left FLAT hand to the right with the palm facing in. Then, with the palm facing down, point the fingertips of the right V hand at the left palm and move the right hand down.

VISUALIZE: Two eyes reading a page of a book.

refuse • will not • won't

HANDSHAPE: Right A hand

POSITION: In front of the right shoulder

MOVEMENT: Hold up the right A hand in front of the right shoulder with the palm facing left. Then move the hand sharply up and over the right shoulder, turning the head to the left at the same time.

VISUALIZE: I refuse to hitchhike.

Curved hand

And hand

Flat hand

V hand

remember • memory • recollect • recall

HANDSHAPE: Right and left A hands

POSITIONS: **1.** On the right side of the forehead **2.** In front of the chest

MOVEMENT: **1.** Touch the thumbtip of the right A hand to the right side of the forehead with the palm facing down. **2.** With the palms facing in, touch the thumbtip of the right A hand to the thumbnail of the left A hand.

VISUALIZE: Securing a memory by pinning it down.

run • sprint • hustle

HANDSHAPE: Left and right L hands

POSITION: In front of the chest

MOVEMENT: Point the left L hand forward with the palm facing right. Hook the index finger of the right L hand around the left thumb. Move both hands forward together quickly while wiggling thumbs and index fingers.

VISUALIZE: Shooting ahead.

say • speak • mention • tell • remark • speech

HANDSHAPE: Right ONE hand

POSITION: In front of the mouth

MOVEMENT: Point the index finger of the right ONE hand to the left in front of the mouth with the palm facing in. Then move the hand forward and away from the mouth in small circles.

VISUALIZE: Words pouring out of the mouth. (Depending on the context in which it is used, this sign is identical to the one that represents a hearing person.)

A hand   L hand   One hand

search

talking with your hands listening with your eyes

search • seek • examine • research

HANDSHAPE: Right C hand

POSITION: In front of the face

MOVEMENT: With the palm facing left, move the right C hand in a circular motion in front of the face from right to left. Repeat a few times.

VISUALIZE: Using binoculars to see far and wide.

send

HANDSHAPES: Left BENT hand and right BENT hand changing to FLAT hand

POSITION: In front of the chest

MOVEMENT: Hold the left BENT hand forward with the palm facing down. Touch the fingertips of the right BENT hand to the back of the left hand; then swing the right hand forward while straightening the fingers.

VISUALIZE: Flicking a bug off the left hand to send it away.

sign

HANDSHAPE: Right and left ONE hands

POSITION: In front of the chest

MOVEMENT: Point the index fingers of the right and left ONE hands up, with the palms facing each other. Then circle the hands alternately back toward the body.

VISUALIZE: Imitating the movements used in signing.

helping hands

100

 C hand

Bent hand

Flat hand

  One hand

sit • be seated • seat

HANDSHAPE: Right and left H hands

POSITION: In front of the chest

MOVEMENT: With the palms facing down, hook the extended fingers of the right H hand over the extended fingers of the left H hand. Then move both hands down slightly.

VISUALIZE: The right H fingers represent a person's legs hanging over the seat of a chair.

stand

HANDSHAPES: Right V hand and left FLAT hand

POSITION: In front of the chest

MOVEMENT: Place the fingertips of the right V hand on the upturned palm of the left FLAT hand.

VISUALIZE: The right V fingers represent a person's legs standing up.

start • begin • commence • initiate

HANDSHAPES: Left OPEN hand and right ONE hand

POSITION: In front of the chest

MOVEMENT: Point the left OPEN hand forward with the palm facing right. Place the index fingertip of the right ONE hand between the left index and middle fingers; then twist the right hand in a clockwise direction.

VISUALIZE: Turning a key to start an engine.

H hand   V hand   Open hand

stay • remain

HANDSHAPE: Right Y hand

POSITION: In front of the chest

MOVEMENT: Hold the right Y hand in front of the top of the chest, with the hand pointing forward and the palm facing down. Firmly move the hand downward to the middle of the chest.

VISUALIZE: Signaling the family dog to stay in place.

stop • halt • cease

HANDSHAPE: Right and left FLAT hands

POSITION: In front of the chest

MOVEMENT: Bring the little finger side of the right FLAT hand sharply down upon the upturned palm of the left FLAT hand.

VISUALIZE: Dropping down a barrier.

surprise • astonish • astound • amaze • startle

HANDSHAPES: Right and left modified X hands changing to L hands

POSITION: Near the temples

MOVEMENT: Hold up the right and left modified X hands near the temples with the palms facing each other; then flick both index fingers up simultaneously, forming L hands.

VISUALIZE: Eyes suddenly widening in surprise.

 Y hand Flat hand X hand L hand

take

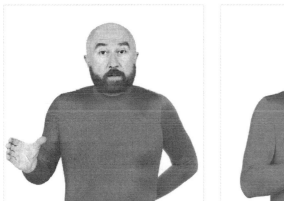

HANDSHAPES: Right CURVED hand changing to s hand

POSITION: In front of the chest

MOVEMENT: Point the right CURVED hand forward with the palm facing left. Then draw the hand in toward the body while changing it to the s handshape.

VISUALIZE: Reaching out and grabbing hold of an object.

talk • communicate • conversation • interview

HANDSHAPE: Right and left ONE hands

POSITION: In front of the mouth

MOVEMENT: Hold up the right and left ONE hands in front of the mouth with the palms facing toward each other; then move the hands alternately back and forth from the lips. To sign *communicate* or *conversation*, use c hands; and for *interview*, use I hands.

VISUALIZE: Words being exchanged.

think • consider • speculate

HANDSHAPE: Right ONE hand

POSITION: Near the right side of the forehead

MOVEMENT: Point the index finger of the right ONE hand toward the right side of the forehead and move the hand in a counterclockwise circle.

VISUALIZE: Wheels turning in the mind.

Curved hand

S hand

One hand

Alexander Graham Bell

Although Alexander Graham Bell is best known for inventing the telephone, he's also celebrated as a pioneer in the education of the deaf. Born in Edinburgh, Scotland, on March 3, 1847, Bell developed an interest in hearing and speech early in his life. His father, Alexander Melville Bell, invented "Visible Speech," a series of symbols that showed the position and action of the throat, tongue, and lips in making sounds; he used these symbols to help deaf people learn to speak. In 1862, Bell began aiding his father in public demonstrations of Visible Speech, and by 1869, he became his father's partner in London. At about this time, he began experimenting with acoustics, which sparked his interest in improving the telegraph to transmit speech—something many inventors had already attempted without success.

Alexander Graham Bell

When both of Bell's brothers died of tuberculosis in 1870, his family moved to Brantford, Ontario, Canada, to take advantage of a healthier climate. Shortly thereafter, in 1872, Bell opened a school for teachers of the deaf in Boston. Through his work in Boston, he became friends with attorney Gardiner Green Hubbard, whose daughter Mabel had been left deaf by scarlet fever as a child. Hubbard was an outspoken critic of the Western Union Telegraph company, and offered Bell financial assistance to help him make improvements to the telegraph.

In September 1875, Bell began to write specifications to patent an instrument that could carry speech by wire—the telephone. His patent was issued on March 7, 1876, and, just three days later, he successfully transmitted human speech for the first time. That same year, Bell married Mabel Hubbard.

Bell was awarded the Volta Prize by the French government in 1880 for his invention of the telephone. He used the 50,000 francs he received to help establish the Volta Laboratory for research, invention, and work for the deaf. In 1890, Bell founded the American Association to Promote the Teaching of Speech to the Deaf, which is now known as the Alexander Graham Bell Association for the Deaf.

Alexander Graham Bell spent most of his later life at his estate in Nova Scotia. He died on August 2, 1922, at the age of seventy-five, surrounded by his family.

throw • toss

HANDSHAPES: Right A hand changing to OPEN hand

POSITION: Starts next to the right side of the head

MOVEMENT: Hold the right A hand next to the right side of the head with the palm facing forward. Then bring the hand forward quickly while opening the fingers.

VISUALIZE: Throwing a ball.

A
hand

Open
hand

understand • comprehend • perceive

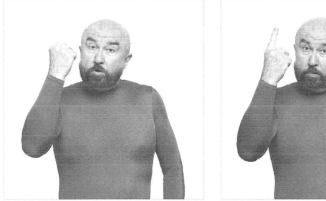

HANDSHAPES: Right S hand changing to ONE hand

POSITION: In front of the forehead

MOVEMENT: Hold up the right S hand in front of the forehead with the palm facing in. Then point the index finger up to form the ONE handshape.

VISUALIZE: A light bulb being turned on in the mind.

use • utilize • useful

HANDSHAPE: Right U hand

POSITION: In front of the right shoulder

MOVEMENT: Hold up the right U hand in front of the right shoulder with the palm facing foward. Then move the hand in a clockwise circular motion.

VISUALIZE: Making use of your U hand around the clock.

walk • step

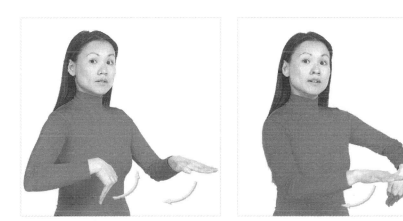

HANDSHAPE: Right and left FLAT hands

POSITION: In front of the chest

MOVEMENT: Point the right and left FLAT hands forward with the palms facing down. Then move the hands foward alternately.

VISUALIZE: The motion of feet when walking forward.

S
hand

One
hand

U
hand

Flat
hand

want • desire

HANDSHAPE: Right and left CLAWED hands

POSITION: In front of the chest

MOVEMENT: Point the right and left CLAWED hands forward with the palms facing up. Then pull both hands in toward the body a few times.

VISUALIZE: Pulling something you want toward yourself.

wash • rub • wipe

HANDSHAPE: Right and left A hands

POSITION: In front of the chest

MOVEMENT: Hold the right and left A hands together with the right palm facing down and the left palm facing up. Rub the right hand in circles on the left hand.

VISUALIZE: Scrubbing something clean.

wish • desire

HANDSHAPE: Right C hand

POSITION: Starts just below the throat

MOVEMENT: Hold the right C hand just below the throat with the palm facing in. Then drop the hand straight down to the center of the chest. (This is also the sign for *hungry*.)

VISUALIZE: Using the sign for *hungry* to indicate a desire for something.

 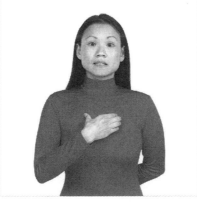

 Clawed hand

A hand

 C hand

worry

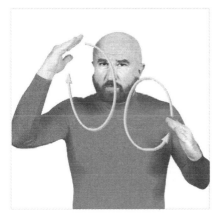

HANDSHAPE: Right and left FLAT hands

POSITION: Starts near the sides of the head

MOVEMENT: Hold up the right and left FLAT hands near the sides of the head with the palms facing each other. Pass the right hand down in front of the face in a circular motion. Then do the same with the left hand. Repeat.

VISUALIZE: Piling up worry upon worry in the mind.

write • edit

HANDSHAPES: Left FLAT hand and right A hand with thumbtip and index fingertip pressed together

POSITION: In front of the chest

MOVEMENT: Point the left FLAT hand to the right with the palm facing in. Then move the thumbtip and index fingertip of the right A hand across the left palm in a wavy motion.

VISUALIZE: Writing on a pad with a pen.

Flat
hand

New Ways to Stay in Touch

For many years, the deaf and hard-of-hearing relied on text telephones, or TTY, to stay in touch with friends, family, and business colleagues. (See the inset on page 116.) Unfortunately, there was a drawback: TTY users could communicate only with other people with TTY devices. Later, the Telecommunications Relay Service (TRS) provided assistants to act as go-betweens for people with text telephones who wished to speak to people without such devices. (See page 8.) Still, communication was awkward, and was impossible for anyone who wanted to send and receive information on the go. While hearing people could keep in touch with cell phones, technology was not helping the hearing-impaired employee who wished to call his office from the road, or the deaf student who needed to contact his parents from his high school campus.

Now, a number of amazing technological devices have made communication fast and easy for individuals with hearing impairments. First among these devices is the two-way pager. A hand-held two-way messaging device with a small keyboard, two-way pagers have provided a simple way to send and receive messages from anywhere.

Two-Way Pager

In essence, these products work like mobile phones, except that text is exchanged rather than voice.

Yet another convenient way to keep in touch is the two-way text-based mobile e-mail service, which offers easy access to e-mail anywhere from virtually any telephone. To send and receive e-mail, the user simply types a message on the device, dials a 1-800 telephone number on almost any phone, and holds the device up to the phone. E-mail can then be sent and received, and can even be retrieved from other e-mail accounts.

Some mobile devices combine a number of services to offer several means of communication. One product, for instance, combines mobile e-mail service with two-way messaging, and even allows the two-way real-time conversations traditionally associated with a "wired" TTY device.

Naturally, both two-way pagers and mobile e-mail services are used by hearing individuals, as well. But for deaf or hard-of-hearing individuals, these portable devices offer a freedom never enjoyed before—the freedom to stay in touch with nearly anyone at any time, no matter where they are.

chapter

5

home
& clothing

This chapter focuses on the signs you need to discuss just about anything in and around the house. With a little practice, you'll soon feel "at home" using these signs to express yourself, whether you want to open a *window,* tidy up the *kitchen,* redecorate your *bedroom,* replace worn-out *furniture,* watch a program on *television,* or just slip into your *pajamas* to go to sleep.

HOME

bed

HANDSHAPE: Right and left FLAT hands

POSITION: On the right cheek

MOVEMENT: Hold the right and left FLAT hands together with the palms touching. Then rest the right cheek on the back of the left hand.

VISUALIZE: Placing your head on a pillow.

SEE HELPING HANDS ON NEXT PAGE.

Feeling at Home in a World Without Sound

Hearing people don't think twice when the doorbell chimes or the telephone rings or the alarm clock buzzes—they answer the door or pick up the phone or hit the snooze button. But these simple actions that hearing people take for granted can offer challenges for people who can't hear or who have trouble hearing. For individuals whose hearing loss is not very severe, extra-loud doorbells, telephone ringers, and alarm-clock buzzers may suffice. However, there are also many alerting devices available for deaf and hard-of-hearing people that make use of the other four senses. These devices use signals that are visual, such as flashing lights, or vibrotactile, meaning that they vibrate. For example, flashing lights can be used to indicate sounds such as the doorbell, the telephone, and even a baby's cry. Sometimes, one flashing light system can alert a deaf person to several different sounds with a simple code that identifies the source of the sound—three slow flashes mean the doorbell is ringing, three quick flashes show that the telephone is ringing, and so forth. Flashing lights can also be used with alarm clocks for people who are very sensitive to light. However, many people prefer to use a vibrating pad placed inside the pillow case to gently shake them awake.

bedroom

HANDSHAPES: **1.** Right FLAT hand **2.** Right and left R hands

POSITIONS: **1.** On the right cheek **2.** In front of the chest

MOVEMENT: **1.** Hold the palm of the right FLAT hand near your right cheek. (This resembles the sign for *bed*.) **2.** Point the right and left R hands forward in front of the chest with the palms facing each other. Then turn both hands so the palms face in and the left hand is closer to the body. (This is the sign for *room*.)

VISUALIZE: Combining the signs for *bed* and *room*.

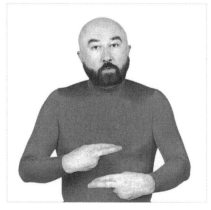

Flat hand

R hand

blanket

HANDSHAPES: Right and left OPEN hands changing to AND hands

POSITION: In front of the chest

MOVEMENT: Point the right and left OPEN hands forward with palms facing down. Then lift both hands up to the shoulders while changing them to the AND handshape.

VISUALIZE: Pulling up a blanket to keep warm.

chair • seat

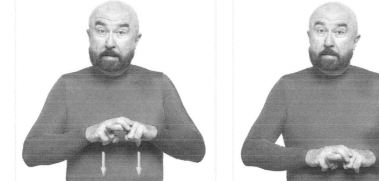

HANDSHAPE: Right and left H hands

POSITION: In front of the chest

MOVEMENT: With the palms facing down, hook the extended fingers of the right H hand over the extended fingers of the left H hand. Then move both hands down slightly.

VISUALIZE: The right H fingers represent a person's legs hanging over the seat of a chair.

door

HANDSHAPE: Right and left B hands

POSITION: In front of the chest

MOVEMENT: Point the right and left B hands up with the index finger sides of the hands touching. Pivot the right hand back and forth from the wrist.

VISUALIZE: Opening one side of a double door.

Open hand

And hand

H hand

B hand

dryer

HANDSHAPES: 1. Right modified X hand
2. Right and left FLAT hands

POSITION: 1. In front of the mouth **2.** Near the sides of the chest

MOVEMENT: 1. With the palm facing down, move the right modified X hand across the lips from left to right. **2.** Point the right and left FLAT hands forward with the palms facing each other, and move them down simultaneously a short distance. (This resembles the *person* ending.)

VISUALIZE: Pulling the moisture out of clothes by placing them in a dryer.

electricity

HANDSHAPE: Right and left X hands with middle fingers bent

POSITION: In front of the chest

MOVEMENT: Point the right and left X hands toward each other with the palms facing in. Then tap the knuckles of the index and middle fingers together a few times.

VISUALIZE: Two electric plugs meeting.

floor

HANDSHAPE: Right and left B hands

POSITION: In front of the chest

MOVEMENT: Point the right and left B hands forward with the palms facing down and the index finger sides of the hands touching. Then move the hands apart to each side of the chest.

VISUALIZE: The flat surface of the floor.

X hand

Flat hand

B hand

furniture

HANDSHAPE: Right F hand

POSITION: In front of the chest

MOVEMENT: Hold up the right F hand in front of the right shoulder with the palm facing forward. Shake the hand back and forth a few times.

VISUALIZE: Moving furniture from one place to another.

home

HANDSHAPE: Right AND hand changing to right FLAT hand

POSITIONS: First on the lips, then on the right cheek

MOVEMENT: Touch the thumbtip and fingertips of the right AND hand to the lips. Then move the hand near your right cheek while changing it to a FLAT hand.

VISUALIZE: Home is where you eat your meals and rest your head.

house • residence

HANDSHAPE: Right and left FLAT hands

POSITION: In front of the chest

MOVEMENT: Touch the fingertips of the right and left FLAT hands together, palms facing each other, to form a triangle below the face. Then move the hands apart and down to either side of the chest, ending with the fingers pointing up.

VISUALIZE: The roof and walls of a house.

F hand

And hand

key • lock • lock up

HANDSHAPES: Right X hand and left FLAT hand

POSITION: In front of the chest

MOVEMENT: Place the index finger of the right X hand in the palm of the left FLAT hand and twist the right hand clockwise.

VISUALIZE: Turning the key to lock the door.

kitchen

HANDSHAPES: Right K hand and left FLAT hand

POSITION: In front of the chest

MOVEMENT: Place the fingertips of the right K hand, palm facing down, on the upturned palm of the left FLAT hand. Then flip the right hand over and place the backs of the K fingers on the left palm.

VISUALIZE: Using the initial K to form a sign similar to *cook*.

lamp

HANDSHAPES: Right AND hand changing to OPEN hand

POSITION: To the right of the head

MOVEMENT: Point the fingertips of the right AND hand toward the right side of the head; then open the fingers.

VISUALIZE: Light streaming from a lamp that's been turned on.

X hand

Flat hand

K hand

And hand

mirror

HANDSHAPE: Right CURVED hand

POSITION: In front of the face

MOVEMENT: Hold up the right CURVED hand in front of the face with the palm facing in. Then twist the hand side to side from the wrist.

VISUALIZE: Gazing into a hand mirror.

radio

HANDSHAPE: Right CLAWED hand

POSITION: Over the right ear

MOVEMENT: Cup the right CLAWED hand over the right ear and twist the hand back and forth a few times.

VISUALIZE: Adjusting a large radio tuning knob.

refrigerator

HANDSHAPE: Right and left R hands

POSITION: In front of the shoulders

MOVEMENT: Hold up the right and left R hands with the palms facing forward and shake them.

VISUALIZE: Using the initial R to form a sign similar to *cold*.

Open hand	Curved hand	Clawed hand	R hand

room

HANDSHAPE: Right and left FLAT hands

POSITION: In front of the chest

MOVEMENT: Point the right and left FLAT hands forward with the palms facing each other. Then turn both hands so the palms face in and the left hand is closer to the body.

VISUALIZE: The four walls of a room.

table

HANDSHAPE: Right and left FLAT hands

POSITION: In front of the chest

MOVEMENT: Fold the arms without crossing them, so that the right forearm rests directly on the left forearm. Then use the right FLAT hand to pat the top of the left elbow several times.

VISUALIZE: Resting both arms on top of a table.

How Do Deaf People Use the Telephone?

People who are deaf or hard of hearing can use a text telephone, or TTY, to communicate by telephone without an interpreter. The TTY device resembles a word processor, with a keyboard and a display screen. Both sender and receiver must have compatible TTYs, because the information is converted to signals that travel over telephone lines.

To place a call, the TTY user turns on the device, dials the number on a regular telephone, and then places the telephone headset on the TTY coupler, which is similar to a computer modem. When a pattern of lights on the display screen shows that someone has answered the TTY, the caller types a greeting. The person receiving the call knows when the phone is ringing because of a flashing signal light. To take an incoming call, the TTY user places the telephone headset on the TTY coupler and turns on the device. The person receiving the call then types his or her greeting—for example, "This is Gabriel"—followed by "GA," which is the abbreviation for "go ahead," prompting the caller to type a response. The caller gives his or her own name, and then conversation can proceed. During the conversation, the participants type "GA" after every sentence to let the other person know that it's his or her turn to respond.

Flat
hand

How Do Deaf People Watch Television?

People who are deaf or hard of hearing can enjoy television programs with the help of closed captioning. Closed captions are hidden in the video signal that the television receives and are invisible without a special caption decoder. When the decoder is turned on, captions appear as text on the television screen, allowing people who can't hear their programs to "read" them instead. About 400 hours worth of television programs are captioned each week, including most network movies.

Caption decoders are available as external devices and are also built into television sets. Since the Television Decoder Circuitry Act went into effect in July 1993, all televisions with screens thirteen inches or larger sold in the United States must contain built-in caption decoders that allow viewers to display closed captions on their sets. In 1996, Congress passed a law requiring video program distributors (cable operators, broadcasters, and satellite distributors) to phase in closed captions of their television programs.

telephone

HANDSHAPE: Right Y hand

POSITION: Next to the right cheek

MOVEMENT: Hold the right Y hand so that the palm faces backwards, with the thumb near the ear and the little finger near the mouth.

VISUALIZE: Talking on the telephone.

television • TV

HANDSHAPES: Right T hand changing to V hand

POSITION: In front of the right shoulder

MOVEMENT: Hold up the right T hand in front of the right shoulder with the palm facing forward. Then move the hand out to the right while changing it to the V handshape.

VISUALIZE: The initials T and V spell out *TV*.

Y hand   T hand   V hand

toilet • bathroom • lavatory

HANDSHAPE: Right T hand

POSITION: In front of the right shoulder

MOVEMENT: Hold up the right T hand in front of the right shoulder with the palm facing forward. Shake the hand back and forth a few times.

VISUALIZE: Raising your T hand in class to get permission to go to the bathroom.

washing machine

HANDSHAPE: Right and left CLAWED hands

POSITION: In front of the chest

MOVEMENT: Point the right and left CLAWED hands forward, palms facing each other, with the right hand above the left. Move the hands in twisting circular motions, rotating them in opposite directions.

VISUALIZE: The twisting motion of a washing machine's agitator.

window

HANDSHAPE: Right and left FLAT hands

POSITION: In front of the chest

MOVEMENT: With the palms facing in, place the little finger side of the right FLAT hand on the thumb side of the left FLAT hand. The draw the right hand up.

VISUALIZE: Opening a window.

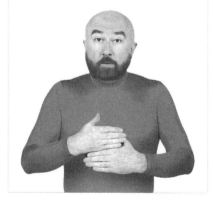 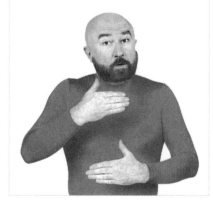

T hand | Clawed hand | Flat hand

CLOTHES & ACCESSORIES

blouse

HANDSHAPE: Right CURVED hand

POSITION: Starts on the right shoulder

MOVEMENT: With the palm facing down, touch the thumb side of the right CURVED hand to the right shoulder. Then turn the hand over and touch the little finger side to the right side of the waist with the palm facing up.

VISUALIZE: Showing that a blouse is loose and flowing.

button

HANDSHAPE: Right F hand

POSITION: On the chest

MOVEMENT: With the palm facing left, touch the index finger side of the right F hand to the center of the chest. Repeat a few more times, moving the hand down each time.

VISUALIZE: Showing the buttons on a shirt.

clothes · dress · suit · costume · wear

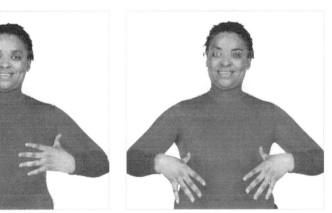

HANDSHAPE: Right and left OPEN hands

POSITION: On the chest

MOVEMENT: With the palms facing in, sweep the fingertips of the right and left OPEN hands down over the chest a few times.

VISUALIZE: Drawing attention to the clothes you're wearing.

Curved hand

F hand

Open hand

coat • overcoat • jacket

HANDSHAPE: Right and left A hands

POSITION: Starts in front of the shoulders

MOVEMENT: Hold the right and left A hands in front of the shoulders with the palms facing in. Then move both hands down in a slight forward curve, stopping in front of the waist.

VISUALIZE: Tracing the shape of coat lapels with your thumbs.

gloves

HANDSHAPE: Right and left OPEN hands

POSITION: In front of the chest

MOVEMENT: Hold up the left OPEN hand with the palm facing in. Then move the right OPEN hand down over the back of the left hand a few times.

VISUALIZE: Pulling on a glove.

hat

HANDSHAPE: Right OPEN hand.

POSITION: On top of the head.

MOVEMENT: Pat the top of the head with the right OPEN hand a few times.

VISUALIZE: Showing where a hat is worn.

A
hand

Open
hand

necktie

HANDSHAPE: Right and left U hands

POSITION: Starts near the top of the chest

MOVEMENT: Point the extended fingers of the right and left U hands in opposite directions near the top of the chest, with the right hand above the left. Rotate the right fingers forward around the left fingers; then bring the right hand down in front of the chest, ending with the extended fingers pointing up.

VISUALIZE: Tying a necktie.

pajamas

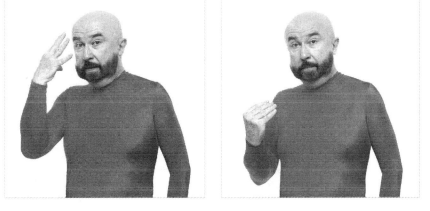

HANDSHAPES: **1.** Right OPEN hand changing to AND hand **2.** Right and left OPEN hands

POSITIONS: **1.** Starts on the forehead
2. On the chest

MOVEMENT: **1.** Touch the fingertips of the right OPEN hand to the forehead; then draw the hand down to the chin while changing it into the AND handshape. (This is the sign for *sleep*.)
2. With the palms facing in, sweep the fingertips of the right and left OPEN hands down over the chest a few times. (This is the sign for *clothes*.)

VISUALIZE: Combining the signs for *sleep* and *clothes* suggests pajamas.

U hand

And hand

pants • trousers • slacks

HANDSHAPES: Right and left OPEN hands changing to AND hands

POSITION: Just below the waist

MOVEMENT: Hang the right and left OPEN hands down just below the waist with the palms facing in. Then move both hands up to the waist while changing them to the AND handshape.

VISUALIZE: Pulling on a pair of pants.

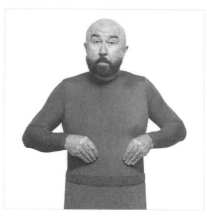 

pocket

HANDSHAPE: Right FLAT hand

POSITION: On the right hip

MOVEMENT: With the fingers pointing down, touch the palm of the right FLAT hand to the right hip. Slide the hand up and down a few times. (The use of the left hand to form a pocket is optional.)

VISUALIZE: Tucking your hand into a pocket.

purse • pocketbook

HANDSHAPE: Right S hand

POSITION: Next to the right side of the waist

MOVEMENT: Hold the right S hand next to the right side of the waist with the palm facing in.

VISUALIZE: Holding the strap of a pocketbook.

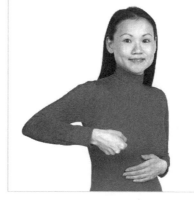

 Open hand   And hand   Flat hand   S hand

ring

HANDSHAPES: Right F hand and left OPEN hand

POSITION: In front of the chest

MOVEMENT: With the palms facing in, slide the thumb and index finger of the right F hand up and down the fourth finger of the left OPEN hand.

VISUALIZE: Slipping a ring onto the left ring finger.

scarf

HANDSHAPE: Right and left modified X hands

POSITION: Starts above the head

MOVEMENT: Hold the right and left modified X hands up above the head with the palms facing each other. Then draw the hands down over the cheeks to the chin and mimic tying two ends together.

VISUALIZE: Tying a scarf under the chin.

shirt

HANDSHAPE: Right F hand

POSITION: On the right shoulder

MOVEMENT: Tug gently upward on the shirt over the right shoulder with the thumb and index finger of the right F hand.

VISUALIZE: Drawing attention to your shirt.

F hand   X hand

shoes

HANDSHAPE: Right and left s hands

POSITION: In front of the chest

MOVEMENT: With the palms facing down, strike the thumb sides of the right and left s hands together a few times.

VISUALIZE: Clicking the heels together.

skirt

HANDSHAPE: Right and left OPEN hands

POSITION: Starts at the waist

MOVEMENT: Brush the fingertips of the right and left OPEN hands down and out from the waist.

VISUALIZE: Smoothing the folds of a skirt.

socks • stockings • hose

HANDSHAPE: Right and left ONE hands

POSITION: In front of the chest

MOVEMENT: Point the index fingertips of the right and left ONE hands down with the palms facing in. Then rub the index finger sides of the hands up and down against each other a few times.

VISUALIZE: Pointing to your socks.

S
hand

Open
hand

One
hand

umbrella

HANDSHAPE: Right and left s hands

POSITION: In front of the chest

MOVEMENT: With the palms facing in, place the right s hand on top of the left s hand. Then raise the right hand up to chin level.

VISUALIZE: Opening up an umbrella.

zipper • zip up

HANDSHAPE: Right and left modified A hands

POSITION: Starts in front of the waist

MOVEMENT: Hold the right and left modified A hands in front of the waist, palms facing in, with the right hand just above the left hand. Then move the right hand up in front of chest.

VISUALIZE: Pulling up a zipper.

A
hand

mealtime & food

A re you hungering for some food for thought? This chapter serves up a smorgasbord of signs that will prepare you for almost any culinary situation—whether you're sitting down to *breakfast, lunch,* or *dinner;* indulging in a sinful *dessert;* or dining at a fine *restaurant.* Just think of it as five-star cuisine for your mind.

MEALTIME

breakfast

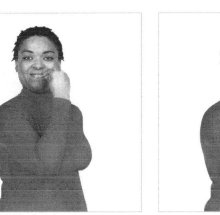 

HANDSHAPES: 1. Right AND hand **2.** Right and left FLAT hands

POSITIONS: 1. On the lips **2.** In front of the chest

MOVEMENT: 1. Tap fingertips of right AND hand on the lips a few times. (The sign for *eat*.)
2. Point right FLAT hand forward with palm facing up; then place little finger side of left FLAT hand in crook of right bent elbow. Bring right hand up toward the body, ending with palm facing in. (The sign for *morning*.)

VISUALIZE: Eating a meal in the morning.

SEE HELPING HANDS ON NEXT PAGE.

127

cook • fry

HANDSHAPE: Right and left FLAT hands

POSITION: In front of the chest

MOVEMENT: Place the palm of the right FLAT hand on the upturned palm of the left FLAT hand. Then flip the right hand over and place the back of the hand on the left palm.

VISUALIZE: Flipping burgers during cooking.

dinner

HANDSHAPES: **1.** Right AND hand **2.** Left FLAT hand and right CURVED hand

POSITIONS: **1.** On the lips **2.** In front of the chest

MOVEMENT: **1.** Tap the fingertips of the right AND hand on the lips a few times. (This is the sign for *eat*.) **2.** Point the left FLAT hand to the right with the palm facing down. Then place the inside wrist of the right CURVED hand, fingertips pointing down, on the back of the left hand. (This is the sign for *evening*.)

VISUALIZE: Eating a meal in the evening.

drink

HANDSHAPE: Right C hand

POSITION: In front of the mouth

MOVEMENT: With the palm facing left, move the right C hand in a short arc toward the mouth.

VISUALIZE: Drinking a glass of a refreshing beverage.

 And hand

 Flat hand

 Curved hand

C hand

eat • consume • dine • food • meal

HANDSHAPE: Right AND hand

POSITION: In front of the mouth

MOVEMENT: Tap the fingertips of the right AND hand on the lips a few times.

VISUALIZE: Bringing food to your mouth.

fork

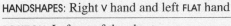

HANDSHAPES: Right v hand and left FLAT hand

POSITION: In front of the chest

MOVEMENT: Tap the fingertips of the right v hand on the upturned palm of the left FLAT hand a few times.

VISUALIZE: Piercing your food with the tines of a fork.

glass

HANDSHAPES: Right C hand and left FLAT hand

POSITION: In front of the chest

MOVEMENT: Place the little finger side of the right C hand on the upturned palm of the left FLAT hand. The move the right hand up a few inches.

VISUALIZE: Sliding your hand up the sides of a glass.

v
hand

hungry • hunger • appetite • crave • famine • starve

HANDSHAPE: Right C hand

POSITION: Starts just below the throat

MOVEMENT: Hold the right C hand just below the throat with the palm facing in. Then drop the hand straight down to the center of the chest.

VISUALIZE: Showing the pathway from the mouth to the stomach.

knife

HANDSHAPE: Right and left H hands

POSITION: In front of the chest

MOVEMENT: Point the left H hand forward with the palm facing right. Then slide the middle finger of the right H hand along the index finger of the left hand and let the right hand drop off the left fingertips.

VISUALIZE: Sharpening a knife.

lunch

HANDSHAPES: **1.** Right AND hand **2.** Left and right FLAT hands

POSITIONS: **1.** On the lips **2.** In front of the chest

MOVEMENT: **1.** Tap the fingertips of the right AND hand on the lips a few times. (This is the sign for *eat*.) **2.** Point the left FLAT hand to the right with the palm facing down. Then place the right bent elbow on the back of the left hand and point the right FLAT hand up with the palm facing left. (This is the sign for *noon*.)

VISUALIZE: Eating a meal at noon.

 C hand

 H hand

 And hand

 Flat hand

napkin

HANDSHAPE: Right FLAT hand

POSITION: On the lips

MOVEMENT: Brush the fingertips of the right FLAT hand across the lips.

VISUALIZE: Using a napkin to wipe your lips.

plate

HANDSHAPE: Right and left OPEN hands

POSITION: In front of the chest

MOVEMENT: With the palms facing each other, touch the thumbtips and middle fingertips of the right and left OPEN hands together to form a circle.

VISUALIZE: Showing the size and shape of a plate.

restaurant

HANDSHAPE: Right R hand

POSITION: In front of the mouth

MOVEMENT: With the palm facing left, touch the index finger side of the right R hand first to the right corner of the mouth, and then to the left corner.

VISUALIZE: Using a linen napkin to pat your mouth while dining in a restaurant.

Open hand

R hand

spoon

HANDSHAPES: Right H hand and left CURVED hand

POSITION: In front of the chest

MOVEMENT: Scoop the fingers of the right H hand into the upturned palm of the left CURVED hand and then up toward the mouth a few times.

VISUALIZE: Scooping up food with a spoon.

thirsty

HANDSHAPE: Right ONE hand

POSITION: Starts under the chin

MOVEMENT: Starting under the chin, trace the index fingertip of the right ONE hand down to the base of the throat.

VISUALIZE: Indicating that your throat is dry.

The Rise of Hearing Loss Among Young People

While it's been well documented that hearing acuity tends to decline with advancing age, researchers now warn of an alarming increase in the number of young Americans with hearing loss. According to government research, an estimated 5.2 million young people—ranging in age from six to nineteen—have some hearing loss resulting from exposure to excessive noise from rock concerts, fireworks, lawnmowers, and other sources. In about 250,000 of those affected, the hearing loss is moderate to profound. These figures, published in the journal *Pediatrics,* are based on a nationally representative survey conducted from 1988 to 1994, in which 5,249 participants were tested for their ability to hear certain decibels and pitches. Researchers say that even one-time exposure to excessive noise can cause hearing loss, and recommend that young people wear ear plugs to protect their hearing.

H
hand

Curved
hand

One
hand

waiter • waitress

HANDSHAPE: Right and left CURVED hands

POSITION: In front of the chest

MOVEMENT: 1. Point the right and left CURVED hands forward with the palms facing up; then move the hands alternately back and forth. **2.** Sign the *person* ending.

VISUALIZE: A waiter or waitress handling plates of food.

FOOD

apple

HANDSHAPE: Right modified X hand

POSITION: On the right cheek

MOVEMENT: Twist the knuckle of the right modified X index finger back and forth on the right cheek a few times. (This sign can also be made with an A hand.)

VISUALIZE: Sinking your teeth into a fresh, crispy apple.

X
hand

bacon

HANDSHAPE: Right and left U hands

POSITION: In front of the chest

MOVEMENT: Touch the fingertips of the right and left U hands together with the palms facing down. Then draw the hands apart while waving the U fingers up and down a few times.

VISUALIZE: Showing the shape of crispy bacon.

banana

HANDSHAPE: Left ONE hand and right OPEN hand with thumbtip and index fingertip touching

POSITION: In front of the chest

MOVEMENT: Point the left ONE hand up in front of the chest with the palm facing in. Make a few grasping downward movements from the left fingertip with the thumb and index finger of the right OPEN hand.

VISUALIZE: Peeling a banana.

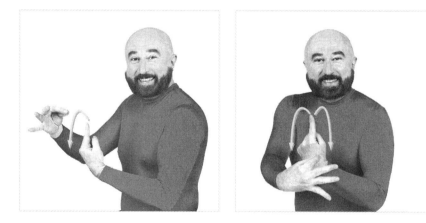

beer

HANDSHAPE: Right B hand

POSITION: On the right corner of the mouth

MOVEMENT: With the palm facing left, touch the index finger side of the right B hand to the right corner of the mouth and then draw the hand down to neck level.

VISUALIZE: Holding the initial B next to the mouth suggests calling out for a brew.

U hand

One hand

Open hand

B hand

bread

HANDSHAPES: Left FLAT hand and right CURVED hand

POSITION: In front of the body

MOVEMENT: Point the left FLAT hand to the right with the palm facing in. Draw the little finger side of the right CURVED hand down over the back of the left hand a few times, moving the right hand to the right each time.

VISUALIZE: Slicing a fresh loaf of bread.

butter

HANDSHAPES: Right H hand and left OPEN hand

POSITION: In front of the chest

MOVEMENT: Brush the fingertips of the right H hand across the upturned palm of the left OPEN hand a few times.

VISUALIZE: Buttering a slice of bread.

cake

HANDSHAPES: Right C hand and left FLAT hand

POSITION: In front of the chest

MOVEMENT: Place the thumbtip and fingertips of the right C hand on the upturned palm of the left FLAT hand near the wrist. Then slide the right hand across the left palm to the fingertips.

VISUALIZE: Sliding a wedge of cake onto a plate.

Flat hand

Curved hand

H hand

C hand

candy

HANDSHAPE: Right U hand

POSITION: On the lips

MOVEMENT: Brush the fingertips of the right U hand down over the lips a few times.

VISUALIZE: Licking something sweet.

cheese

HANDSHAPE: Right and left OPEN hands

POSITION: In front of the chest

MOVEMENT: Twist the heel of the right OPEN hand back and forth on the heel of the left OPEN hand a few times.

VISUALIZE: Squishing cheese flat between the heels of your palms.

chicken • bird

HANDSHAPE: Right Q hand

POSITION: In front of the mouth

MOVEMENT: Point the extended fingers of the right Q hand forward in front of the mouth. Then close and open the Q fingers a few times.

VISUALIZE: The opening and closing of a chicken's beak.

 U hand Open hand Q hand

coffee

HANDSHAPE: Right and left s hands

POSITION: In front of the chest

MOVEMENT: With the palms facing in, move the right s hand in a counterclockwise circle above the left s hand.

VISUALIZE: Grinding coffee beans in a mill.

cookie

HANDSHAPES: Right CLAWED hand and left FLAT hand

POSITION: In front of the chest

MOVEMENT: Twist the thumbtip and fingertips of the right CLAWED hand on the upturned palm of the left FLAT hand. Repeat a few times.

VISUALIZE: The right hand acting as a cookie cutter.

corn

HANDSHAPE: Right ONE hand

POSITION: In front of the mouth

MOVEMENT: With the palm facing down, point the index finger of the right ONE hand to the left in front of the mouth. Twist the hand back and forth slightly from the wrist a few times.

VISUALIZE: Eating corn on the cob.

cracker

HANDSHAPE: Right s hand

POSITION: In front of the chest

MOVEMENT: Strike the index finger side of the right s hand on the left arm near the elbow.

VISUALIZE: A cracking noise coming from your elbow.

dessert

HANDSHAPE: Right and left D hands

POSITION: In front of the chest

MOVEMENT: Hold up the right and left D hands and tap the thumbtips together several times.

VISUALIZE: The initial D suggests a delicious dessert after dinner.

egg

HANDSHAPE: Right and left H hands

POSITION: In front of the chest

MOVEMENT: Strike the middle finger of the right H hand against the index finger of the left H hand. Then move both hands down and apart.

VISUALIZE: Cracking an egg against a bowl and pulling the halves apart.

 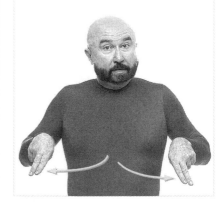

S
hand

D
hand

H
hand

fish

HANDSHAPE: Right and left OPEN hands

POSITION: In front of the chest

MOVEMENT: Point the right OPEN hand forward with palm facing left. Then, with the palm facing in, touch the fingertips of the left OPEN hand to the right wrist and swing the right hand back and forth a few times.

VISUALIZE: The movement of a fish when swimming.

French fries

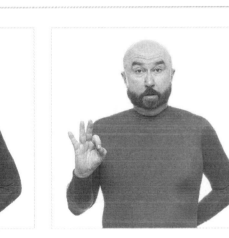

HANDSHAPE: Right F hand

POSITION: In front of the right shoulder

MOVEMENT: Sign the letter F in front of the right shoulder. Then move the hand slightly to the right and sign the F again.

VISUALIZE: Signing the initial F twice suggests French fries.

fruit

HANDSHAPE: Right F hand

POSITION: On the right cheek

MOVEMENT: Twist the thumbtip and index fingertip of the right F hand back and forth on the right cheek a few times.

VISUALIZE: Using the initial F to form a sign similar to *apple*.

Open hand

F hand

grapes

HANDSHAPES: Right O hand and left FLAT hand

POSITION: In front of the chest

MOVEMENT: With the palms facing down, place the fingertips of the right O hand on the back of the left FLAT hand near the wrist. Then move the right hand in a hopping motion a few times across the back of the left hand toward the fingertips.

VISUALIZE: Bunches of grapes sitting on a plate.

hamburger

HANDSHAPE: Right and left CURVED hands

POSITION: In front of the chest

MOVEMENT: Place the right CURVED hand on top of the left CURVED hand with the palms facing each other. Then reverse the motion by placing the left hand on top of the right.

VISUALIZE: Shaping a hamburger patty.

ice cream

HANDSHAPE: Right S hand

POSITION: In front of the mouth

MOVEMENT: With the palm facing left, move the right S hand toward the mouth and down a few times.

VISUALIZE: Licking an ice cream cone.

O hand

Flat hand

Curved hand

S hand

juice

HANDSHAPE: Right J hand

POSITION: In front of the right shoulder

MOVEMENT: Sign the letter J twice in front of the right shoulder.

VISUALIZE: The initial J suggests *juice*.

meat • beef • flesh

HANDSHAPES: Right F hand and left FLAT hand

POSITION: In front of the chest

MOVEMENT: Using the thumb and index finger of the right F hand, pinch the skin between the thumb and index finger of the left FLAT hand.

VISUALIZE: Drawing attention to the fleshy part of the hand.

melon • watermelon

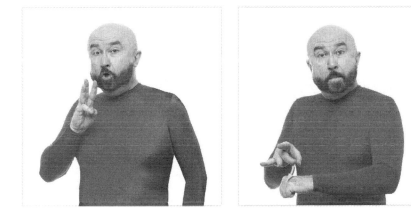

HANDSHAPES: **1.** Right W hand **2.** Right CURVED hand and left S hand

POSITIONS: **1.** On the lips **2.** In front of the chest

MOVEMENT: **1.** With the fingertips pointing up, tap the index finger side of the right W hand on the lips a few times. (This is the sign for *water*.) **2.** With the palms facing down, flick the middle fingertip of the right CURVED hand against the back of the left S hand a few times.

VISUALIZE: Thumping a melon to see if it's ripe.

J hand   F hand   W hand

milk

HANDSHAPES: Right and left slightly open s hands changing to closed s hands

POSITION: In front of the chest

MOVEMENT: Move the right and left slightly open s hands alternately up and down, squeezing them closed during the downward motion.

VISUALIZE: Milking a cow.

nuts • peanuts

HANDSHAPE: Right A hand

POSITION: Starts behind the upper front teeth

MOVEMENT: Place the thumbtip of the right A hand behind the upper front teeth with the palm facing left; then move the hand forward quickly.

VISUALIZE: Using the teeth to crack the shell of a nut.

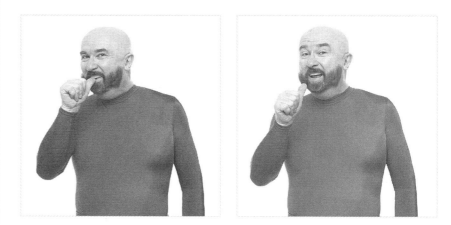

peach

HANDSHAPES: Right OPEN hand changing to AND hand

POSITION: On the right cheek

MOVEMENT: Touch the fingertips of the right OPEN hand to the right cheek. Then draw the hand down while closing it into the AND handshape.

VISUALIZE: Running your fingers over peach fuzz.

S hand

A hand

Open hand

And hand

pepper

HANDSHAPE: Right F hand

POSITION: In front of the chest

MOVEMENT: Hold the right F hand forward with the palm facing down. Then shake the hand down to the left a few times. (This is sometimes done with an O hand.)

VISUALIZE: A pinch of pepper shaken over food.

pineapple

HANDSHAPE: Right P hand

POSITION: On the right cheek

MOVEMENT: Twist the middle fingertip of the right P hand back and forth on the right cheek a few times.

VISUALIZE: Using the initial P in forming a sign similar to *apple*.

pizza

HANDSHAPE: Right P hand

POSITION: In front of the chest

MOVEMENT: Hold up the right P hand in front of the chest and trace the letter "Z" in the air.

VISUALIZE: The initial P plus "Z" suggests pizza.

F hand

P hand

potato

HANDSHAPES: Right v hand and left s hand

POSITION: In front of the chest

MOVEMENT: With the palms facing down, tap the fingertips of the right v hand on the back of the left s hand a few times.

VISUALIZE: Sticking a fork into a baking potato.

salt

HANDSHAPES: Right v hand and left h hand

POSITION: In front of the chest

MOVEMENT: With the palms facing down, tap the fingertips of the right v hand on the extended fingers of the left h hand a few times.

VISUALIZE: Tapping a salt shaker against your finger and onto your food.

sandwich

HANDSHAPE: Right and left FLAT hands

POSITION: In front of the mouth

MOVEMENT: Hold the right and left FLAT hands together so the palms are touching and point the fingers toward the mouth.

VISUALIZE: A hand sandwich about to be eaten.

 V hand

 S hand

H hand

Flat hand

soda • pop • soda water

HANDSHAPES: Right OPEN hand and left O hand

POSITION: In front of the chest

MOVEMENT: Point the middle finger of the right OPEN hand down into the opening of the left O hand. Then pull the right hand up, straighten the fingers, and bring the palm of the right OPEN hand down onto the left O hand.

VISUALIZE: Putting the cap back on a bottle of soda.

soup

HANDSHAPES: Right H hand and left CURVED hand

POSITION: In front of the chest

MOVEMENT: Scoop the fingers of the right H hand into the upturned palm of the left CURVED hand and then up toward the mouth a few times.

VISUALIZE: Eating soup with a spoon.

 Open hand

 O hand

 Curved hand

sour • bitter • tart • acid

HANDSHAPE: Right ONE hand

POSITION: On the chin

MOVEMENT: Place the index fingertip of the right ONE hand on the chin and twist it several times.

VISUALIZE: Pursing your lips when tasting a tart twist of lemon.

spaghetti

HANDSHAPE: Right and left I hands

POSITION: In front of the chest

MOVEMENT: Touch the fingertips of the right I hands together with the palms facing in; then draw the hands apart to the sides a few times, moving them in small spiral motions.

VISUALIZE: Using two forks to twirl spaghetti.

strawberry

HANDSHAPES: Right C hand and left ONE hand

POSITION: In front of the chest

MOVEMENT: Grasp the index finger of the left ONE hand with the thumbtip and fingertips of the right C hand. Twist the right hand back and forth a few times.

VISUALIZE: Twisting the stem and leaves off a strawberry.

One hand

I hand

C hand

sweet • sugar

HANDSHAPE: Right FLAT hand

POSITION: On the lips

MOVEMENT: Brush the fingertips of the right FLAT hand down over the lips a few times.

VISUALIZE: Licking sugar off your fingertips.

tea

HANDSHAPES: Right F hand and left O hand

POSITION: In front of the chest

MOVEMENT: Point the thumb and index finger of the right F hand down into the opening of the left O hand and move the right hand in a few small circles.

VISUALIZE: Stirring a cup of tea.

toast

HANDSHAPES: Right bent V hand and left FLAT hand

POSITION: In front of the chest

MOVEMENT: Touch the fingertips of the right bent V hand to the upturned palm of the left FLAT hand. Then touch the V fingertips to the back of the left hand.

VISUALIZE: Toasting a slice of bread on the top and then on the bottom.

Flat hand

F hand

O hand

V hand

tomato

HANDSHAPES: **1.** Right ONE hand **2.** Left AND hand and right ONE hand

POSITIONS: **1.** On the lips **2.** In front of the chest

MOVEMENT: **1.** Brush the index fingertip of the right ONE hand down over the lips. (This is the sign for *red*.) **2.** Point the left AND hand to the right and brush the right ONE fingertip down across the left fingertips.

VISUALIZE: Slicing a red tomato.

water

HANDSHAPE: Right w hand

POSITION: On the lips

MOVEMENT: With the fingertips pointing up, tap the index finger side of the right w hand on the lips a few times.

VISUALIZE: Having to drink three glasses of water a day.

wine

HANDSHAPE: Right w hand

POSITION: On the right cheek

MOVEMENT: Touch the fingertips of the right w hand to the right cheek and move the hand in a forward circular motion against the cheek.

VISUALIZE: Using the initial w to suggest the cheeks reddening from the alcohol in wine.

 One hand

 And hand

 W hand

numbers, math terms, quantity & money

You don't have to be a math whiz to master the numbers and related signs included in this chapter. Whether you want to jog *five* miles, *count* your blessings, *divide* the last cupcake, *buy* a present, write a *check*, or meet *some* friends for dinner, these signs will help you get your message across clearly and effectively. In fact, with a little practice, you'll find it's as easy as 1, 2, 3!

NUMBERS

number

HANDSHAPE: Right and left AND hands

POSITION: In front of the chest

MOVEMENT: Touch the fingertips of the right and left AND hands together with the right palm facing down and the left palm facing up; then twist both hands from the wrists so the right palm faces up and the left palm faces down. Repeat a few times.

VISUALIZE: Combining one set of numbers with another.

SEE HELPING HANDS ON NEXT PAGE.

zero

HANDSHAPE: Right O hand

POSITION: In front of the right shoulder

MOVEMENT: Hold up the right O hand with the palm facing left.

one

POSITION: In front of the right shoulder

MOVEMENT: Hold up the right hand, palm facing forward, with the index finger extended and the other fingers closed.

two

POSITION: In front of the right shoulder

MOVEMENT: Hold up the right hand, palm facing forward, with the index and middle fingers extended and the other fingers closed.

And
hand

0
hand

three

POSITION: In front of the right shoulder

MOVEMENT: Hold up the right hand, palm facing forward, with the thumb, index and middle fingers extended and the other fingers closed.

four

POSITION: In front of the right shoulder

MOVEMENT: Hold up the right hand, palm facing forward, with four fingers extended and the thumbtip touching the palm.

five

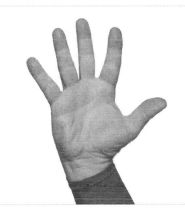

HANDSHAPE: Right OPEN hand

POSITION: In front of the right shoulder

MOVEMENT: Hold up the right OPEN hand with the palm facing forward.

Open hand

six

HANDSHAPE: Right OPEN hand

POSITION: In front of the right shoulder

MOVEMENT: Hold up the right OPEN hand, palm facing forward, with the thumbtip and little fingertip touching.

seven

HANDSHAPE: Right OPEN hand

POSITION: In front of the right shoulder

MOVEMENT: Hold up the right OPEN hand, palm facing forward, with the thumbtip and ring fingertip touching.

eight

HANDSHAPE: Right OPEN hand

POSITION: In front of the right shoulder

MOVEMENT: Hold up the right OPEN hand, palm facing forward, with the thumbtip and middle fingertip touching.

Open hand

nine

HANDSHAPE: Right OPEN hand

POSITION: In front of the right shoulder

MOVEMENT: Hold up the right OPEN hand, palm facing forward, with the thumbtip and index fingertip touching.

ten

HANDSHAPE: Right A hand

POSITION: In front of the right shoulder

MOVEMENT: Hold up the right A hand with the thumb extended and the palm facing left. Shake the hand side to side from the wrist a few times.

eleven

HANDSHAPE: Right S hand

POSITION: In front of the right shoulder

MOVEMENT: Hold up the right S hand, palm facing in, and flick the index finger up sharply.

A
hand

S
hand

twelve

HANDSHAPE: Right s hand

POSITION: In front of the right shoulder

MOVEMENT: Hold up the right s hand, palm facing in, and flick the index and middle fingers up sharply at the same time.

thirteen

HANDSHAPE: Right THREE hand

POSITION: In front of the right shoulder

MOVEMENT: Hold up the right THREE hand, palm facing in, and bend and straighten the index and middle fingers quickly a few times.

fourteen

HANDSHAPE: Right FOUR hand

POSITION: In front of the right shoulder

MOVEMENT: Hold up the right FOUR hand, palm facing in, and bend and straighten the four fingers quickly a few times.

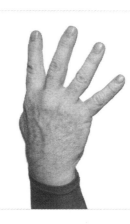

S
hand

Three
hand

Four
hand

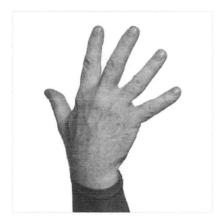

fifteen

HANDSHAPE: Right FIVE hand

POSITION: In front of the right shoulder

MOVEMENT: Hold up the right FIVE hand, palm facing in, and bend and straighten the four fingers quickly a few times.

sixteen

HANDSHAPE: Right A hand with thumb extended, changing to SIX hand

POSITION: In front of the right shoulder

MOVEMENT: Hold up the right A hand with the thumb extended and the palm facing left. Then sharply twist the wrist forward while changing the hand to the SIX handshape.

seventeen

HANDSHAPE: Right A hand with thumb extended, changing to SEVEN hand

POSITION: In front of the right shoulder

MOVEMENT: Hold up the right A hand with the thumb extended and the palm facing left. Then twist the wrist forward while changing the hand to the SEVEN handshape.

 Five
hand

 A
hand

 Six
hand

Seven
hand

eighteen

HANDSHAPE: Right A hand with thumb extended, changing to EIGHT hand

POSITION: In front of the right shoulder

MOVEMENT: Hold up the right A hand with the thumb extended and the palm facing left. Then twist the wrist forward while changing the hand to the EIGHT handshape.

nineteen

HANDSHAPE: Right A hand with thumb extended, changing to NINE hand

POSITION: In front of the right shoulder

MOVEMENT: Hold up the right A hand with the thumb extended and the palm facing left. Then twist the wrist forward while changing the hand to the NINE handshape.

twenty

HANDSHAPE: Right G hand

POSITION: In front of the right shoulder

MOVEMENT: Point the extended fingers of the right G hand forward; then move the hand slightly to the right while touching the thumbtip and index fingertip together a few times.

A hand

Eight hand

Nine hand

G hand

one hundred

HANDSHAPES: Right ONE hand changing to C hand

POSITION: In front of the right shoulder

MOVEMENT: Point the right ONE hand up with the palm facing forward; then move the hand slightly to the right while changing it to the C handshape.

VISUALIZE: The C represents the Roman numeral for hundred.

one thousand

HANDSHAPES: **1.** Right ONE hand **2.** Right M hand with index, middle, and ring fingers extended, and left FLAT hand

POSITION: In front of the chest

MOVEMENT: **1.** Point the right ONE hand up with the palm facing forward. **2.** Touch the fingertips of the right M hand once to the upturned palm of the left FLAT hand.

VISUALIZE: The M represents the Roman numeral for thousand.

one million

HANDSHAPES: **1.** Right ONE hand **2.** Right M hand with index, middle, and ring fingers extended, and left FLAT hand

POSITION: In front of the chest

MOVEMENT: **1.** Point the right ONE hand up with the palm facing forward. **2.** Tap the extended fingers of the right M hand twice on the upturned palm of the left FLAT hand.

VISUALIZE: Tapping the M hand twice on the left palm represents 1,000 multiplied by 1,000 — one million.

One hand   C hand   M hand   Flat hand

one fourth

HANDSHAPES: Right ONE hand changing to FOUR hand

POSITION: In front of the right shoulder

MOVEMENT: Point the right ONE hand up with the palm facing forward. Then draw the hand down slightly while changing it to the FOUR handshape.

VISUALIZE: Signing the numerator above the denominator.

one half

HANDSHAPES: Right ONE hand changing to TWO hand

POSITION: In front of the right shoulder

MOVEMENT: Point the right ONE hand up with the palm facing forward. Then draw the hand down slightly while changing it to the TWO handshape.

VISUALIZE: Signing the numerator above the denominator.

MATH TERMS

add • add up

HANDSHAPES: Right OPEN hand changing to AND hand and left AND hand

POSITION: In front of the chest

MOVEMENT: Hold the right OPEN hand and left AND hand apart in front of the chest with the right palm facing left and the left palm facing down. Then swing the right hand toward the left while changing it to the AND handshape and touch the fingertips of the right and left AND hands together.

VISUALIZE: The right hand adding to the quantity in the left hand.

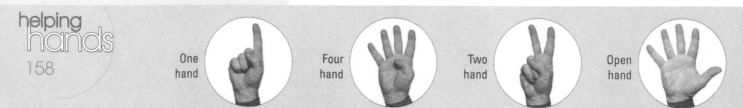

One hand   Four hand   Two hand   Open hand

count

HANDSHAPE: Left FLAT hand and right F hand

POSITION: In front of the chest

MOVEMENT: Hold up the left FLAT hand with the palm facing right. Starting near the wrist, slide the thumbtip and index fingertip of the right F hand up along the left palm to the fingertips.

VISUALIZE: Moving the beads on an abacus.

divide • split up

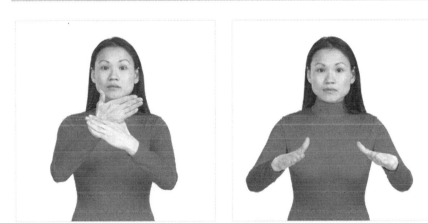

HANDSHAPE: Right and left FLAT hands

POSITION: Starts in front of the chest

MOVEMENT: Place the little finger side of the right FLAT hand across the index finger side of the left FLAT hand. Then move both hands down and apart to the sides, ending with the palms facing down.

VISUALIZE: Dividing something in half.

increase • add

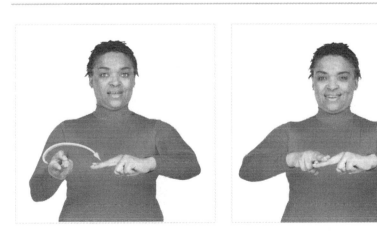

HANDSHAPE: Right and left H hands

POSITION: In front of the chest

MOVEMENT: Point the right H hand forward and the left H hand to the right with the left palm facing down. Then turn the right hand over and place the right H fingers on the back of the left H fingers.

VISUALIZE: Adding more weight to a surface.

And
hand

Flat
hand

F
hand

H
hand

mathematics • algebra • geometry • statistics

HANDSHAPE: Right and left M hands with index, middle, and ring fingers extended

POSITION: In front of the chest

MOVEMENT: Hold the right and left M hands with the fingers pointing upward and the palms facing in. Then cross the hands so that the palm of the left hand passes across the back of the right. To sign *algebra,* use A hands; to sign *geometry,* use G hands; to sign *statistics,* use S hands.

VISUALIZE: The "M" formed by the arms repesents the multiplication symbol, and the initial hands represent the specific word.

multiply

HANDSHAPE: Right and left V hands

POSITION: Starts in front of the shoulders

MOVEMENT: Hold up the right and left V hands in front of the shoulders with the palms facing in. Then move both hands toward each other and cross the right hand behind the left.

VISUALIZE: The "X" formed by the hands represents the multiplication symbol.

subtract • deduct • remove • eliminate

HANDSHAPES: Right CURVED hand and left FLAT hand

POSITION: In front of the chest

MOVEMENT: Point the left FLAT hand forward with the palm facing right. Then, with the palm facing down, brush the fingertips of the right CURVED hand straight down across the left palm.

VISUALIZE: The right hand taking some amount away from the left hand.

M hand

V hand

Curved hand

Flat hand

than

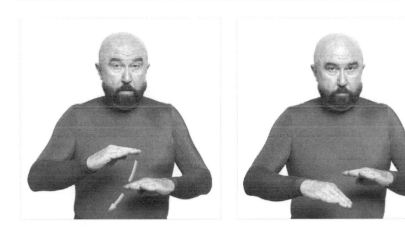

HANDSHAPE: Right and left FLAT hands

POSITION: In front of the chest

MOVEMENT: With the palms of the right and left FLAT hands facing down, brush the index finger edge of the right hand against the fingertips of the left hand and continue the downward motion a few inches.

VISUALIZE: Noting the placement of your right hand—first higher than, then lower than your left.

total • amount • sum

HANDSHAPES: Right and left CLAWED hands changing to AND hands

POSITION: In front of the chest

MOVEMENT: Hold the right and left CLAWED hands apart in front of the chest, palms facing each other, with the left hand above the right. Then bring the hands toward each other while changing them to the AND handshape and touch the fingertips together.

VISUALIZE: Bringing two separate quantities together to find the total.

QUANTITY

all • whole • entire

HANDSHAPE: Right and left FLAT hands

POSITION: In front of the chest

MOMENT: Hold the left FLAT hand forward, with the palm facing in. Hold the right FLAT hand behind the left hand, with the palm facing out, and circle it over the left hand, rotating the right wrist so that the left hand ends up in front of the right, with the palm facing in.

VISUALIZE: A sweeping motion that pulls in the whole and locks it in.

Clawed hand

And hand

almost • nearly

HANDSHAPE: Right and left CURVED hands

POSITION: In front of the chest

MOVEMENT: Hold the right and left CURVED hands forward, palms facing in, with the right hand slightly lower than the left. Then brush the little finger side of the right hand up against the left fingertips.

VISUALIZE: The right hand almost joining with the left—and then moving past it.

both • pair

HANDSHAPES: Left C hand and right V hand

POSITION: In front of the chest

MOVEMENT: Hold the left C hand forward with the palm facing in. Then, with the palm facing in, draw the fingers of the right V hand down through the left C hand, closing the right V fingers together as they pass through.

VISUALIZE: Two separate fingers uniting to form a pair.

decrease • diminish • shrink • less • lessen

HANDSHAPE: Right and left CURVED hands

POSITION: In front of the chest

MOVEMENT: Hold the right and left CURVED hands apart in front of the chest, palms facing each other, with the right hand above the left. Then move the hands toward each other.

VISUALIZE: Decreasing the space between the hands.

 Curved hand

 C hand

 V hand

each • every

HANDSHAPE: Right and left A hands with thumbs slightly extended

POSITION: In front of the chest

MOVEMENT: Hold the left A hand forward with the palm facing right. Then stroke the knuckles and thumb of the right A hand downward against the left thumb several times.

VISUALIZE: The left hand making contact with each and every knuckle of the right.

enough • plenty • adequate • sufficient • ample

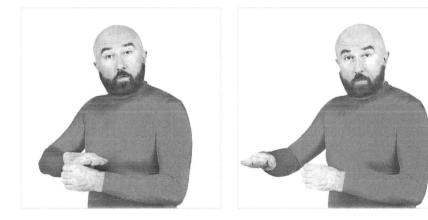

HANDSHAPES: Left S hand and right FLAT hand

POSITION: In front of the chest

MOVEMENT: Hold the left S hand forward with the palm facing right. Then brush the palm of the right FLAT hand forward across the thumb side of the left hand a few times.

VISUALIZE: A full cup that's starting to overflow.

equal • even • fair

HANDSHAPE: Right and left BENT hands

POSITION: In front of the chest

MOVEMENT: Bring the right and left BENT hands together, palms facing each other, until the fingertips touch. Repeat a few times.

VISUALIZE: Showing that the hands are even with each other.

A hand   S hand   Flat hand   Bent hand

few • several

HANDSHAPE: Right A hand changing to OPEN hand

POSITION: In front of the chest

MOVEMENT: Hold the right A hand forward with the palm facing up. Open the hand slowly while passing the thumb lightly across the inside of the fingers, from the index finger to the little finger.

VISUALIZE: Showing a small number by touching the fingers one by one.

many • lots • numerous • plural

HANDSHAPES: Right and left S hands changing to OPEN hands

POSITION: In front of the chest

MOVEMENT: Hold the right and left S hands forward with the palms facing up. Then sharply flick the fingers and thumbs open a few times.

VISUALIZE: Many fingers popping up.

measure

HANDSHAPE: Right and left Y hands

POSITION: In front of the chest

MOVEMENT: Hold the right and left Y hands forward with the palms facing down and touch the thumbtips together a few times.

VISUALIZE: A tape measure showing the distance between two points.

 A hand
Open hand
S hand
 Y hand

more

HANDSHAPE: Right and left AND hands

POSITION: In front of the chest

MOVEMENT: Touch the fingertips of the right and left AND hands together. Repeat the motion once or twice.

VISUALIZE: Resembles the sign for *add* to suggest that one hand is adding more to the other.

most

HANDSHAPE: Right and left A hands with thumbs extended

POSITION: In front of the chest

MOVEMENT: Hold the right and left A hands close together in front of the chest, with the palms facing each other, the thumbs pointing up, and the knuckles of the right hand slightly below the knuckles of the left. Then sharply move the right hand up past the left hand.

VISUALIZE: Thumbs up! You are the most!

much • lot • a lot

HANDSHAPE: Right and left CLAWED hands

POSITION: Starts in front of the chest

MOVEMENT: Hold up the right and left CLAWED hands with the fingertips touching. Then move both hands apart to the sides.

VISUALIZE: Holding a small balloon as it inflates and gets much larger.

 And hand Clawed hand

nothing · none

HANDSHAPES: Right and left O hands changing to OPEN hands

POSITION: Starts in front of the chest

MOVEMENT: Hold up the right and left O hands side by side with the palms facing forward. Then move both hands out to the sides while opening the fingers.

VISUALIZE: Showing that there's nothing in your hands.

some · part · portion · section

HANDSHAPES: Left FLAT hand and right CURVED hand changing to FLAT hand

POSITION: In front of the chest

MOVEMENT: Point the left FLAT hand forward with the palm facing up. Place the little finger side of the right CURVED hand on the left palm; then move the right hand toward the body while forming a FLAT hand.

VISUALIZE: Pulling your portion towards you.

than

HANDSHAPE: Right and left FLAT hands

POSITION: In front of the chest

MOVEMENT: With the palms of the right and left FLAT hands facing down, brush the index finger edge of the right hand against the fingertips of the left hand and continue the downward motion a few inches.

VISUALIZE: Noting the placement of your right hand—first higher than, then lower than your left.

O hand

Open hand

Flat hand

Curved hand

too • also

HANDSHAPE: Right and left ONE hands

POSITION: In front of the chest

MOVEMENT: Point the right and left ONE hands forward with the palms facing down and bring the hands together until the index finger sides touch. (This is the sign for *same*.) Move the hands to the left and repeat the sign.

VISUALIZE: When the left hand moves, the right hand moves too.

MONEY

cent • cents • penny

HANDSHAPE: Right ONE hand

POSITION: On the forehead

MOVEMENT: Touch the index fingertip of the right ONE hand to the center of the forehead.

VISUALIZE: The more "sense" you have, the more "cents" you have.

check

HANDSHAPES: Right C hand and left FLAT hand

POSITION: In front of the chest

MOVEMENT: Slide the thumbtip and fingertips of the right C hand across the upturned palm of the left FLAT hand from the heel of the hand to the fingertips.

VISUALIZE: Using the initial C to outline the shape of a check.

One hand

C hand

cost • price • expense • charge • fine • tax

HANDSHAPES: Left FLAT hand and right X hand

POSITION: In front of the chest

MOVEMENT: Point the left FLAT hand forward with the palm facing right. Then strike the index finger of the right X hand down across the left palm a few times.

VISUALIZE: Moving your hand down an invoice to check the costs.

credit card

HANDSHAPES: Right S hand and left FLAT hand

POSITION: In front of the chest

MOVEMENT: Brush the little finger side of the right S hand back and forth across the upturned palm of the left FLAT hand.

VISUALIZE: Imprinting credit card information using a credit card machine.

dollars • bills • bucks

HANDSHAPES: Left FLAT hand and right C hand

POSITION: In front of the chest

MOVEMENT: Point the left FLAT hand to the right with the palm facing in. Grasp the left fingertips with the thumbtip and fingertips of the right hand. Then pull the right hand away to the right.

VISUALIZE: Pulling cash out of an ATM machine.

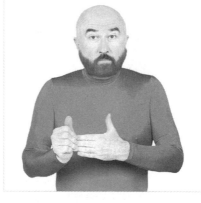

Flat hand

X hand

S hand

C hand

expensive • costly

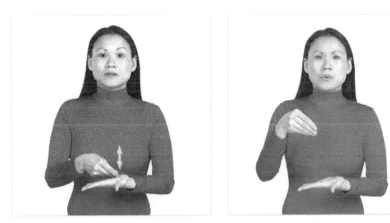

HANDSHAPES: Right AND hand changing to OPEN hand and left FLAT hand

POSITION: In front of the chest

MOVEMENT: Tap the back of the right AND hand against the upturned palm of the left FLAT hand a few times. (This is the sign for *money*.) Then lift the right hand while opening the fingers and twist the hand to the right.

VISUALIZE: Throwing money away on something expensive.

inexpensive • cheap

HANDSHAPE: Left and right FLAT hands

POSITION: In front of the chest

MOVEMENT: Hold up the left FLAT hand with the palm facing forward. Then brush the index finger side of the right FLAT hand down across the left palm.

VISUALIZE: Showing that the costs are low.

And hand

Open hand

money • cash • capital • finances

HANDSHAPES: Right AND hand and left FLAT hand

POSITION: In front of the chest

MOVEMENT: Tap the back of the right AND hand against the upturned palm of the left FLAT hand a few times.

VISUALIZE: Counting loose change into the left hand.

owe • due • debt • afford

HANDSHAPES: Right ONE hand and left FLAT hand

POSITION: In front of the chest

MOVEMENT: Tap the index fingertip of the right ONE hand on the upturned palm of the left FLAT hand a few times.

VISUALIZE: Asking for money to be placed in your hand.

pay

HANDSHAPES: Right ONE hand and left FLAT hand

POSITION: In front of the chest

MOVEMENT: Place the index fingertip of the right ONE hand on the upturned palm of the left FLAT hand. Then move the right hand up and away from the body, ending with the index finger pointing forward.

VISUALIZE: Showing that payment will be made to you.

 And hand

 Flat hand

 One hand

save • store • economize

HANDSHAPES: Right v hand and left s hand

POSITION: In front of the chest

MOVEMENT: With the palms facing in, hold the extended fingers of the right v hand upright against the back of the left s hand.

VISUALIZE: Showing that savings will remain in your hand.

spend • waste • squander

HANDSHAPES: Right AND hand changing to OPEN hand and left FLAT hand

POSITION: In front of the chest

MOVEMENT: Tap the back of the right AND hand against the upturned palm of the left FLAT hand a few times. (This is the sign for *money*.) Then open the right hand and slide it off the fingertips of the left hand.

VISUALIZE: Throwing money away.

V hand   S hand   Open hand

days of the week & time

There's no time like the present to learn the signs you'll find in this chapter. Soon you'll be reminiscing about the *past* and making plans for the *future*, greeting the *morning* and wondering where the *day* went, even fretting about *Monday* and looking forward to *Friday* with confidence and pride in your signing abilities. So why not seize the moment and get started?

DAYS OF THE WEEK

Sunday

HANDSHAPE: Right and left FLAT hands

POSITION: In front of the shoulders

MOVEMENT: Hold up the right and left FLAT hands in front of the shoulders with the palms facing forward and move both hands in outward circles.

VISUALIZE: Church doors opening on Sunday morning.

SEE HELPING HANDS ON NEXT PAGE.

Monday

HANDSHAPE: Right M hand

POSITION: In front of the right shoulder

MOVEMENT: With the palm facing forward, move the right M hand in a small clockwise circle in front of the right shoulder.

VISUALIZE: The initial M indicates Monday, while the circular motion shows the continuity of the week.

Tuesday

HANDSHAPE: Right T hand

POSITION: In front of the right shoulder

MOVEMENT: With the palm facing forward, move the right T hand in a small clockwise circle in front of the right shoulder.

VISUALIZE: The initial T indicates Tuesday, while the circular motion shows the continuity of the week.

Wednesday

HANDSHAPE: Right W hand

POSITION: In front of the right shoulder

MOVEMENT: With the palm facing forward, move the right W hand in a small clockwise circle in front of the right shoulder.

VISUALIZE: The initial W indicates Wednesday, while the circular motion shows the continuity of the week.

 Flat hand | M hand | T hand | W hand

Thursday

HANDSHAPE: Right H hand

POSITION: In front of the chest

MOVEMENT: Point the extended fingers of the right H hand to the left, palm facing in, and move the hand in a small clockwise circle. *Thursday* can also be signed by circling the initial T into the H.

VISUALIZE: The H indicates Thursday, while the circular motion shows the continuity of the week.

Friday

HANDSHAPE: Right F hand

POSITION: In front of the right shoulder

MOVEMENT: With the palm facing forward, move the right F hand in a small clockwise circle in front of the right shoulder.

VISUALIZE: The initial F indicates Friday, while the circular motion shows the continuity of the week.

Saturday

HANDSHAPE: Right S hand

POSITION: In front of the right shoulder

MOVEMENT: With the palm facing forward, move the right S hand in a small clockwise circle in front of the right shoulder.

VISUALIZE: The initial S indicates Saturday, while the circular motion shows the continuity of the week.

H hand

F hand

S hand

TIME

after • afterward • beyond

HANDSHAPE: Right and left CURVED hands

POSITION: In front of the chest

MOVEMENT: Hold the right and left CURVED hands forward, palms facing in, with the palm of the right hand on the back of the left hand. Then move the right hand forward and away from the left hand.

VISUALIZE: Moving the right hand beyond the left.

afternoon

HANDSHAPE: Left and right FLAT hands

POSITION: In front of the chest

MOVEMENT: Point the left FLAT hand to the right with the palm facing down. Place the right forearm on the back of the left hand at an angle, with the fingertips of the right FLAT hand pointing slightly upward.

VISUALIZE: The sun going down.

always • constantly • ever

HANDSHAPE: Right ONE hand

POSITION: In front of the chest

MOVEMENT: Point the right ONE hand forward at a slight angle with the palm facing up and move the hand in a clockwise circular motion.

VISUALIZE: The hand constantly moving in a circle.

 Curved hand

 Flat hand

One hand

before • prior

HANDSHAPE: Right and left FLAT hands

POSITION: In front of the chest

MOVEMENT: Hold the right and left FLAT hands forward, palms facing in, with the back of the right FLAT hand touching the left palm. Then move the right hand in toward the body.

VISUALIZE: Moving the right hand *before* moving the left hand.

day • all day

HANDSHAPE: Left and right ONE hands

POSITION: In front of the chest

MOVEMENT: Point the left ONE hand to the right with the palm facing down. Place the right bent elbow on the left index finger, pointing the right ONE hand up. Then move the right hand down across the body toward the left elbow.

VISUALIZE: The sun's arc across the sky.

during • while • in the meantime

HANDSHAPE: Right and left ONE hands

POSITION: In front of the chest

MOVEMENT: Hold the right and left ONE hands in front of the chest with the palms facing in, and the index fingers pointing slightly downward. Then simultaneously move both hands in an upward curve until the index fingertips are pointing directly forward.

VISUALIZE: The parallel movement of the hands suggests two things happening simultaneously.

early

HANDSHAPES: Right OPEN hand and left A hand

POSITION: In front of the chest

MOVEMENT: With the palms facing down, place the middle fingertip of the right OPEN hand on the index finger side of the left A hand. Then slide the right hand across the back of the left hand toward the little finger side.

VISUALIZE: Making an early-day adjustment to your watch.

evening • night

HANDSHAPES: Left FLAT hand and right CURVED hand

POSITION: In front of the chest

MOVEMENT: Point the left FLAT hand to the right with the palm facing down. Then place the inside wrist of the right CURVED hand, fingertips pointing down, on the back of the left hand.

VISUALIZE: The sun setting as evening approaches.

first

HANDSHAPES: Left A hand with thumb pointing up, and right ONE hand

POSITION: In front of the chest

MOVEMENT: Hold the left A hand forward with the thumb pointing up and the palm facing right. Strike the index fingertip of the right ONE hand against the left thumbtip.

VISUALIZE: Showing the first and most important digit of the hand.

Open hand

A hand

Flat hand

Curved hand

future • someday • later on • will

HANDSHAPE: Right FLAT hand

POSITION: Starts next to the right temple

MOVEMENT: Hold up the right FLAT hand next to the right temple with the palm facing left. Then move the hand in a forward and upward arc away from the face. To suggest a time further into the future, make the arc bigger with a slower motion.

VISUALIZE: Your hand thrusting forward into the future.

hour

HANDSHAPES: Left FLAT hand and right ONE hand

POSITION: In front of the chest

MOVEMENT: Hold up the left FLAT hand with palm facing right. Touch the index finger side of the right ONE hand, palm facing forward, to the left palm. Then move the right hand in a clockwise circle by twisting the hand from the wrist.

VISUALIZE: The movement of a minute hand on a clock over a full hour.

last • final • end

HANDSHAPES: Left S hand with little finger extended, and right ONE hand

POSITION: In front of the chest

MOVEMENT: Hold the left S hand forward with the palm facing in. Strike the index fingertip of the right ONE hand against the extended little finger of the left hand.

VISUALIZE: Showing the last finger of the hand.

One hand

S hand

late • tardy • not yet • not done

HANDSHAPE: Right FLAT hand

POSITION: Above the right hip

MOVEMENT: Hang the right FLAT hand down above the right hip with the palm facing back. Then swing the hand back and forth from the wrist a few times.

VISUALIZE: Time is passing, making you later and later for events.

minute

HANDSHAPES: Left FLAT hand and right ONE hand

POSITION: In front of the chest

MOVEMENT: Hold up the left FLAT hand with palm facing right. Touch the index finger side of the right ONE hand, palm facing forward, to the left palm. Then move the right index finger forward past the little finger of the left hand.

VISUALIZE: The movement of a minute hand on a clock.

month • monthly

HANDSHAPE: Left and right ONE hands

POSITION: In front of the chest

MOVEMENT: Hold up the left ONE hand with the palm facing right. Then slide the index fingertip of the right ONE hand down the left index finger from the fingertip to the base. To indicate *monthly*, repeat the sign.

VISUALIZE: Sliding your finger down the page of a calendar.

 Flat hand

 One hand

morning

HANDSHAPE: Right and left FLAT hands

POSITION: In front of the chest

MOVEMENT: Point the right FLAT hand forward with the palm facing up. Place the little finger side of the left FLAT hand in the crook of the right bent elbow; then bring the right hand up toward the body, ending with the palm facing in.

VISUALIZE: The sun coming up.

never

HANDSHAPE: Right FLAT hand

POSITION: Starts in front of the right shoulder

MOVEMENT: With the palm facing down, trace a clockwise half-circle in the air with the right FLAT hand. Then sharply drop the hand down to the right side.

VISUALIZE: An emphatic gesture showing that this will *never* happen.

noon

HANDSHAPE: Left and right FLAT hands

POSITION: In front of the chest

MOVEMENT: Point the left FLAT hand to the right with the palm facing down. Then place the right bent elbow on the back of the left hand and hold the right FLAT hand upright with the palm facing left.

VISUALIZE: The sun shining directly overhead at noon.

now · present · immediate · current

HANDSHAPE: Right and left CURVED hands

POSITION: In front of the chest

MOVEMENT: Hold both CURVED hands forward with the palms facing up. Then sharply drop the hands downward a short distance.

VISUALIZE: Bearing the burden of present events right now.

often · frequent

HANDSHAPES: Right BENT hand and left FLAT hand

POSITION: In front of the chest

MOVEMENT: Touch the fingertips of the right BENT hand to the upturned palm of the left FLAT hand. Move the left hand forward and repeat.

VISUALIZE: The same thing occurring often.

past · ago · formerly · previously · used to

HANDSHAPE: Right OPEN hand

POSITION: Starts in front of the right shoulder

MOVEMENT: Hold up the right OPEN hand in front of the right shoulder with the palm facing in. Then move the hand up and back over the shoulder.

VISUALIZE: Events having moved into the past.

 Curved hand   Bent hand   Flat hand    Open hand

recently • a short time ago • lately

HANDSHAPE: Right X hand with index finger curved

POSITION: On the right cheek

MOVEMENT: Touch the curved index finger of the right X hand to the right cheek with the palm facing back. Then move the index finger up and down a few times.

VISUALIZE: Scratching your cheek as you try to recall something that happened just a short time ago.

then

HANDSHAPES: Right ONE hand and left L hand

POSITION: In front of the chest

MOVEMENT: Point the left L hand forward with the palm facing right. Then touch the index finger of the right ONE hand first to the thumb of the left hand, and then to the index finger of the left hand.

VISUALIZE: Pointing to one finger and then another.

time • clock • watch

HANDSHAPES: Right ONE hand with index finger curved, and left S hand

POSITION: In front of the chest

MOVEMENT: With the palms facing down, tap the curved index finger of the right ONE hand on the wrist of the left S hand a few times.

VISUALIZE: Pointing to a wristwatch.

 X hand   One hand   L hand   S hand

today

HANDSHAPES: **1.** Right and left CURVED hands
2. Right and left ONE hands

POSITIONS: **1.** Starts in front of the shoulders
2. In front of the chest

MOVEMENT: **1.** With the palms facing up, drop the right and left CURVED hands downward a short distance. (This is the sign for *now*.)
2. Point the left ONE hand to the right with the palm facing down. Place the right bent elbow on the left index finger, holding the right ONE hand upright. Then move the right hand down across the body toward the left elbow. (This is the sign for *day*.)

VISUALIZE: Combining the signs for *now* and *day*.

tomorrow

HANDSHAPE: Right A hand

POSITION: Starts near the right side of the chin

MOVEMENT: Hold the thumbtip of the right A hand next to the right side of the chin with the palm facing left. Then move the hand in a small forward arc away from the face.

VISUALIZE: Moving the hand slightly forward, only into the near future—tomorrow.

Curved hand

One hand

A hand

until

HANDSHAPE: Right and left ONE hands

POSITION: In front of the chest

MOVEMENT: Hold the left ONE hand with the index finger pointing up and the palm facing in. Then move the index finger of the right ONE hand in a slow forward arc until it touches the tip of the left index finger.

VISUALIZE: Moving your finger until it reaches its destination.

was

HANDSHAPES: Right w hand changing to s hand

POSITION: Starts near the side of the chin

MOVEMENT: Hold the right w hand at the side of the face, near the chin, with the palm facing left. The move it backwards toward the side of the neck while changing it to the s handshape.

VISUALIZE: Moving the hand backwards suggests a time in the past, and the signed letters indicate the specific word.

week • next week

HANDSHAPES: Right ONE hand and left FLAT hand

POSITION: In front of the chest

MOVEMENT: Slide the index fingertip of the right ONE hand across the palm of the left FLAT hand from the heel of the hand to the fingertips. To sign *next week,* move the right hand beyond the fingertips of the left hand, ending with the right index finger pointing forward.

VISUALIZE: Sliding your finger across a row of days on a calendar.

W hand

S hand

Flat hand

were

HANDSHAPES: Right w hand changing to R hand

POSITION: Starts near the side of the chin

MOVEMENT: Hold the right w hand at the side of the face, near the chin, with the palm facing left. Then move it backwards toward the side of the neck while changing it to the R handshape.

VISUALIZE: Moving the hand backwards suggests a time in the past, and the initials indicate the specific word.

year

HANDSHAPE: Right and left s hands

POSITION: In front of the chest

MOVEMENT: Hold the right and left s hands forward, palms facing in, with the right hand above the left. Then move the right hand forward in a full circle around the left hand and place the right hand on top of the left.

VISUALIZE: The earth's yearly movement around the sun.

yesterday

HANDSHAPE: Right y hand

POSITION: Starts on the right side of the chin

MOVEMENT: Touch the thumbtip of the right y hand to the right side of the chin with the palm facing forward. Then move the hand up and back across the right cheek toward the ear.

VISUALIZE: Moving the hand backwards suggests a time in the past, and the initial indicates the specific word.

W hand   R hand   S hand   Y hand

seasons,
animals,
nature
& weather

E ven if you're not the outdoor type, you'll feel at one with nature when you use the signs from this chapter in conversation. The next time you're inspired to gaze at the *stars,* climb the highest *mountain,* or catch a *butterfly,* or you have to mow the *grass,* weed the *garden,* or walk the *dog,* you'll be ready to show off what you've learned. With practice, signing these words will come "naturally."

SEASONS

season

HANDSHAPES: Left FLAT hand and right S hand

POSITION: In front of the chest

MOVEMENT: Hold up the left FLAT hand with the palm facing forward. Move the thumb side of the right S hand in a circle on the left palm.

VISUALIZE: The yearly cycle of seasons.

SEE HELPING HANDS ON NEXT PAGE.

winter

HANDSHAPE: Right and left s hands

POSITION: In front of the shoulders

MOVEMENT: Hold up the right and left s hands with the palms facing each other and shake them.

VISUALIZE: Shivering from the cold.

spring · grow · mature

HANDSHAPES: Left c hand and right AND hand changing to OPEN hand

POSITION: In front of the chest

MOVEMENT: Hold the left c hand forward with the fingers pointing right. Push the right AND hand up through the left c hand, opening the right hand as it passes through.

VISUALIZE: Spring flowers sprouting from the earth.

summer

HANDSHAPE: Right x hand

POSITION: Starts on the left side of the forehead

MOVEMENT: With the palm facing down, draw the index finger of the right x hand across the forehead from left to right.

VISUALIZE: Wiping perspiration from the forehead.

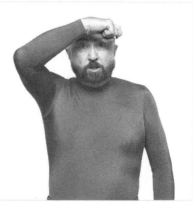

 Flat
hand

S
hand

C
hand

 And
hand

fall • autumn

HANDSHAPE: Left FLAT hand and right OPEN hand

POSITION: In front of the chest

MOVEMENT: Hold up the left FLAT hand, palm facing in, with the forearm tilted slightly to the right. Then move the index finger side of the right OPEN hand down along the outside of the left forearm while wiggling the fingers of the right OPEN hand.

VISUALIZE: Leaves tumbling gently from a tree.

ANIMALS

animals

HANDSHAPE: Right and left CLAWED hands

POSITION: On the chest

MOVEMENT: Holding the fingertips of the right and left CLAWED hands on the chest, rock both hands forward and back.

VISUALIZE: Showing the claws of an animal.

bear

HANDSHAPE: Right and left CLAWED hands

POSITION: In front of the chest

MOVEMENT: Cross the right and left CLAWED hands at the wrists with the palms facing in and make a few downward clawing motions with both hands simultaneously.

VISUALIZE: A grizzly bear showing his powerful claws.

Upen hand

X hand

Clawed hand

bird

HANDSHAPE: Right Q hand

POSITION: In front of the mouth

MOVEMENT: Point the extended fingers of the right Q hand forward in front of the mouth. Then close and open the Q fingers a few times.

VISUALIZE: The opening and closing of a bird's beak.

bug • insect

HANDSHAPE: Right THREE hand

POSITION: On the tip of the nose

MOVEMENT: Place the thumbtip of the right THREE hand on the tip of the nose with the palm facing left. Then bend and straighten the index and middle fingers a few times.

VISUALIZE: A bug's antennae twitching in the air.

butterfly

HANDSHAPE: Right and left OPEN hands

POSITION: In front of the chest

MOVEMENT: Hold up the right and left OPEN hands with the palms facing in and the thumbs interlocked. Wiggle the fingers.

VISUALIZE: The fluttering motion of a butterfly's wings.

Q
hand

Three
hand

Open
hand

cat

HANDSHAPE: Right and left F hands

POSITION: Starts near the corners of the mouth

MOVEMENT: Hold up the right and left F hands near the corners of the mouth with the palms facing each other. Then draw both hands out to the sides.

VISUALIZE: A cat's whiskers.

cow • bull

HANDSHAPE: Right and left Y hands

POSITION: On the temples

MOVEMENT: Touch the thumbtips of the right and left Y hands to the temples with the palms facing down. Then twist the hands up so the little fingers point up.

VISUALIZE: A bull's horns.

dinosaur

HANDSHAPES: Left FLAT hand and right AND hand

POSITION: In front of the chest

MOVEMENT: Point the left FLAT hand to the right with palm facing down. Place the right bent elbow, forearm upright, on the back of the left hand; then twist the right AND hand back and forth from the wrist a few times.

VISUALIZE: The shape and motion of a dinosaur's neck and head.

F
hand

Y
hand

Flat
hand

And
hand

dog

HANDSHAPE: Right FLAT hand

POSITION: Next to the right side

MOVEMENT: Pat the right side with the right FLAT hand, then snap the fingers. Repeat a few times.

VISUALIZE: A familiar way to call a dog.

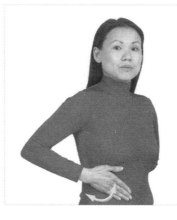 

duck

HANDSHAPE: Right N hand with thumb, index, and middle fingers extended

POSITION: In front of the mouth

MOVEMENT: Hold right N hand in front of the mouth with the extended thumb and fingers pointing forward. Then close and open the N fingers a few times.

VISUALIZE: The opening and closing of a duck's bill.

Hearing Ear Dogs for the Deaf

Did you know that dogs can be trained to assist people who are deaf or hard of hearing? Hearing ear dogs—also called service dogs, signal dogs, or hearing guide dogs—are similar to seeing eye dogs, but act as "ears" for people with hearing difficulties. The dogs are trained to distinguish between sounds such as a siren, a crying baby, a car horn, or a ringing telephone, and to alert their owners. Currently, forty-nine states allow hearing ear dogs to enter public places and ride on public transportation with their owners.

Dogs of many different breeds can perform well as hearing ear dogs, as long as they are intelligent and show good concentration. They are trained by professionals for anywhere from three to five months to learn basic obedience and response to sounds; and to respond to voice and hand signals. Once a dog has been trained, it's ready to be matched with an owner.

A candidate for a hearing ear dog doesn't immediately own the dog. First, the candidate must go through a week-long training period with the dog so that they can learn to work together, and so the potential owner can build a rapport with the dog. The candidate becomes the dog's owner only if the pair establishes a good relationship.

Flat hand

N hand

elephant

HANDSHAPE: Right B hand

POSITION: Starts on the lips

MOVEMENT: Place the back of the right B hand on the lips with fingertips pointing forward. Then swoop the hand down and forward.

VISUALIZE: The shape and motion of an elephant's trunk.

frog

HANDSHAPES: Right S hand changing to V hand

POSITION: In front of the throat

MOVEMENT: Hold the right S hand in front of the throat with the palm facing in. Then flick the index and middle fingers out straight to form the V handshape.

VISUALIZE: A frog croaking and then jumping.

horse

HANDSHAPE: Right U hand

POSITION: Next to the right temple

MOVEMENT: Hold up the right U hand next to the right temple with the palm facing forward. Then bend and straighten the U fingers a few times.

VISUALIZE: A horse's ears twitching.

B
hand

S
hand

V
hand

U
hand

lion

HANDSHAPE: Right CLAWED hand

POSITION: Above the head

MOVEMENT: Hold the right CLAWED hand above the head with the palm facing down. Shake the hand while moving it back over the head.

VISUALIZE: The movement of a lion's mane as he shakes his head.

monkey • ape

HANDSHAPE: Right and left CURVED hands

POSITION: On the sides of the chest

MOVEMENT: Scratch the sides of the chest with the fingertips of the right and left CURVED hands.

VISUALIZE: A monkey scratching its sides.

Internet Users Go Bananas for Koko

On April 27, 1998, H.E.A.V.E.N. and The EnviroLink Network, in collaboration with the Internet provider America Online, sponsored the first-ever interspecies online chat between humans and a gorilla. Koko, then twenty-six years old, is a lowland gorilla who understands more than 2,000 words of spoken English and has a working sign language vocabulary of 500 signs. During the live chat, Koko's tutor, Dr. Francine Patterson, signed questions posted to Koko, who signed her responses back to the doctor. A typist then posted Koko's responses on the Internet.

H.E.A.V.E.N. (Helping Educate, Activate, Volunteer and Empower via the Net) is a nonprofit organization that uses the Internet to foster activism. The EnviroLink Network is an online community that provides environmental news, information, and resources. The event sponsors hoped to raise awareness about the plight of gorillas as an endangered species. Lowland gorillas are threatened by human interference—such as expansive logging—in their natural habitat, which stretches from Cameroon to Zaire in central Africa.

Clawed hand

Curved hand

mouse

HANDSHAPE: Right ONE hand

POSITION: On the right side of the nose

MOVEMENT: Brush the index fingertip of the right ONE hand across the right side of the nose a few times.

VISUALIZE: A mouse's nose as it twitches and sniffs.

pig • hog

HANDSHAPE: Right FLAT hand

POSITION: Under the chin

MOVEMENT: Point the right FLAT hand to the left under the chin with the palm facing down. Then bend and straighten the fingers a few times.

VISUALIZE: A pig bending its snout into a food trough.

rabbit

HANDSHAPE: Right and left H hands

POSITION: In front of the chest

MOVEMENT: Cross the right and left H hands at the wrists with the palms facing in. Then bend and straighten the H fingers a few times.

VISUALIZE: A rabbit's ears twitching.

One hand   Flat hand   H hand

snake

HANDSHAPES: Right ONE hand and left FLAT hand

POSITION: In front of the chest

MOVEMENT: With the index finger pointing forward, move the right ONE hand forward in small circles and pass it under the down-turned palm of the left FLAT hand.

VISUALIZE: A snake wriggling out from its hiding place.

squirrel • chipmunk

HANDSHAPE: Right and left V hands

POSITION: In front of the chest

MOVEMENT: Hold up the right and left V hands with the palms facing each other. Tap the V fingertips of both hands together a few times.

VISUALIZE: A squirrel's front paws.

tiger

HANDSHAPE: Right and left CLAWED hands

POSITION: Starts in front of the face

MOVEMENT: Hold the fingers of the right and left CLAWED hands in front of the face with the palms facing in. Then pull the hands apart to the sides of the face while bending the fingers.

VISUALIZE: A tiger's claws moving to reveal its face.

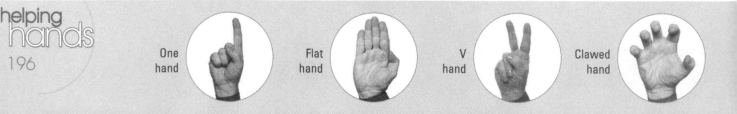

One hand   Flat hand   V hand   Clawed hand

turtle · tortoise

HANDSHAPES: Right A hand and left CURVED hand

POSITION: In front of the chest

MOVEMENT: Hold the right A hand under the downturned palm of the left CURVED hand. Then poke the right thumbtip out from under the little finger side of the left hand and wiggle the thumb up and down.

VISUALIZE: A turtle's head peeking out from its shell.

worm

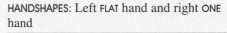

HANDSHAPES: Left FLAT hand and right ONE hand

POSITION: In front of the chest

MOVEMENT: Point the left FLAT hand forward with the palm facing right. Touch the index fingertip of the right ONE hand to the left palm. Then wiggle the right index finger while moving it across the left palm to the fingertips.

VISUALIZE: A worm squirming across a leaf.

NATURE

earth · globe · terrestrial · geography

HANDSHAPES: Right OPEN hand and left S hand

POSITION: In front of the chest

MOVEMENT: With the palms facing down, place the thumbtip and middle fingertip of the right OPEN hand on the sides of the left S hand. Then rock the right hand forward and back a few times, first toward the left fingers, then toward the left wrist.

VISUALIZE: A globe spinning on its axis.

A
hand

Curved
hand

Open
hand

S
hand

fire • flame • burn

HANDSHAPE: Right and left OPEN hands

POSITION: In front of the chest

MOVEMENT: Hold up the right and left OPEN hands with the palms facing in. Then move both hands alternately up and down while wiggling the fingers.

VISUALIZE: The flickering flames of a bonfire.

garden • yard

HANDSHAPES: **1.** Right and left OPEN hands **2.** Right AND hand

POSITIONS: **1.** In front of the chest **2.** Under the nose

MOVEMENT: **1.** Hold up the right and left OPEN hands with the palms facing in. Move the hands in a half circle until they face each other. **2.** Touch the fingertips of the right AND hand under the right nostril, then under the left. (This is the sign for *flower*.)

VISUALIZE: A fence surrounding flowers.

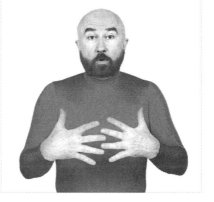

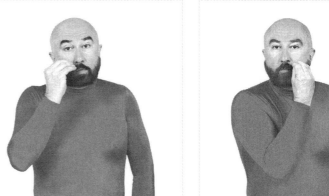

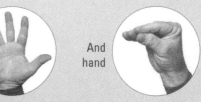

Open hand

And hand

grass

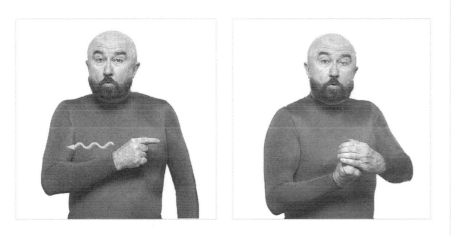

HANDSHAPES: 1. Right G hand **2.** Right AND hand and left C hand

POSITION: In front of the body

MOVEMENT: 1. Point the right G hand to the left; then move the hand to the right while shaking it from the wrist. (This is the sign for *green*.) **2.** Hold the left C hand forward with the fingers pointing right. Push the right AND hand up through the left C hand, opening the right hand as it passes through. (This is the sign for *grow*.)

VISUALIZE: Green grass growing.

flower • blossom

HANDSHAPE: Right AND hand

POSITION: Under the nose

MOVEMENT: Touch the fingertips of the right AND hand under the right nostril, then under the left.

VISUALIZE: Smelling a flower.

G hand

C hand

moon

HANDSHAPE: Right C hand

POSITION: In front of the right eye

MOVEMENT: Hold up the right C hand in front of the right eye with the fingers pointing left.

VISUALIZE: A crescent moon hanging in the sky.

mountain • hill

HANDSHAPES: **1.** Right and left S hands **2.** Right and left OPEN hands

POSITION: In front of the chest

MOVEMENT: **1.** With the palms facing down, place the right S hand on the back of the left S hand. (This resembles the sign for *rock*.) **2.** Hold up the right and left OPEN hands with the palms facing forward and move both hands upward and to the left with a wavy motion.

VISUALIZE: Rocks piled to form a mountain slope.

nature • natural

HANDSHAPES: Right N hand with index and middle fingers extended, and left S hand

POSITION: In front of the chest

MOVEMENT: With the palms facing down, move the right N hand in a small clockwise circle above the left S hand. Then touch the N fingertips to the back of the left hand.

VISUALIZE: The initial N resting on a firm foundation.

C hand   S hand   Open hand   N hand

ocean • sea

HANDSHAPES: **1.** Right W hand **2.** Right and left CURVED hands

POSITIONS: **1.** On the lips **2.** In front of the chest

MOVEMENT: **1.** With the fingertips pointing up, tap the index finger side of the right W hand on the lips a few times. (This is the sign for *water*.) **2.** Then point the right and left CURVED hands forward with the palms facing down and the left hand slightly behind the right; move both hands forward with a wavy motion.

VISUALIZE: Water flowing towards the shore in waves.

river

HANDSHAPES: **1.** Right W hand **2.** Right and left OPEN hands

POSITIONS: **1.** On the lips **2.** In front of the chest

MOVEMENT: **1.** With the fingertips pointing up, tap the index finger side of the right W hand on the lips a few times. (This is the sign for *water*.) **2.** Point the right and left OPEN hands forward with the palms facing down; then move the hands to the left while wiggling the fingers.

VISUALIZE: Water flowing along a river bank.

rock • stone

HANDSHAPES: **1.** Right and left A hands **2.** Right and left C hands

POSITION: In front of the chest

MOVEMENT: **1.** With the palms facing down, tap the knuckles of the right A hand on the back of the left A hand. **2.** Hold both C hands in front of the chest with the palms facing each other.

VISUALIZE: The hardness and roundness of a rock.

W hand   Curved hand   A hand

sky • heavens • space

HANDSHAPE: Right FLAT hand

POSITION: Above the forehead

MOVEMENT: With the palm facing out, move the right OPEN hand in an arc from left to right above the forehead.

VISUALIZE: The sweep of sky above your head.

star • starry

HANDSHAPE: Right and left ONE hands

POSITION: In front of the face

MOVEMENT: Hold up the right and left ONE hands in front of the face with the palms facing forward. Then move both hands up alternately, brushing the side of one index finger against the other.

VISUALIZE: A shooting star in the sky.

sun

HANDSHAPE: Right ONE hand

POSITION: Above the right side of the head

MOVEMENT: Hold up the right ONE hand above the right side of the head with the palm facing forward. Trace a small clockwise circle in the air.

VISUALIZE: A round sun blazing in the sky.

Flat hand

One hand

tree • woods • forest • branch

HANDSHAPES: Right OPEN hand and left S hand

POSITION: In front of the chest

MOVEMENT: Place the bent right elbow, forearm upright, on the back of the left S hand. Then twist the right OPEN hand from the wrist while wiggling the fingers.

VISUALIZE: A tree moving in the wind.

WEATHER

cloud • gale • storm

HANDSHAPE: Right and left CURVED hands

POSITION: In front of the forehead

MOVEMENT: Hold up the right and left CURVED hands in front of the forehead with the palms facing each other. Move the hands gently from side to side while making small circular motions from the wrists. For *gale* and *storm*, use more forceful movements.

VISUALIZE: Clouds forming in the sky.

cold • chilly • frigid • shiver

HANDSHAPE: Right and left S hands

POSITION: In front of the shoulders

MOVEMENT: Hold up the right and left S hands with the palms facing each other and shake them.

VISUALIZE: Shivering from the cold.

Open hand

S hand

Curved hand

cool • refresh

HANDSHAPE: Right and left OPEN hands

POSITION: Above the shoulders

MOVEMENT: Hold up the right and left OPEN hands above the shoulders with the palms facing back. Wiggle the fingers of both hands a few times.

VISUALIZE: Cooling yourself down by creating your own breeze.

dry • parched • drought

HANDSHAPE: Right X hand

POSITION: On the lips

MOVEMENT: With the palm facing down, draw the index finger of the right X hand across the lips from left to right.

VISUALIZE: Rubbing your hand across parched lips.

flood

HANDSHAPES: **1.** Right W hand **2.** Right and left OPEN hands

POSITIONS: **1.** On the lips **2.** In front of the chest

MOVEMENT: **1.** With the fingertips pointing up, tap the index finger side of the right W hand on the lips a few times. (This is the sign for *water*.) **2.** Point the right and left OPEN hands forward with the palms facing down. Pull both hands up while wiggling the fingers.

VISUALIZE: Flood waters rising around you.

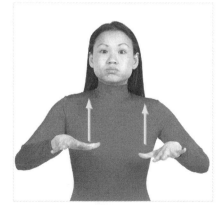

Open hand

X hand

W hand

hot • heat

HANDSHAPE: Right CLAWED hand

POSITION: Starts on the corners of the mouth

MOVEMENT: Hold the thumbtip and fingertips of the right CLAWED hand on the corners of the mouth. Then twist the hand forward sharply, ending with the palm facing down.

VISUALIZE: Pulling a hot tamale out of your mouth and throwing it away.

ice • freeze • frost • frozen • rigid

HANDSHAPE: Right and left OPEN hands

POSITION: In front of the chest

MOVEMENT: Point the right and left OPEN hands forward with the palms facing down. Pull up both hands simultaneously while curving the fingers in toward the palms.

VISUALIZE: Your hands becoming stiff and rigid after being dunked in icy water.

lightning

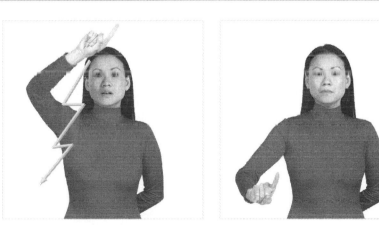

HANDSHAPE: Right ONE hand

POSITION: Near the forehead

MOVEMENT: Hold up the right ONE hand near the forehead with the palm facing forward. Then move the hand downward with a quick, jagged motion.

VISUALIZE: A flash of lightning in the sky.

Clawed hand

One hand

rain

HANDSHAPES: **1.** Right W hand **2.** Right and left CLAWED hands

POSITIONS: **1.** On the lips **2.** In front of the chest

MOVEMENT: **1.** With the fingertips pointing up, tap the index finger side of the right W hand on the lips a few times. (This is the sign for *water.*) **2.** Point the right and left CLAWED hands forward with the palms facing down. Move both hands up and down several times in quick movements while wiggling the fingers.

VISUALIZE: Water falling from the sky.

rainbow

HANDSHAPE: **1.** Right OPEN hand **2.** Right and left OPEN hands

POSITIONS: **1.** In front of the mouth **2.** In front of the chest

MOVEMENT: **1.** Hold up the right OPEN hand in front of the mouth with the palm facing in and wiggle the fingers. (This is the sign for *color.*) **2.** Hold the right and left OPEN hands in front of the chest with the fingertips touching. Then move the right OPEN hand in an arc from left to right above the forehead.

VISUALIZE: A rainbow arcing across the sky.

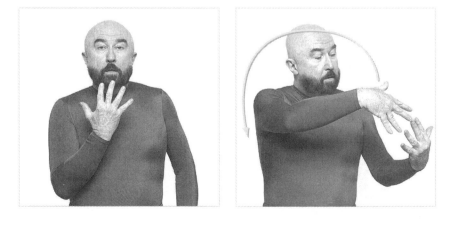

W hand   Clawed hand   Open hand

snow

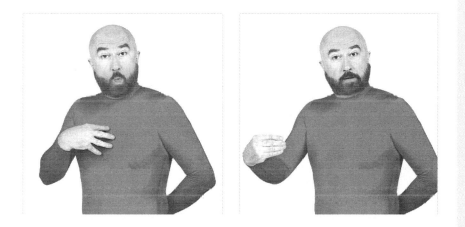

HANDSHAPES: **1.** Right OPEN hand changing to AND hand **2.** Right and left CLAWED hands

POSITION: In front of the chest

MOVEMENT: **1.** Touch the thumbtip and finger-tips of the right OPEN hand to the chest; then bring the hand forward a few inches while changing it to the AND handshape. (This is the sign for *white*.) **2.** Point the right and left CLAWED hands forward with the palms facing down. Drop both hands down while wiggling the fingers. (This is part of the sign for *rain*.)

VISUALIZE: Snow, or "white rain," falling gently from the sky.

temperature • thermometer • fever

HANDSHAPE: Right and left ONE hands

POSITION: In front of the chest

MOVEMENT: Slide the index fingertip of the right ONE hand up and down the upright index finger of the left ONE hand.

VISUALIZE: The mercury in a thermometer rising and falling with the temperature.

warm • warmth • heat

HANDSHAPES: Right AND hand changing to OPEN hand

POSITION: Starts in front of the mouth

MOVEMENT: Point the right AND hand toward the mouth; then move the hand upward and forward while opening it, ending with the palm facing up.

VISUALIZE: Warm breath coming from your mouth.

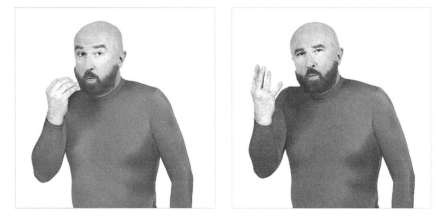

Understanding Usher's Syndrome

Usher's syndrome is a hereditary condition that causes loss of both hearing and eyesight. Although very rare, affecting about 3 babies out of every 1,000,000 born, Usher's is the cause of approximately 10 percent of all hereditary deafness.

There are three types of Usher's syndrome. People with type I are profoundly deaf at birth and typically experience an onset of vision loss by age five or six. Type II is characterized by a milder hearing loss that grows progressively worse over time, and an onset of vision loss usually starting at age ten or later. Type III is similar to type I, but the hearing deteriorates more quickly.

The gradual vision loss that's part of Usher's syndrome progresses from night blindness to blind spots to tunnel vision and, eventually, results in total blindness. Naturally, vision loss presents special problems for people with Usher's who use sign language. One solution has been to confine the signing space to a small area near the face, which helps people to see the entire sign in their central vision. People with Usher's syndrome have also developed a variation on sign language called "tactile signing": as they lose their vision over time, they begin to rely more on the sense of touch to understand the signs.

One hand

And hand

Open hand

weather

HANDSHAPE: Right and left w hands

POSITION: In front of the chest

MOVEMENT: Point the right and left w hands forward with the palms facing each other and twist both hands up and down from the wrists.

VISUALIZE: Using the initial w in forming a sign similar to *change* suggests that the weather is always changing.

wet • drench • soak • saturate

HANDSHAPES: **1.** Right w hand **2.** Right and left CLAWED hands changing to AND hands

POSITIONS: **1.** On the lips **2.** In front of the chest

MOVEMENT: **1.** With the fingertips pointing up, tap the index finger side of the right w hand on the lips a few times. (This is the sign for *water*.) **2.** Point the right and left CLAWED hands forward with the palms facing up. Pull both hands down slowly while changing them to the AND handshape. (This is the sign for *soft*.)

VISUALIZE: Water falling and soaking into the ground.

W hand   Clawed hand

wind • breeze • blow

HANDSHAPE: Right and left OPEN hands

POSITION: In front of the forehead

MOVEMENT: Hold up the right and left OPEN hands in front of the forehead with the palms facing each other. Sweep both hands gently from side to side a few times.

VISUALIZE: The blowing and shifting of wind.

Alerting the Hard of Hearing About the Weather

Among the many challenges that deaf and hard-of-hearing people face, one that might not immediately come to mind is the danger of being unprepared for hazardous weather conditions. But for people with hearing impairments, being caught unaware of approaching tornadoes, flash floods, high winds, and other weather emergencies is a very real and frightening problem. That's why meteorologist Vincent "Bim" Wood—a research meteorologist at the National Oceanic and Atmospheric Administration's National Severe Storms Laboratory (NSSL) in Norman, Oklahoma—pioneered the Hazardous Weather Pager Program, the first of its kind to directly transmit National Weather Service alerts to people with hearing impairments. Weather warnings are sent via pagers to deaf and hard-of-hearing subscribers, who would otherwise need access to a television or computer to learn of severe weather warnings. The pagers vibrate when a weather alert has been issued and display a text readout indicating the specific warning, whether a tornado, a severe thunderstorm, a snow storm, a flash flood, or dangerously high winds. In addition,

three warning lights indicate the level of alert, ranging from Statement, to Watch, to Warning.

Wood, who has been deaf since infancy, recognized the need for an early warning system after a series of tornadoes touched down in Oklahoma in May of 1999. In the months that followed, Wood interviewed many deaf and hard-of-hearing Oklahomans to learn more about the kinds of access they had to weather alerts. Of the individuals he surveyed, 81 percent were fearful about being unprepared for weather emergencies due to limited links to critical weather information. Unable to hear either standard radio reports or even the loudest of storm sirens, one couple Wood interviewed said they had no knowledge of an approaching tornado until they happened to look outside and see neighbors fleeing their homes! Everyone interviewed expressed the need to receive the same vital information that hearing people receive via radio broadcasts. Hopefully, Wood's program will serve as a model for other states so that many more people with hearing impairments will have access to lifesaving weather alerts.

Open
hand

school & education

10

Y ou can go straight to the head of the class with these "educational" signs. It doesn't matter if you're a timid *freshman* or a super-confident *senior,* or if you've already earned your *diploma* and left *school* behind. If you *study* hard and *learn* the signs in this chapter, you should give yourself an A!

book • textbook • volume

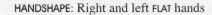

HANDSHAPE: Right and left FLAT hands

POSITION: In front of the chest

MOVEMENT: Hold the right and left FLAT hands together with the palms touching and the fingers pointing forward. Then pull the hands apart so the palms face up, keeping the little finger sides together.

VISUALIZE: Opening a book.

SEE HELPING HANDS ON NEXT PAGE.

class

HANDSHAPE: Right and left C hands

POSITION: In front of the chest

MOVEMENT: Hold up the right and left C hands with the fingers pointing toward each other. Then move the hands in an outward circle until the little finger sides touch.

VISUALIZE: The movement traces a roomful of people, and the initial indicates the word.

college

HANDSHAPE: Right and left FLAT hands

POSITION: In front of the chest

MOVEMENT: Place the palm of the right FLAT hand on the upturned palm of the left FLAT hand. Then lift the right hand slightly and make a small counterclockwise circle above the left hand.

VISUALIZE: Resembles the sign for *school* to suggest a school that's on a higher level.

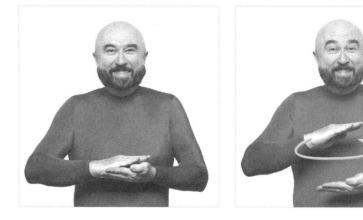

course • lesson

HANDSHAPES: Right C hand and left FLAT hand

POSITION: In front of the chest

MOVEMENT: Touch the little finger side of the right C hand to the upturned palm of the left FLAT hand near the fingers. Then move the right hand in a small arc down to the heel of the left hand.

VISUALIZE: Running your hand down a printed lesson plan.

 Flat hand

 C hand

 F hand

degree • diploma

HANDSHAPE: Right and left F hands

POSITION: In front of the chest

MOVEMENT: Touch the index finger sides of the right and left F hands together with the palms facing forward. Then move the hands apart to the sides. (In common usage, this sign is often made with O hands.)

VISUALIZE: Running your hands along the length of a diploma.

education • educate

HANDSHAPE: Right and left E hands changing to D hands

POSITION: Near the sides of the forehead

MOVEMENT: Hold up the right and left E hands near the sides of the forehead with the palms facing each other. Move both hands forward while changing to D hands.

VISUALIZE: Using the initial E to form a sign similar to *teach*.

examination • test • quiz

HANDSHAPES: Right and left ONE hands changing to OPEN hands

POSITION: Starts in front of the shoulders

MOVEMENT: Hold up the right and left ONE hands in front of the shoulders with the palms facing forward and trace the shape of question marks in opposite directions in the air. Then open both hands and move them forward with the palms facing down.

VISUALIZE: Directing questions toward others in the classroom.

E hand   D hand   One hand 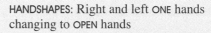   Open hand

fail

HANDSHAPES: Right v hand and left OPEN hand

POSITION: In front of the chest

MOVEMENT: With the palms facing up, place the extended fingers of the right v hand on the palm of the left OPEN hand. Then slide the right hand forward along the fingers of the left hand and drop it off the end of the left fingertips.

VISUALIZE: Falling grades leading to failure.

Building Brain Power With Sign Language

While babies typically say their first words between one and two years of age, it's clear that they want to communciate long before they're physically able to speak—which can be frustrating for parents and children alike. Now, sign language is being used as a way to help babies communicate before they have the motor skills to form words. Signing can help babies express specific needs, without whining or crying. And exciting new research suggests that teaching babies to sign may actually increase their IQs.

In a study that began in 1989, psychology professors Linda Acredolo of the University of California-Davis and Susan Goodwyn of California State University tracked the development of 120 children, 40 of whom learned simple signs starting at eleven months. When the children who could sign were three years old, their verbal ability was about four months ahead of the children who had not learned to sign. By the time they had finished second grade, the signing children had an average IQ of 114, compared with 102 for the other children.

Although these results are encouraging, some parents are hesitant to try signing with their babies, usually because of fear that the children won't feel the need to talk if they learn to use sign language. However, it seems that the reverse might be the case—research suggests that babies who learn to sign tend to speak earlier than children who don't sign. Signing seems to create a more verbal environment, and earlier exposure to successful communication encourages babies to speak.

Signing can help babies express their needs.

V hand

Open hand

freshman

HANDSHAPES: Right ONE hand and left OPEN hand

POSITION: In front of the chest

MOVEMENT: Touch the index fingertip of the right ONE hand to the ring fingertip of the left OPEN hand.

VISUALIZE: Pointing to the fourth finger shows that a freshman has four years until graduation.

Gallaudet University

HANDSHAPE: Right G hand

POSITION: Starts near the outside corner of the right eye

MOVEMENT: Point the right G hand to the left near the outside corner of the right eye. Then move the hand back toward the right ear while touching the thumbtip and index fingertip together.

VISUALIZE: Symbolizes the rimless eyeglasses worn by Dr. Thomas Hopkins Gallaudet, the founder of Gallaudet University.

graduate • graduation

HANDSHAPES: Right G hand and left OPEN hand

POSITION: In front of the chest

MOVEMENT: Move the right G hand in a small clockwise circle above the upturned palm of the left OPEN hand. Then touch the little finger side of the right hand to the left palm.

VISUALIZE: Using the initial G to place a seal on a diploma.

One hand

G hand

junior

HANDSHAPES: Right ONE hand and left OPEN hand

POSITION: In front of the chest

MOVEMENT: Touch the index fingertip of the right ONE hand to the index fingertip of the left OPEN hand.

VISUALIZE: Pointing to the second finger shows that a junior has two years until graduation.

learn • student

HANDSHAPES: Right CURVED hand changing to AND hand and left FLAT hand

POSITION: Starts in front of the chest

MOVEMENT: Touch the fingertips of the right CURVED hand to the upturned palm of the left FLAT hand. Then lift the right hand while changing it to the AND handshape and touch the fingertips to the center of the forehead. To sign *student*, add the *person* ending. (See page 18.)

VISUALIZE: Pulling information out of a book and placing it in the brain.

library

HANDSHAPE: Right L hand

POSITION: Above the right shoulder

MOVEMENT: Hold up the right L hand in front of the right shoulder with the palm facing forward and trace a small clockwise circle in the air.

VISUALIZE: Signaling a librarian to ask for help.

One hand Open hand Curved hand And hand

major • area • specialty • field

HANDSHAPE: Right and left B hands

POSITION: In front of the chest

MOVEMENT: Point the left B hand forward with the palm facing right. Then, with the palm facing left, slide the little finger side of the right B hand forward along the left index finger.

VISUALIZE: Following a chosen path.

pass

HANDSHAPE: Right and left A hands

POSITION: In front of the chest

MOVEMENT: Hold the right and left A hands forward, palms facing each other, with the right hand slightly behind the left. Then bring the right hand forward past the left.

VISUALIZE: One hand passing the other

principal

HANDSHAPES: Right P hand and left FLAT hand

POSITION: In front of the chest

MOVEMENT: With the palms facing down, move the right P hand in a small counter-clockwise circle above the left FLAT hand, ending with the P hand touching the FLAT hand.

VISUALIZE: Taking charge over a group of people.

Flat hand — L hand — B hand — A hand — P hand

program

HANDSHAPES: Left FLAT hand and right P hand

POSITION: In front of the chest

MOVEMENT: Hold up the left FLAT hand with the palm facing right. Slide the middle fingertip of the right P hand down over the left palm from the fingertips to the wrist. Then twist the left hand slightly and slide the middle P fingertip down the back of the left hand.

VISUALIZE: Showing a program that has printing on the front and back.

read

HANDSHAPES: Left FLAT hand and right V hand

POSITION: In front of the chest

MOVEMENT: Point the left FLAT hand to the right with the palm facing in. Then, with the palm facing down, point the fingertips of the right V hand at the left FLAT palm and move the right hand down.

VISUALIZE: Two eyes scanning the page of a book.

register • sign • signature

HANDSHAPES: Right H hand and left FLAT hand

POSITION: In front of the chest

MOVEMENT: Touch the fingertips of the right H hand to the upturned palm of the left FLAT hand.

VISUALIZE: Showing where the signature belongs on a register.

Flat hand   P hand   V hand   H hand

schedule

HANDSHAPE: Left and right OPEN hands

POSITION: In front of the chest

MOVEMENT: Point the left OPEN hand forward with the palm facing right. Then, with the palm facing down, brush the fingertips of the right OPEN hand down across the left palm. Next, turn the right hand so the palm faces in and brush the back of the right fingertips across the left palm from the heel of the hand to the fingertips.

VISUALIZE: Tracing the columns and rows of a train schedule.

school

HANDSHAPE: Right and left FLAT hands

POSITION: In front of the chest

MOVEMENT: Clap the right and left FLAT hands together a few times.

VISUALIZE: A teacher clapping to get the attention of her students.

senior

HANDSHAPES: Right ONE hand and left OPEN hand

POSITION: In front of the chest

MOVEMENT: Touch the index fingertip of the right ONE hand to the thumbtip of the left OPEN hand.

VISUALIZE: Pointing to the thumb shows that a senior has one year until graduation.

Open hand   One hand

sophomore

HANDSHAPES: Right ONE hand and left OPEN hand

POSITION: In front of the chest

MOVEMENT: Touch the index fingertip of the right ONE hand to the middle fingertip of the left OPEN hand.

VISUALIZE: Pointing to the third finger shows that a sophomore has three years until graduation.

study

HANDSHAPES: Left FLAT hand and right OPEN hand

POSITION: In front of the chest

MOVEMENT: Point the left FLAT hand to the right with the palm facing in. Then, with the palm facing down, point the fingertips of the right OPEN hand toward the left palm. Move the right hand toward and then away from the left hand while wiggling the right fingers.

VISUALIZE: Studying the page of a book.

teach • instruct • educate • teacher • professor

HANDSHAPES: Right and left open AND hands changing to closed AND hands

POSITION: **1.** Near the sides of the forehead **2.** At the shoulders

MOVEMENT: Hold the right and left open AND hands near the sides of the forehead with the palms facing each other. Move both hands forward while changing them to the closed AND handshape. To sign *teacher* or *professor*, add the *person* ending. (See page 18.)

VISUALIZE: A teacher taking information from the mind and giving it to others.

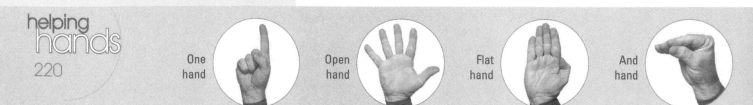

One hand   Open hand   Flat hand   And hand

How Do Hearing Tests Work?

Your hearing test actually begins with a medical case history, during which the audiologist asks a number of questions to determine if you are at risk for hearing loss or have already lost some hearing. For example, you may be asked if you've noticed difficulty with your hearing, and for how long; if you have a family history of hearing loss; what kinds of noise levels you've been exposed to; and if you've had any illnesses or taken any medications that may have affected your hearing. Next, the audiologist will examine the inside of your ear with an otoscope, a cone-shaped instrument with a magnifying lens and light, to see if there are any abnormalities in your ear canal or eardrum.

A pure tone test is used to determine the threshold at which you hear different frequencies. You will be asked to put earplugs into your ears or to place headphones over your ears. Then the audiologist will use an audiometer to present several tones at different pitches and intensity levels, which you hear through the earplugs or head-phones. The pitch of the sound is measured in Hertz (Hz), and the intensity of the sound is measured in decibels (dB). You'll be instructed to raise your hand or push a button whenever you hear a pure tone.

Speech tests include the speech recognition threshold (SRT) and the word recognition score. The SRT is used to determine the lowest level at which you can identify speech at least half the time. For the SRT, you'll be instructed to repeat a series of words after you hear them. Words may have one or two syllables, and become softer during the test. For the word recognition score, on the other hand, all of the words have one syllable, and are presented at a comfortable loudness level, sometimes with background noise. This test helps evaluate how well you understand what you have heard; a score of 0% indicates no understanding of the words, and a score of 100% indicates that all of the words were correctly identified.

Your responses to these hearing tests will be recorded on a chart called an audiogram. Frequency numbers run across the top or bottom of the audiogram, and range from high to low tones—125 Hz to 8,000 Hz. The numbers that run down the side of the graph show hearing level. Marks near the top of the graph indicate better hearing, and marks near the bottom of the graph indicate poorer hearing.

word

HANDSHAPES: Left ONE hand and right Q hand

POSITION: In front of the chest

MOVEMENT: Hold up the left ONE hand in front of the chest with the palm facing right. Tap the thumbtip and index fingertip of the right Q hand on the left index finger a few times.

VISUALIZE: A small piece of a sentence—a word.

Q hand

write • edit

HANDSHAPES: Left FLAT hand and right A hand with thumbtip and index fingertip pressed together

POSITION: In front of the chest

MOVEMENT: Point the left FLAT hand to the right with the palm facing in. Then move the thumbtip and index fingertip of the right A hand across the left palm in a wavy motion.

VISUALIZE: Writing with a pen.

Websites to Rely On

The Internet is an ever-expanding source of information about sign language and deaf culture. In fact, sometimes the most difficult part of finding what you're looking for is wading through all the websites! To help make your research easier, I've sifted through the sites and come up with the following list of select resources. Turn to them for articles, reading lists, and links to important information about deafness and sign language.

American Sign Language Browser •
http://commtechlab.msu.edu/sites/aslweb/
Offered by Michigan State University, the American Sign Language Browser presents clear videos of thousands of ASL signs. Each video is accompanied by explanatory text that further clarifies the desired movement.

ASLinfo.com • www.aslinfo.com
With its focus on American Sign Language, plus links to sites about education and deaf culture, this is one of the most complete sign language resources. Plus, it provides a helpful outline of Federal laws concerning deafness, and a time line of events in deaf history and culture.

Deaf Mall's Deaf Linx • deafmall.net/deaflinx
The "ultimate guide to deafness Internet links," this website offers resources about deaf culture, as well as material on sign language, organizations for the deaf, and legal issues. Also featured are online sites, suggested reading and video lists, and information on sign language classes.

The Deaf Resource Library • www.deaflibrary.org
A collection of resources and links about deaf culture, this site offers information on periodicals by and for deaf people, material on sign language interpreting and captioning, and a list of organizations for the deaf. A special section includes resources for deaf children and their parents.

Deaf World Web's Deaf Encyclopedia Online •
www.deafworldweb.org/pub
This online "encyclopedia" provides hundreds of links to sites on deafness, deaf culture, and sign language. Also included is an overview of deaf education, as well as insight into controversial topics such as oralism.

Laurent Clerc National Deaf Education Center •
clerccenter.gallaudet.edu
Designed to benefit people from all walks of life—both hearing individuals who wish to learn about the deaf and deaf people—this site provides links to information on topics such as sign language and assistive listening devices. In addition, its online exhibit "History Through Deaf Eyes" showcases the historic achievements of deaf people.

Flat
hand

A
hand

careers, jobs & the workplace

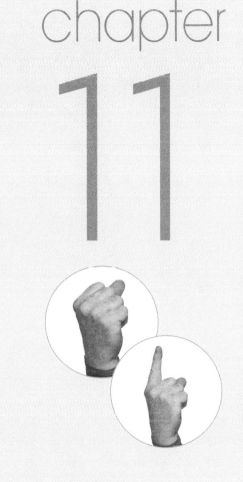

A re you ready to get down to business? Put these career-oriented signs to work for you, and you'll be a success! Whether you're a *doctor*, a *secretary*, or a *photographer*, or you've yet to choose your *profession* or even *apply* for a job, you're sure to *profit* from the signs included in this chapter.

CAREERS & JOBS

actor • actress • drama • perform • show

HANDSHAPES: 1. Right and left A hands
2. Right and left FLAT hands

POSITION: In front of the chest

MOVEMENT: 1. Hold the right and left A hands forward with the palms facing each other; then circle both hands alternately up and toward the body. (This is the sign for *drama*.) **2.** Sign the *person* ending.

VISUALIZE: An actor's "Hey, look at me" pose while onstage.

SEE HELPING HANDS ON NEXT PAGE.

Marlee Matlin

Acclaimed actress Marlee Matlin was born in Morton Grove, Illinois, on August 24th, 1965. Although she was born with normal hearing, she became deaf after a bout with German measles when she was just 18 months old. As a young child, she learned to communicate with her family and friends using sign language.

Undaunted by her inability to hear, Matlin started acting at a children's theater company in Chicago when she was seven years old. She was a star from the beginning—her first-ever acting role was that of Dorothy in *The Wizard of Oz*. But it was her later role as a minor character in a stage production of Mark Medoff's *Children of a Lesser God* that won her the role of "Sara" in the film version, starring opposite William Hurt. Her impressive motion picture debut earned her the Academy Award for Best Actress in 1987, when she was only twenty-one years old. She also received the Golden Globe Award for Best Actress in a Drama that same year.

Matlin has numerous other movie roles to her credit, as well, including *Walker,* co-starring Ed Harris; *The Man in the Golden Mask* with Jean Reno; and Robert Altman's *The*

Marlee Matlin

Player. In 1989, she made her television debut in *Bridge to Silence* with Lee Remick. Since then, she was twice nomiated for a Golden Globe as Best Actress in a Dramatic Television Series for her starring role in *Reasonable Doubts,* and was also nominated for two Emmy Awards in 1994 for performances in episodes of *Picket Fences* and *Seinfeld.* Matlin also appears in *The West Wing.*

Despite her busy acting career, Matlin has managed to devote much time and energy to various charitable causes. In 1994, she was appointed to the Board of Directors of the Corporation for National Service, which oversees the volunteer organization Americorps. Then, in 1995, she served as Honorary Chairperson for National Volunteer Week. Currently, she is the national spokesperson for VITAC, which provides closed captioning for television, and has helped promote closed captioning around the world.

Matlin lives in California with her husband, law enforcement officer Kevin Grandalski, and her children, Sarah Rose and Brandon Joseph.

artist

HANDSHAPES: **1.** Left FLAT hand and right I hand **2.** Right and left FLAT hands

POSITION: In front of the chest

MOVEMENT: **1.** Point the left FLAT hand forward with the palm facing right. Then slide the little fingertip of the right I hand down across the left palm with a wavy motion. (This is the sign for *art*.) **2.** Sign the *person* ending.

VISUALIZE: A person who draws or paints.

A
hand

Flat
hand

I
hand

dentist

HANDSHAPE:	Right D hand
POSITION:	On the teeth
MOVEMENT:	Tap the thumbtip and middle fingertip of the right D hand lightly against the teeth a few times.
VISUALIZE:	Working on a patient's teeth.

doctor • physician • surgeon

HANDSHAPES:	Right D hand and left A hand
POSITION:	In front of the chest
MOVEMENT:	Tap the thumbtip of the right D hand on the upturned wrist of the left A hand a few times.
VISUALIZE:	The motion suggests checking a patient's pulse, and the initial indicates the word *doctor*.

Ludwig van Beethoven

Who *hasn't* heard of the famous composer Ludwig van Beethoven? While he lived, Beethoven had a reputation among patrons and colleagues as a difficult man who was prone to moodiness and fits of temper. Today he's widely regarded as a musical genius—the last of the classic and the first of the romantic composers.

Born in Bonn, Germany, on December 16, 1770, Beethoven began his career as a pianist and composer early in his childhood. But as the years passed, his growing deafness made a career as a virtuoso impossible. Yet, despite the deterioration of his hearing, Beethoven continued to write music, including his celebrated Ninth Symphony and the Missa Solemnis, which were composed in total deafness.

After a prolonged illness, Beethoven died on March 26, 1827, during a violent thunderstorm. Roused by a brilliant flash of light, he lifted his right hand in a fist and shouted, "I shall hear in heaven!" He then fell back dead.

D
hand

Technology Opens Career Doors

Just a few decades ago, deaf people didn't have many career choices. Most found their options limited to trade jobs, non-profit work, or teaching positions at schools for the deaf. When the Americans with Disabilities Act made discrimination against people with disabilities illegal, a great many doors were opened. (See page 290 for more information.) Yet, because communication in the workplace was often challenging, many deaf people remained frustrated by obstacles. Well, times have changed—and we have technology to thank for that.

The 1990s saw a veritable explosion in technological innovations that made communication between deaf and hearing coworkers easy and convenient. Today, vibrating pagers let deaf people receive messages on the go. Real-time captioning, in which spoken words are displayed on a television or computer screen, enables instantaneous communication. Video-relay interpreting allows deaf and hearing people to "talk" with the aid of a remote sign language interpreter, who transmits the content of the conversation through video. And, of course, the Internet and e-mail have virtually leveled the playing field, providing direct exchanges between deaf and hearing peers.

Such a proliferation of options in communications technology means that more and more deaf people are being hired based on what they *can* do, instead of being regarded merely as deaf in a hearing world. And with future technological advances, there will soon be no limit to what they can achieve.

farmer

HANDSHAPES: **1.** Right OPEN hand **2.** Right and left FLAT hands

POSITIONS: **1.** Starts on the left side of the chin **2.** In front of the chest

MOVEMENT: **1.** Touch the thumbtip of the right OPEN hand to the left side of the chin with the palm facing left; then slide the right thumbtip across the chin to the right. **2.** Sign the *person* ending.

VISUALIZE: The bushy beard of a farmer.

Open hand   Flat hand

judge · court · trial · judgment · justice

HANDSHAPES: 1. Right ONE hand **2.** Right and left F hands

POSITIONS: 1. On the forehead **2.** In front of the chest

MOVEMENT: 1. Touch the index fingertip of the right ONE hand to the center of the forehead. **2.** Point the right and left F hands forward with the palms facing each other, and move the hands alternately up and down a few times.

VISUALIZE: A judge considering both sides of a case before coming to a decision.

lawyer · attorney · law

HANDSHAPES: 1. Left FLAT hand and right L hand **2.** Right and left FLAT hands

POSITION: In front of the chest

MOVEMENT: 1. Hold up the left FLAT hand with the palm facing forward. Place the thumb and index finger side of the right L hand on the left hand near the fingertips; then move the right hand down in an arc to the heel of the left hand. (This is the sign for *law*.) **2.** Sign the *person* ending.

VISUALIZE: The initial L being imprinted on an official document.

One hand   F hand   L hand

nurse

HANDSHAPES: Right N hand with index and middle fingers extended, and left S hand

POSITION: In front of the chest

MOVEMENT: Place the extended fingertips of the right N hand on the upturned wrist of the left S hand.

VISUALIZE: The motion suggests checking a patient's pulse, and the initial indicates the word *nurse*.

photographer

HANDSHAPES: 1. Right C hand and left FLAT hand **2.** Right and left FLAT hands

POSITIONS: 1. Starts next to the right cheek **2.** In front of the chest

MOVEMENT: 1. Hold the right C hand next to the right cheek with the fingers pointing forward. Then move the right hand down and place the thumb and index finger side on the palm of the upright left FLAT hand. (This is the sign for *photograph*.) **2.** Sign the *person* ending.

VISUALIZE: A person who takes photographs.

N
hand

S
hand

C
hand

Flat
hand

pilot

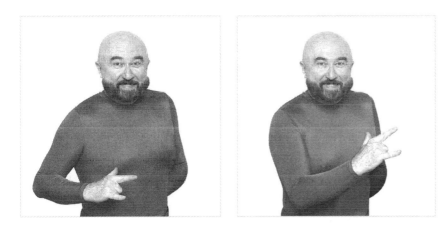

HANDSHAPES: 1. Right Y hand with index finger extended **2.** Right and left FLAT hands

POSITION: In front of the chest

MOVEMENT: 1. With the palm facing down, move the right Y hand forward and upward away from the body. (This is the sign for *airplane*.) **2.** Sign the *person* ending.

VISUALIZE: An airplane taking off and the person who's flying it.

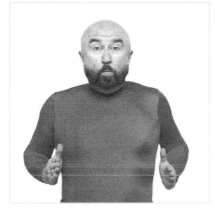

police officer • sheriff • marshal • security • badge

HANDSHAPE: Right C hand

POSITION: On the left shoulder

MOVEMENT: Tap the thumb side of the right C hand on the left shoulder a few times.

VISUALIZE: The badge on the chest of an officer of the law.

Y
hand

Becoming a
Sign Language Interpreter

Sign language interpreters help bridge the communication gap between deaf or hard-of-hearing people who use only sign language and people who don't know sign language, such as hearing people who use only a spoken language. Interpreters are often needed in schools, hospitals and clinics, government agencies, legal and court settings, and theaters, just to name a few places.

People who are interested in becoming sign language interpreters must have excellent sign language and fingerspelling skills. Some people begin developing signing skills at a young age through communication with relatives who are deaf or hard-of-hearing. Others take an interest in learning to sign later in life, and study sign language at the high school or college level, or through adult education courses or local agencies.

Of course, becoming a qualified sign language interpreter goes beyond learning to sign fluently.

Individuals who are committed to pursuing this type of work must complete an interpreter education program, which covers important aspects of the profession such as the role of an interpreter, situations in which an interpreter might function, the history of the profession, and public speaking techniques. Interpreter education programs also help students develop an understanding of the deaf community, and guide them in practicing the skills involved in interpreting.

Once a student completes an interpreter education program, he or she must pass written and performance tests administered by the Registry of Interpreters for the Deaf, Inc., in order to become a certified interpreter. Certified interpreters are bound by the Registry's Code of Ethics to conduct themselves professionally and appropriately on the job, by keeping all information pertaining to the discussion strictly confidential and refraining from giving advice or expressing a personal opinion.

president • superintendent

HANDSHAPES: Right and left C hands changing to S hands

POSITION: Starts on the temples

MOVEMENT: Hold the right and left C hands on the temples with the fingers pointing forward. Then move the hands out and away from the head while changing them to the S handshape.

VISUALIZE: Showing the "big horns" that symbolize authority.

C hand

S hand

psychiatrist

HANDSHAPES: Right P hand and left S hand	
POSITION: In front of the chest	
MOVEMENT: Place the middle fingertip of the right P hand on the upturned wrist of the left S hand.	
VISUALIZE: The motion suggests checking a patient's pulse, and the initial indicates the word *psychiatrist*.	

psychologist • psychology

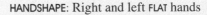

HANDSHAPE: Right and left FLAT hands	
POSITION: In front of the chest	
MOVEMENT: 1. Tap the little finger side of the right FLAT hand in the space between the thumb and index finger of the left FLAT hand a few times. **2.** Sign the *person* ending.	
VISUALIZE: A psychologist dividing the mind in order to analyze it.	

Ear Cell Transplants

Researchers have shown that engineered ear cells—nerve cells that are actually grown outside of the body—can be transplanted into humans to arrest hearing loss or even regenerate lost hearing.

Clinical trials with transplanted nerve cells will likely be conducted initially in participants with cochlear implants, devices that bypass the ear's damaged cochlea and directly stimulate the nerve of hearing in the ear. (For more information on cochlear implants, see page 303.) Although cochlear implants have been used with some success in certain deaf individuals, they are generally not helpful in people with long-term deafness because of the extent of the damage to the sensory nerves in the ear. As a result of the pioneering work of Dr. Matthew Holley of the University of Bristol in England, researchers believe that transplanted cells have the potential to improve the transmissions between the cochlear implant and the nerve of hearing, thereby making the implant more effective and broadening the range of candidates who can benefit from the device.

P hand

Flat hand

secretary

HANDSHAPES: **1.** Right U hand **2.** Left FLAT hand and right A hand with thumbtip and index fingertip pressed together

POSITIONS: **1.** Starts below the right earlobe **2.** In front of the chest

MOVEMENT: **1.** Starting below the right earlobe, slide the index finger side of the right U hand down along the jawbone to the chin. **2.** Point the left FLAT hand forward with the palm facing right. Then move the thumbtip and index fingertip of the right A hand across the left palm in a wavy motion. (This is the sign for *write*.)

VISUALIZE: Listening and taking messages.

teacher • professor

HANDSHAPES: **1.** Right and left open AND hands changing to closed AND hands **2.** Right and left FLAT hands

POSITIONS: **1.** Near the sides of the forehead **2.** In front of the chest

MOVEMENT: **1.** Hold the right and left open AND hands near the sides of the forehead with the palms facing each other. Point both hands forward while changing them to the closed AND handshape. **2.** Sign the *person* ending.

VISUALIZE: A teacher taking information from the mind and giving it to others.

U
hand

Flat
hand

A
hand

And
hand

waiter • waitress

HANDSHAPE: Right and left slightly CURVED hands

POSITION: In front of the chest

MOVEMENT: 1. Point the right and left CURVED hands forward with the palms facing up; then move the hands alternately back and forth. **2.** Sign the *person* ending.

VISUALIZE: A waiter or waitress handling plates of food.

writer • reporter • journalist • playwright

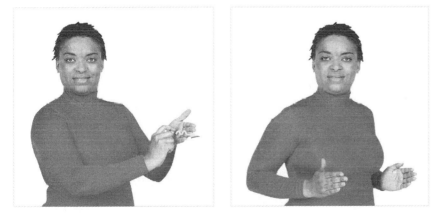

HANDSHAPES: 1. Left FLAT hand and right A hand with thumbtip and index fingertip pressed together **2.** Right and left FLAT hands

POSITION: In front of the chest

MOVEMENT: 1. Hold the left FLAT hand forward with the palm facing in. Move the right A hand, with the thumbtip and index fingertip pressed together, across the left palm in a wavy motion. (This is the sign for *write*.) **2.** Sign the *person* ending.

VISUALIZE: A person who writes to earn a living.

Curved hand

233

THE WORKPLACE

advertise • publicize • commercial • publicity

HANDSHAPE: Right and left S hands

POSITION: In front of the mouth

MOVEMENT: Hold the right and left S hands in front of the mouth, palms facing in opposite directions, with the right hand in front of the left. Move the right hand toward and then away from the left hand a few times.

VISUALIZE: Blowing your own horn for publicity.

apply • volunteer • candidate

HANDSHAPE: Right OPEN hand

POSITION: On the chest

MOVEMENT: Grasp the right coat lapel, or shirt fabric near the lapel area, with the thumb and index finger of the right OPEN hand. Pull the fabric forward a few times.

VISUALIZE: Picking yourself as a candidate.

appointment • engagement • reservation

HANDSHAPES: Right A hand and left S hand

POSITION: In front of the chest

MOVEMENT: With the palms facing down, move the right A hand in a small counter-clockwise circle above the left S hand. Then place the right wrist on the back of the left wrist and move both hands down together.

VISUALIZE: Showing that your hands are tied due to an obligation.

S hand

Open hand

A hand

beeper • pager

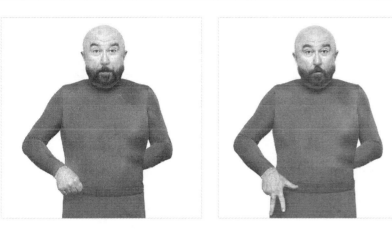

HANDSHAPES: Right S hand changing to a THREE hand.

POSITION: The right side of the waist

MOVEMENT: Hold the right S hand with the palm facing in, the fingers pointing down, and the thumb touching the right side of the waist. Then flick out the thumb, index, and middle fingers into a THREE hand.

VISUALIZE: A pulsating beeper worn on a belt at your waist.

boss • chairman • captain • general

HANDSHAPE: Right CLAWED hand

POSITION: On the right shoulder

MOVEMENT: Tap the fingertips of the right CLAWED hand on the right shoulder a few times.

VISUALIZE: A person who shoulders responsibility.

business

HANDSHAPES: Left S hand and right B hand

POSITION: In front of the chest

MOVEMENT: Point the left S hand to the right with the palm facing down. Then, with the palm facing forward, strike the wrist of the right B hand on the side of the left wrist.

VISUALIZE: Putting up a sign to show you're open for business.

Three hand

Clawed hand

B hand

computer

HANDSHAPE: Right C hand and left S hand

POSITION: In front of the chest

MOVEMENT: Hold up the left arm with elbow bent, and the left S hand facing right with the palm facing down. Hold the right C hand with the palm facing forward, and bounce the hand from the left wrist to the left elbow a few times.

VISUALIZE: The movement of a computer cursor across the screen.

department

HANDSHAPE: Right and left D hands

POSITION: In front of the chest

MOVEMENT: Hold up the right and left D hands with the thumbtips touching. Then move both hands in an outward circular motion until the little finger sides of the hands are touching.

VISUALIZE: The movement traces a group of people, and the initial indicates the word.

dismiss • lay off

HANDSHAPE: Left and right FLAT hands

POSITION: In front of the chest

MOVEMENT: Point the left FLAT hand forward with the palm facing up. Brush the fingertips of the right FLAT hand, palm facing down, across and off the little finger side of the left palm.

VISUALIZE: Workers being pushed off a job site.

 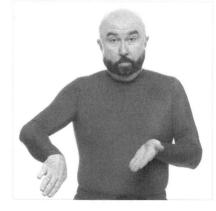

C
hand

S
hand

D
hand

Flat
hand

earn • salary • collect • wages • accumulate

HANDSHAPES: Right CURVED hand and left FLAT hand

POSITION: In front of the chest

MOVEMENT: Brush the little finger side of the right CURVED hand over the upturned palm of the left FLAT hand from the fingertips to the wrist.

VISUALIZE: Scooping wages into your hand.

employ • hire • invite • greet • welcome

HANDSHAPE: Right FLAT hand

POSITION: In front of the chest

MOVEMENT: Hold the right OPEN hand forward with the palm facing up. Then swing the hand down and in toward the chest. To sign *hire*, use the H hand.

VISUALIZE: Inviting someone to come inside your workplace or home.

e-mail

HANDSHAPES: Right E hand and left ONE hand

POSITION: In front of the chest

MOVEMENT: Hold the left ONE hand forward, with the index finger pointing right and the palm facing in. Then slide the fingertips of the right E hand quickly across the left index finger from the base to the fingertip.

VISUALIZE: The lightning speed of an e-mail message.

 Curved hand • E hand • One hand

fax

HANDSHAPES: Right F hand changing to X hand, and left FLAT hand

POSITION: In front of the chest

MOVEMENT: Quickly slide the right F hand, palm down, across the upturned palm of the left FLAT hand from the wrist to the fingertips, at the same time changing the F hand into an X hand.

VISUALIZE: The motion shows something going from one place to another, while the initials indicate the word.

internet

HANDSHAPE: Right and left OPEN hands

POSITION: In front of the chest

MOVEMENT: Hold the right and left OPEN hands in front of the chest and slightly to the left, with the palms facing in and the middle fingertips touching. Then rotate the hands in half twists while moving them across the chest to the right.

VISUALIZE: Information moving through wires from one place to another.

letter

HANDSHAPES: Right A hand and left FLAT hand

POSITION: Starts on the lips

MOVEMENT: Touch the thumbtip of the right A hand to the lips. Then bring the right hand down and touch the thumbtip to the upturned palm of the left FLAT hand.

VISUALIZE: Licking a stamp and sticking it on an envelope.

F hand   X hand   Flat hand   Open hand

meeting • assemble • gather • conference

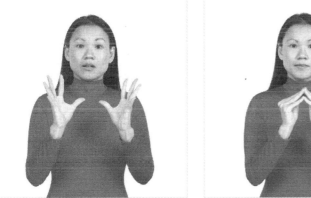

HANDSHAPES: Right and left OPEN hands changing to AND hands

POSITION: Starts near the sides of the chest

MOVEMENT: Hold up the right and left OPEN hands near the sides of the chest with the palms facing each other. Then bring the hands toward each other while changing them into the AND handshape and touch the fingertips together.

VISUALIZE: Gathering people together in a steepled meeting place.

offer • present • suggest • propose • submit

HANDSHAPE: Right and left FLAT hands

POSITION: In front of the chest

MOVEMENT: Point the right and left FLAT hands forward with the palms facing up. Then move both hands upward and forward.

VISUALIZE: Offering a gift to someone.

office

HANDSHAPE: Right and left O hands

POSITION: In front of the chest

MOVEMENT: Hold the right and left O hands forward, palms facing in, with the right hand closer to the chest. Then move both hands out to the sides, ending with the palms facing each other.

VISUALIZE: The movement suggests the walls of a room, and the initial indicates the word.

A
hand

And
hand

O
hand

239

plan • arrange • order • prepare • system

HANDSHAPE: Right and left FLAT hands

POSITION: In front of the chest

MOVEMENT: Hold the right and left FLAT hands to the left with the palms facing each other and fingers pointing forward. Move both hands simultaneously to the right in several small arcs.

VISUALIZE: Putting things in order.

profession • professional

HANDSHAPES: Left FLAT hand and right P hand

POSITION: In front of the chest

MOVEMENT: Point the left FLAT hand forward with the palm facing right. Then slide the middle fingertip of the right P hand forward along the left index finger.

VISUALIZE: Advancing in a career.

profit

HANDSHAPE: Right F hand

POSITION: Below the left shoulder

MOVEMENT: Hold the right F hand below the left shoulder with the thumb and index finger pointing down; then move the hand down slightly.

VISUALIZE: Tucking money into a shirt pocket.

Flat hand

P hand

F hand

promotion • advanced • high

HANDSHAPE: Right and left BENT hands

POSITION: In front of the chest

MOVEMENT: Point the fingertips of the right and left BENT hands toward each other and move both hands upward in stages.

VISUALIZE: Climbing the ladder to success.

resign • quit

HANDSHAPES: Left C hand and right U hand

POSITION: In front of the chest

MOVEMENT: Hold the left C hand forward with the fingers pointing to the right. Place the extended fingers of the right U hand in the opening of the left C hand; then pull the U fingers out.

VISUALIZE: Getting out of a tight place.

responsibility • obligation • burden

HANDSHAPE: Right and left R hands

POSITION: On the left shoulder

MOVEMENT: Tap the fingertips of the right and left R hands on the left shoulder a few times.

VISUALIZE: Shouldering the burden of obligation.

Bent hand

C hand

U hand

  R hand

The Warmth and Openness of the Deaf

While the students in my sign language classes at New School University generally begin signing without hesitation during class sessions, many say they are reluctant to engage a deaf person in conversation. When I ask them why, most admit that as "novices," they are nervous about communicating with native signers. This is a shame, since the New York area has the largest concentration of hard-of-hearing and deaf people in America, creating an environment ripe with real-world situations in which students can gain confidence in their skills.

It's been my experience that the deaf are usually delighted to converse with people who are trying to learn their language, and will respond with warmth and encouragement. Most deaf people will take the time to ask beginning signers why they became interested in sign language, and will help them expand their vocabulary. So if you have the opportunity to talk with a native signer, don't hesitate! You'll surely come away from the conversation feeling that you made the right choice to explore the language and culture of the deaf.

supervise • take care of • care

HANDSHAPE: Right and left κ hands

POSITION: In front of the body

MOVEMENT: With the palms facing down, cross the right and left κ hands at the wrists with the right wrist on top of the left. Then move both hands together in a counter-clockwise circle.

VISUALIZE: The watchful eyes of a person in authority.

work • labor • job

HANDSHAPE: Right and left s hands

POSITION: In front of the chest

MOVEMENT: With the palms facing down, tap the wrist of the right s hand against the wrist of the left s hand.

VISUALIZE: Using a hammer to pound on a nail.

K
hand

S
hand

sports
& leisure

All work and no play makes for a dull life indeed—so let's kick back and relax with some signs that are all about recreation. Do you enjoy watching *baseball,* playing *soccer, swimming* a few laps, going to the *movies,* listening to *music,* or *dancing* the night away? With the signs in this chapter, you'll be ready to exercise your signing know-how when it's time to play.

SPORTS

ball • round • sphere

HANDSHAPE: Right and left C hands

POSITION: In front of the chest

MOVEMENT: Hold up the right and left C hands with the thumbtips and fingertips touching.

VISUALIZE: Showing the round shape of a ball.

SEE HELPING HANDS ON NEXT PAGE.

William Hoy

William Ellsworth Hoy made history as the first deaf player in major league baseball, but it was his remarkable talent both at bat and on the field that made him famous.

Born in Houckstown, Ohio, on May 23, 1862, Bill Hoy lost his hearing due to an illness during childhood. He wasn't about to let his inability to hear keep him from achieving his dream. After graduating from the Ohio School for the Deaf, he began his professional career in Oshkosh, Wisconsin, in 1886. From there, Hoy went on to play as an outfielder for five different major league teams over fifteen years, and racked up some impressive statistics. As a rookie in the majors, he led the National League in stolen bases with 82 steals. Playing with the Chicago White Sox in 1901, he hit a grand-slam home run—the first ever in the American League.

Hoy is widely credited as the creator of the hand signals still used in baseball today. When he began his professional career, all of the umpires' calls were shouted. As the story goes, he asked his third-

William Hoy

base coach to raise his left arm to indicate a ball and his right arm to indicate a strike when Hoy was at bat. Soon, the coach was also signaling the opposing players' balls and strikes to Hoy while he played the outfield. And gradually, hand signals came into common use in baseball among umpires, managers, and players.

Hoy even inspired a kind of sign language among the crowds. An outstanding outfielder, a consistently good hitter, and an exciting base-stealer, Hoy was a favorite, and whenever he made a great play, his fans would cheer by standing up and wildly waving their arms.

After playing 1,792 games in the major leagues, Hoy finished his career in Los Angeles in the Pacific Coast winter league. His very last play clinched the 1903 pennant for his team.

In 1951, William Hoy was the first player to be enshrined in the American Athletic Association of the Deaf's Hall of Fame. Hoy died in 1961 at the age of ninety-nine.

baseball • softball • bat

HANDSHAPE: Right and left s hands

POSITION: Starts in front of the right shoulder

MOVEMENT: Hold up the right and left s hands in front of the right shoulder with the right hand on top of the left; then swing both hands forward to the front of the chest.

VISUALIZE: Swinging a baseball bat.

C
hand

S
hand

basketball

HANDSHAPE: Right and left CLAWED hands

POSITION: Just above eye level

MOVEMENT: Hold the left CLAWED hand up above the head as if holding a basketball; steady the "basketball" with the right CLAWED hand. Then thrust the right hand forward in an upward arc. (Common usage sign.)

VISUALIZE: Taking a jump shot with a basketball.

bicycle • tricycle • cycle

HANDSHAPE: Right and left S hands

POSITION: In front of the chest

MOVEMENT: Hold the right and left S hands side by side in front of the chest with the palms facing down; then move the hands alternately in forward circles.

VISUALIZE: Pedaling a bicycle.

boxing • fighting

HANDSHAPE: Right and left S hands

POSITION: In front of the chin

MOVEMENT: Hold up the right S hand close to the chin and the left S hand several inches in front of the chin. Then reverse positions. Repeat a few times.

VISUALIZE: Throwing punches in a boxing match.

Clawed hand

fishing

HANDSHAPE: Right and left A hands

POSITION: In front of the chest

MOVEMENT: Hold the right and left A hands forward with the right hand above the left. Pivot both hands quickly up and backward from the wrists.

VISUALIZE: Pulling up on a fishing line.

football

HANDSHAPE: Right and left OPEN hands

POSITION: In front of the chest

MOVEMENT: Hold up the right and left OPEN hands with the palms facing each other; then angle the hands down toward each other and lock the fingers together a few times.

VISUALIZE: Two teams clashing at the line of scrimmage.

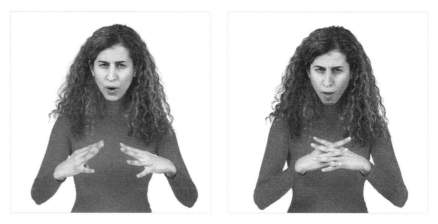

In the Huddle

Did you know that the football huddle actually originated at Gallaudet University in Washington, D.C.? The huddle was said to have been "invented" by Paul Hubbard, quarterback for the Gallaudet University Bisons, from 1892 to 1895. Because Hubbard used sign language to call plays during football games, deaf players on opposing teams were able to read the signs and prepare to stop the plays. In order to shield their strategies from their opponents, the Bisons gathered in a huddle around the quarterback so his signs were hidden from anyone who could intercept them.

A
hand

Open
hand

game • challenge

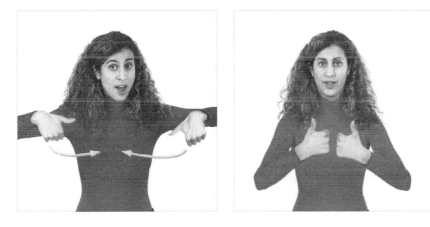

HANDSHAPE: Right and left A hands with thumbs extended

POSITION: Starts in front of the shoulders

MOVEMENT: Hold up the right and left A hands in front of the shoulders with palms facing in. Then bring the hands up toward the center of the chest and touch the knuckles together.

VISUALIZE: A hand-to-hand competition.

golf

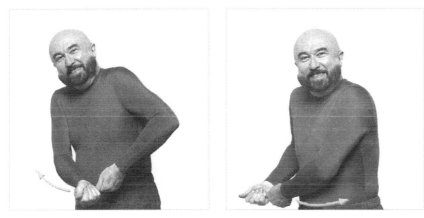

HANDSHAPE: Right and left A hands

POSITION: In front of the waist

MOVEMENT: Hold the right and left A hands down in front of the waist with little finger side of the right hand against the thumb side of the left hand. Swing both hands to the right and then to the left.

VISUALIZE: Swinging a golf club.

race • contest • competition • rivalry

HANDSHAPE: Right and left A hands

POSITION: In front of the chest

MOVEMENT: Hold the right and left A hands forward with the palms facing each other. Move the hands forward and back alternately.

VISUALIZE: Two runners racing against each other.

skiing

HANDSHAPE: Right and left S hands

POSITION: Near the sides of the chest

MOVEMENT: Hold the right and left S hands out near the sides of the chest with palms facing each other; then simultaneously push both hands down and back.

VISUALIZE: Using ski poles.

soccer • kick

HANDSHAPE: Right and left B hands

POSITION: In front of the chest

MOVEMENT: Point the left B hand to the right with the palm facing in. Tap the index finger side of the right B hand against the little finger side of the left hand a few times.

VISUALIZE: Kicking a ball.

swimming

HANDSHAPE: Right and left OPEN hands

POSITION: In front of the chest

MOVEMENT: Point the right and left OPEN hands forward with the backs of the hands facing each other; then move both hands simultaneously forward and out to the sides of the chest a few times.

VISUALIZE: Swimming the breaststroke.

S
hand

B
hand

Open
hand

team

HANDSHAPE: Right and left T hands

POSITION: In front of the chest

MOVEMENT: Hold up the right and left T hands with the palms facing each other. Move both hands in an outward circular motion, ending with the little finger sides of the hands touching.

VISUALIZE: The movement traces a group of people, and the initial indicates the word.

tennis

HANDSHAPE: Right A hand

POSITION: Starts in front of the right shoulder

MOVEMENT: Hold up the right A hand in front of the right shoulder. Swing the hand across the front of the chest to the left shoulder, then back to the right.

VISUALIZE: Swinging a tennis racquet.

throw • toss

HANDSHAPES: Right A hand changing to OPEN hand

POSITION: Starts next to the right side of the head

MOVEMENT: Hold up the right A hand next to the right side of the head with the palm facing forward; then bring the hand forward quickly while opening it.

VISUALIZE: Throwing a ball.

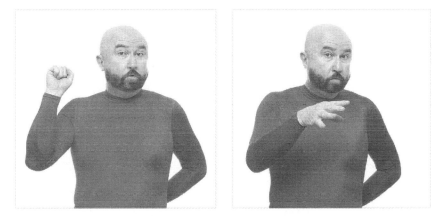

T hand

A hand

win • triumph

HANDSHAPE: Right modified x hand

POSITION: Next to the right side of the head

MOVEMENT: Hold up the right modified x hand next to the right side of the head and move the hand in small circles a few times.

VISUALIZE: Waving a noisemaker at a victory celebration.

LEISURE

art • design • draw

HANDSHAPES: Left FLAT hand and right I hand

POSITION: In front of the chest

MOVEMENT: Point the left FLAT hand forward with the palm facing right; then slide the little finger of the right I hand down across the left palm with a wavy motion.

VISUALIZE: Drawing with a pencil.

book • textbook • volume

HANDSHAPE: Right and left FLAT hands

POSITION: In front of the chest

MOVEMENT: Hold the right and left FLAT hands together with the palms touching and the fingertips pointing forward. Then pull the hands apart so the palms face up, keeping the little finger sides together.

VISUALIZE: Opening a book.

X
hand

Flat
hand

I
hand

camping

HANDSHAPES: Right and left A hands with index and little fingers extended

POSITION: In front of the chest

MOVEMENT: Touch the extended fingertips of the right and left A hands together with the palms facing each other, forming the top of a triangle. Then move the hands down and apart a couple of times.

VISUALIZE: The triangular shape of a tent.

dance • ball

HANDSHAPES: Right V hand and left FLAT hand

POSITION: In front of the chest

MOVEMENT: Point the extended fingers of the right V hand toward the upturned palm of the left FLAT hand; then swing the right hand from side to side.

VISUALIZE: Kicking up your heels at a ball.

magazine • booklet • brochure • catalog • bulletin

HANDSHAPES: Right C hand and left FLAT hand

POSITION: In front of the chest

MOVEMENT: Slide the thumbtip and index fingertip of the right C hand forward along the little finger side of the left FLAT hand from the heel of the hand to the fingertip.

VISUALIZE: Running your fingers up the thin spine of a magazine.

A hand V hand C hand

movie • film • cinema • show

HANDSHAPE: Right and left OPEN hands

POSITION: In front of the chest

MOVEMENT: Hold up the right and left OPEN hands, palms touching, with the left palm facing partly forward; then slide the right hand from side to side across the left palm a few times, pivoting the right hand from the wrist.

VISUALIZE: Moving images on a movie screen.

music • hymn • sing • melody • song • poetry

HANDSHAPE: Left and right FLAT hands

POSITION: In front of the chest

MOVEMENT: Point the left FLAT hand forward with the palm facing right. Then point the fingers of the right FLAT hand toward the left palm and sweep the right hand forward and back. The P handshape can be used to sign *poetry*.

VISUALIZE: A conductor directing musicians.

paint

HANDSHAPE: Right and left FLAT hands

POSITION: In front of the chest

MOVEMENT: Brush the fingertips of the right FLAT hand across the palm of the left FLAT hand from the wrist to the fingertips and then back to the wrist.

VISUALIZE: Painting with a wide brush.

Open hand

Flat hand

party

HANDSHAPE: Right and left Y hands

POSITION: In front of the chest

MOVEMENT: With the hands side by side and the palms facing in opposite directions, swing the right and left Y hands from side to side in front of the chest while rotating the wrists. P hands can also be used for this sign.

VISUALIZE: The Y hands swinging to the lively sounds of a party.

play · recreation

HANDSHAPE: Right and left Y hands

POSITION: In front of the chest

MOVEMENT: Hold up the right and left Y hands with the palms facing in and twist them back and forth from the wrists a few times.

VISUALIZE: The Y hands playing around with each other.

The USA Deaf Sports Federation

When Ohio's Akron Club of the Deaf sponsored its first national basketball tournament in 1945, few people realized that the event would be the start of an internationally renowned athletic association. But out of those humble beginnings grew today's USA Deaf Sports Federation (USADSF), which gives deaf and hard-of-hearing athletes the opportunity to compete with their peers in a variety of sports on regional, national, and international levels. The USADSF aims to help participants develop not only physically, but socially and psychologically as well, through an environment that promotes equality, respect, and a positive image of all that deaf and hard-of-hearing people can achieve.

Over the decades since its establishment, the Deaf Sports Federation has produced highly competitive United States teams at the World Games for the Deaf, including American athletes who continue to set new national and world records. Today, the USADSF is affiliated with both the Comité International des Sports des Sourds (CISS) and the United States Olympic Committee (USOC). It is currently the only athletic association that coordinates international competition for deaf and hard-of-hearing athletes.

Y
hand

The National Theater of the Deaf

For more than three decades, the National Theater of the Deaf has delighted deaf and hearing audiences alike with its unique visual performances of original works and adaptations of classical literature. Founded in 1967 by David Hays, a Broadway scenic designer, through funds from the U.S. Department of Health, Education, and Welfare, the NTD has produced sixty-four national tours and thirty-one international tours to date, and has performed in all fifty states and, remarkably, on all seven continents. The company's resounding success within its first year also led to the creation of The Little Theatre of the Deaf, a troupe that performs for young audiences.

The NTD has done a great deal to promote social change through the art of theater, staying true to its mission to inform even as it entertains. The troupe's uncommon blend of sign language, mime, dance, and even narration and music, continues to enlighten hearing members of the audience and to serve as a source of pride in the culture of the deaf. Among its many honors, the NTD received the Tony Award for Theatrical Excellence in 1977 and the National Association for the Deaf Award in 1980, and was invited to perform at the White House in 1993.

stage

HANDSHAPES: Right S hand and left FLAT hand

POSITION: In front of the chest

MOVEMENT: With the palms facing down, slide the right S hand across the back of the left FLAT hand from the wrist to the fingertips.

VISUALIZE: An actor moving across the flat surface of a stage floor.

television • TV

HANDSHAPES: Right T hand changing to V hand

POSITION: In front of the right shoulder

MOVEMENT: Hold up the right T hand in front of the right shoulder with the palm facing forward; then move the hand to the right while changing it to the V handshape.

VISUALIZE: The initials T and V spell out *TV*.

 S hand   Flat hand   T hand   V hand

theater

HANDSHAPES: 1. Right and left A hands
2. Right and left FLAT hands

POSITIONS: 1. In front of the chest **2.** In front of the face

MOVEMENT: 1. Hold the right and left A hands forward with the palms facing each other; then move the hands toward the body in alternating circles. (This is the sign for *drama*.) **2.** Touch the fingertips of the right and left FLAT hands together, palms facing each other, to form a triangle below the face. Move the hands apart and down to the sides of the chest, ending with the fingers pointing up. (This is the sign for *house*.)

VISUALIZE: A building where dramas are enacted.

vacation • holiday • leisure

HANDSHAPE: Right and left OPEN hands

POSITION: In front of the shoulders

MOVEMENT: With the palms facing forward, touch the thumbtips of the right and left OPEN hands to the sides of the chest near the armpits and wiggle the fingers.

VISUALIZE: Tucking the thumbs under suspenders while relaxing on vacation.

A
hand

Open
hand

The World of the Deaf in Movies

Gaining skill in sign language is obviously the first important step in learning to communicate with deaf individuals. But if you're not in surroundings that enable you to interact frequently with the deaf, you may feel that you don't have a real sense of their unique challenges and triumphs. One great way to gain valuable insight into their world is through films. Today, there are a variety of movies that present an honest, accurate view of the experiences of deaf people. Some of these films are based on the real lives of individuals who have had a major impact on deaf culture. Others document some of the issues and even controversies that have been—and continue to be—central to the lives of deaf people and their friends and families. And still other films, while fictional, nevertheless tell realistic, often moving stories of the intricate connections between the worlds of the deaf and the hearing.

Once you start looking, you'll undoubtedly find that the number of excellent movies is quite overwhelming. To help you begin, I've compiled a list of some of my personal favorites.

❑ *Children of a Lesser God* **(1986).** Speech therapist James Leeds (William Hurt) has just started his assignment at a school for the deaf, where he quickly shows he has a knack for inspiring even the most challenging students. But he can't seem to reach Sarah Norman (Marlee Matlin), a beautiful and intelligent graduate of the school who chose to stay on as a cleaning woman.

❑ *The Heart Is a Lonely Hunter* **(1968).** Alan Arkin and Sondra Locke both received Oscar nominations for their performances in this film based on a Carson McCullers' story. When John Singer (Arkin), who is deaf and mute, moves to a small town in Alabama, he meets and befriends a lonely teenage girl named Mick Kelly (Locke)— and the friendship changes both their lives.

❑ *Johnny Belinda* **(1948).** This Oscar-winning film explores the ties between Belinda (Jane Wyman), a deaf woman who cannot speak, and Robert (Lew Ayres), the hearing man who teaches her to sign. As the unwed mother of an infant, Belinda faces harsh judgment from the local town gossips, and soon finds she's in danger of losing custody of her child because she is deaf.

❑ *Man of a Thousand Faces* **(1957).** Silent film legend Lon Chaney—portrayed by James Cagney—was the son of deaf parents who could not speak, and learned early in life to respect people's differences. This film takes us through the life of the "master of disguise" on his journey from the vaudeville stage to silver screen stardom.

❑ *The Miracle Worker* **(1962).** Deaf and blind since infancy, Helen Keller (Patty Duke) lives in her own isolated world until her parents hire Annie Sullivan (Anne Bancroft) to teach her to communicate. This inspiring story examines the complex, uniquely challenging relationship between teacher and student.

❑ *Mr. Holland's Opus* **(1995).** Glenn Holland (Richard Dreyfuss) dreams of writing a memorable piece of music, but fears that his dreams will be put on hold when he accepts a position as a music teacher. Instead, he finds that life holds unexpected joys as he learns how to share his love of music with his students and, most important, discovers that music is the key to connecting with his son, who has been deaf since birth.

❑ *Sound and Fury* **(2001).** This Academy Award nominee for Best Documentary Feature gives stunning insight into one of the most controversial issues affecting the deaf community today—the use of cochlear implants. As one family struggles to decide whether two children should undergo the surgery, we gain an understanding of the arguments both for and against the device.

❑ *The Story of Alexander Graham Bell* **(1939).** This drama stars Don Ameche as the indefatigable inventor Alexander Graham Bell. The story begins in the 1870s, at which time Bell was already teaching deaf students how to speak and, in his spare time, tinkering with an innovation that could send speech over wires—the telephone.

location, direction & travel

Y ou'll really go places with a little "direction" from this chapter. If you want to get *ahead* in the world, move *away* from home, live *near* a city, head *south* for the winter, *travel* to a foreign land, or *visit* your grandparents, you'll find that learning these signs is the ticket to expressing yourself effectively.

LOCATION

---

above • over

HANDSHAPE: Right and left FLAT hands

POSITION: In front of the chest

MOVEMENT: With the palms facing down, move the right FLAT hand in a counterclockwise circle above the left FLAT hand.

VISUALIZE: A flying saucer circling above the ground.

SEE HELPING HANDS ON NEXT PAGE.

257

across • cross • over

HANDSHAPE: Left and right FLAT hands

POSITION: In front of the chest

MOVEMENT: Point the left FLAT hand to the right with the palm facing down; then slide the little finger side of the right FLAT hand forward over the left knuckles.

VISUALIZE: Crossing over a bridge.

against • oppose

HANDSHAPES: Left and right FLAT hands

POSITION: In front of the chest

MOVEMENT: Point the left FLAT hand forward with the palm facing right. Then, with the palm facing in, strike the fingertips of the right FLAT hand against the left palm.

VISUALIZE: Bumping against a wall.

ahead

HANDSHAPE: Right and left A hands

POSITION: In front of the chest

MOVEMENT: Hold the right and left A hands forward with the palms facing each other; then move the right hand forward and in front of the left hand.

VISUALIZE: The race begins; the right hand pulls ahead of the left.

 Flat hand

A hand

among

HANDSHAPES: Right ONE hand and left OPEN hand

POSITION: In front of the chest

MOVEMENT: Move the index finger of the right ONE hand in and out among the fingers of the upright left OPEN hand.

VISUALIZE: One person weaving his way among a group of people.

around

HANDSHAPES: Left AND hand and right ONE hand

POSITION: In front of the chest

MOVEMENT: Hold the left AND hand forward with the fingertips pointing up; then move the index finger of the right ONE hand in a counterclockwise circle around the left fingers.

VISUALIZE: The moon circling around the earth.

at

HANDSHAPES: Left FLAT hand and right BENT hand

POSITION: In front of the chest

MOVEMENT: Hold the left FLAT hand forward at an angle with the fingertips pointing slightly upward. Then, with the palm facing down, touch the fingertips of the right BENT hand to the back of the left hand. (This sign is often fingerspelled.)

VISUALIZE: The right and left hands meeting at one point.

One hand   Open hand   And hand   Bent hand

away

HANDSHAPES: Right CURVED hand changing to FLAT hand

POSITION: Starts near the right side of the chest

MOVEMENT: Hold the right CURVED hand near the right side of the chest with the palm facing down. Then swing the hand away from the body to the right while changing it to the FLAT handshape.

VISUALIZE: Shooing something away from you.

behind

HANDSHAPE: Right and left A hands

POSITION: In front of the chest

MOVEMENT: Hold the right and left A hands forward with the palms facing each other; then move the right hand back toward the body and behind the left hand.

VISUALIZE: One racer falling behind the other.

below • beneath • under • bottom

HANDSHAPE: Right and left FLAT hands

POSITION: In front of the chest

MOVEMENT: With the palms facing down, move the right FLAT hand in a counter-clockwise circle below the left FLAT hand.

VISUALIZE: A submerged submarine circling beneath a ship.

 Curved hand

Flat hand

 A hand

by • near • close to • adjacent

HANDSHAPE: Right and left CURVED hands

POSITION: In front of the chest

MOVEMENT: Hold the right and left CURVED hands forward, palms facing in, with the left hand farther away from the body than the right. Then move the right hand toward the left palm without touching it.

VISUALIZE: Two objects moving close to each other.

far • distant • remote

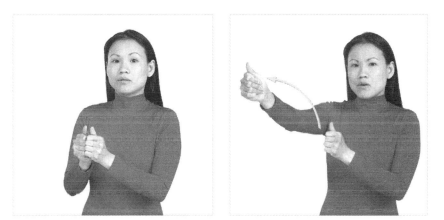

HANDSHAPE: Right and left A hands

POSITION: In front of the chest

MOVEMENT: Hold the right and left A hands together with the palms facing each other. Then move the right hand forward in a large arc.

VISUALIZE: Moving the right hand far from the left hand.

from

HANDSHAPES: Right X hand and left ONE hand

POSITION: In front of the chest

MOVEMENT: Hold up the right X hand and left ONE hand, palms facing in, with the right index finger touching the left index fingertip. Then move the right hand down and back toward the body.

VISUALIZE: Moving the right hand away from the left hand.

X hand   One hand

here • present

HANDSHAPE: Right and left OPEN hands

POSITION: In front of the chest

MOVEMENT: Point the right and left OPEN hands forward with the palms facing up; then circle both hands simultaneously forward and outward.

VISUALIZE: Showing that which is right here, in front of the body.

in

HANDSHAPES: Left C hand and right AND hand

POSITION: In front of the chest

MOVEMENT: Hold the left C hand forward with the fingers pointing right. Then place the fingers of the right AND hand in the opening of the left C hand.

VISUALIZE: Making a hole in one.

off

HANDSHAPES: Right BENT hand changing to A hand and left S hand

POSITION: In front of the chest

MOVEMENT: Hold the right BENT hand and left S hand forward, palms facing down, with the right hand on the back of the left; then lift the right hand while changing it to the A handshape.

VISUALIZE: Peeling off a label.

Open hand   C hand   And hand   Bent hand

on

HANDSHAPE: Right and left FLAT hands

POSITION: In front of the chest

MOVEMENT: With the palms facing down, place the right FLAT hand on the back of the left FLAT hand.

VISUALIZE: The laying on of hands.

out

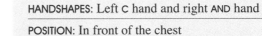

HANDSHAPES: Left C hand and right AND hand

POSITION: In front of the chest

MOVEMENT: Hold the left C hand forward with the fingers pointing right. Tuck the fingers of the right AND hand down into the left C hand; then pull the right fingers out.

VISUALIZE: Pulling a rabbit out of a hat.

there

HANDSHAPE: Right ONE hand

POSITION: In front of the chest

MOVEMENT: To indicate a specific location, point with the index finger of the right ONE hand. To make a general reference, hold up the right OPEN hand in front of the chest with the palm facing forward; then move the hand to the right.

VISUALIZE: Pointing to something "over there."

A hand	S hand	Flat hand	One hand

through • via • by way of

HANDSHAPE: Left and right FLAT hands

POSITION: In front of the chest

MOVEMENT: Hold up the left FLAT hand with the palm facing in. Then slide the little finger side of the right FLAT hand forward between the index and middle fingers of the left hand.

VISUALIZE: Passing through an obstacle.

to • toward

HANDSHAPE: Right and left ONE hands

POSITION: In front of the chest

MOVEMENT: Point the left ONE hand up with the palm facing right; then touch the index fingertip of the right ONE hand to the index fingertip of the left hand.

VISUALIZE: One object moving toward another.

DIRECTION

down

HANDSHAPE: Right ONE hand

POSITION: In front of the chest

MOVEMENT: Point the right ONE hand down with the palm facing in and move it up and down a few times.

VISUALIZE: Pointing down.

Flat hand

One hand

east

HANDSHAPE: Right E hand

POSITION: In front of the right shoulder

MOVEMENT: With the palm facing forward, move the right E hand to the right from the right shoulder.

VISUALIZE: The initial E showing east on a wall map.

left

HANDSHAPE: Right L hand

POSITION: In front of the right shoulder

MOVEMENT: With the palm facing forward, move the right L hand to the left from the right shoulder.

VISUALIZE: Moving the initial L to the left.

north

HANDSHAPE: Right N hand

POSITION: Starts in front of the right shoulder

MOVEMENT: With the palm facing forward, move the right N hand upward from the right shoulder.

VISUALIZE: The initial N showing north on a wall map.

 E hand
 L hand
 N hand

right

HANDSHAPE: Right R hand

POSITION: In front of the right shoulder

MOVEMENT: With the palm facing forward, move the right R hand to the right from the right shoulder.

VISUALIZE: Moving the initial R to the right.

south

HANDSHAPE: Right S hand

POSITION: Starts in front of the right shoulder

MOVEMENT: With the palm facing forward, move the right S hand downward from the right shoulder.

VISUALIZE: The initial S showing south on a wall map.

up

HANDSHAPE: Right ONE hand

POSITION: In front of the right shoulder

MOVEMENT: Point the right ONE hand up with the palm facing forward and move it up and down a few times.

VISUALIZE: Pointing up.

R
hand

S
hand

One
hand

west

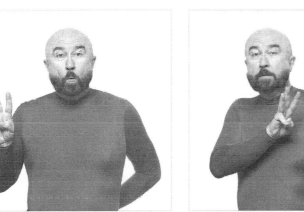

HANDSHAPE: Right W hand

POSITION: In front of the right shoulder

MOVEMENT: With the palm facing forward, move the right W hand to the left from the right shoulder.

VISUALIZE: The initial W showing west on a wall map.

TRAVEL

airplane · jet · airport

HANDSHAPE: Right Y hand with index finger extended

POSITION: In front of the chest

MOVEMENT: With the palm facing down, move the right Y hand forward and upward away from the body in a sweeping gesture.

VISUALIZE: An airplane taking off.

arrive · reach · get to

HANDSHAPE: Right and left CURVED hands

POSITION: In front of the chest

MOVEMENT: Hold the right and left CURVED hands forward, palms facing in, with the right hand closer to the chest. Then move the right hand forward until it touches the left palm.

VISUALIZE: The right hand arriving at the left hand.

 W hand   Y hand   Curved hand

Is Sign Language Universal?

Although American Sign Language is one of the most complete signing systems in the world, it's not universal. Just as no single spoken language is used worldwide, no single form of sign language is understood in every country. Interestingly, even countries that use the same spoken language may have developed very different sign languages; for example, ASL is more like French Sign Language than it is like British Sign Language, because many American signs were derived from the French. (See "The History of Sign Language" on page 1.) However, even though different sign languages are used in different countries, people who know how to sign often find they can communicate across sign language barriers more easily than hearing people can across spoken language barriers.

boat • cruise • sail

HANDSHAPE: Right and left CURVED hands

POSITION: In front of the chest

MOVEMENT: Point the right and left CURVED hands forward with the palms facing up and the little finger sides touching. Then move the hands forward with a wavy motion.

VISUALIZE: A boat sailing over the waves of the ocean.

bridge

HANDSHAPES: Left s hand and right v hand

POSITION: In front of the chest

MOVEMENT: Hold the left s hand in front of the chest with the palm facing down. Touch the fingertips of the right v hand first to the underside of the left wrist, then under the forearm.

VISUALIZE: The supports of a suspension bridge.

Curved
hand

S
hand

V
hand

camera

HANDSHAPE: Right and left L hands

POSITION: In front of the face

MOVEMENT: Hold up the right and left L hands in front of the face with the palms facing each other and the index fingers slightly curved. Move the right index finger down and up a few times.

VISUALIZE: Taking pictures with a camera.

car • automobile • drive

HANDSHAPE: Right and left S hands

POSITION: In front of the chest

MOVEMENT: Hold the right and left S hands forward with the palms facing each other. Twist both hands to the left and then to the right.

VISUALIZE: Driving a car along a winding road.

depart • leave • retire • withdraw

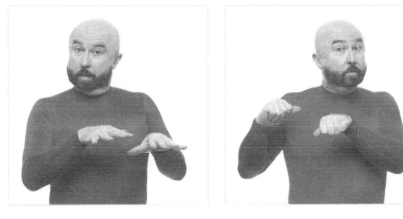

HANDSHAPES: Right and left OPEN hands changing to A hands

POSITION: Starts near the left side of the chest

MOVEMENT: With the palms facing down, point the right and left OPEN hands forward near the left side of the chest. The bring both hands up and toward the right side of the chest simultaneously while changing them to the A handshape.

VISUALIZE: Pulling your hands away.

L hand   Open hand   A hand

gasoline

HANDSHAPES: Right A hand and left O hand

POSITION: In front of the chest

MOVEMENT: Point the thumb of the right A hand down into the opening of the left O hand.

VISUALIZE: Filling up a gas tank.

hotel

HANDSHAPES: Left ONE hand and right H hand

POSITION: In front of the chest

MOVEMENT: Point the left ONE hand up with the palm facing in. Place the little finger side of the right H hand on the index fingertip of the left hand and wiggle the right H fingers back and forth a few times.

VISUALIZE: Using the initial H to represent the sign in front of a hotel.

photograph

HANDSHAPES: Right C hand and left FLAT hand

POSITIONS: Starts next to the right cheek

MOVEMENT: Hold up the right C hand next to the right cheek with the fingers pointing forward. Move the right hand down and place the thumb and index finger side on the palm of the upright left FLAT hand.

VISUALIZE: Copying the face onto a photograph.

A hand

O hand

One hand

H hand

place • area • location • site

HANDSHAPE: Right and left P hands

POSITION: In front of the chest

MOVEMENT: Hold the right and left P hands about a foot in front of the chest with the middle fingertips touching. Then move both hands back toward the body with an outward circular motion and touch the middle fingertips together again. To sign *area*, use A hands; for *location*, use L hands; and for *site*, use S hands.

VISUALIZE: Showing the boundaries of a particular location.

street • road • avenue • way • highway • route

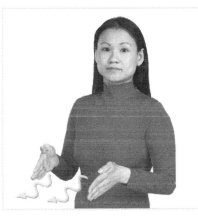

HANDSHAPE: Right and left FLAT hands

POSITION: In front of the chest

MOVEMENT: Point the right and left FLAT hands forward with the palms facing each other. Then move both hands forward in a wavy motion. To sign *road*, use R hands; to sign *avenue*, use A hands; to sign *way*, use W hands; etc.

VISUALIZE: A winding road.

suitcase • luggage

HANDSHAPE: Right S hand

POSITION: Next to the right hip

MOVEMENT: Hang the right S hand down next to the right hip. Then pull the hand up a short distance.

VISUALIZE: Picking up a suitcase by its handle.

C hand   Flat hand   P hand   S hand

ticket

HANDSHAPES: Right V hand with index and middle fingers curved, and left FLAT hand

POSITION: In front of the chest

MOVEMENT: Squeeze the little finger side of the left FLAT hand between the curved index and middle fingers of the right V hand.

VISUALIZE: A train conductor punching a ticket.

traffic

HANDSHAPE: Right and left OPEN hands

POSITION: In front of the chest

MOVEMENT: Hold up the right and left OPEN hands in front of the chest with the palms facing each other. Move the hands alternately back and forth.

VISUALIZE: Cars passing in opposite directions.

train • railroad

HANDSHAPE: Right and left H hands

POSITION: In front of the chest

MOVEMENT: With the palms facing down, slide the extended fingers of the right H hand forward and back along the extended fingers of the left H hand.

VISUALIZE: The movement of the pistons on an old steam locomotive.

 V hand

 Flat hand

 Open hand

 H hand

travel • trip • journey • tour

HANDSHAPE: Right v hand with index and middle fingers curved

POSITION: In front of the chest

MOVEMENT: With the palm facing down, move the right v hand forward with a wavy motion.

VISUALIZE: A person traveling down a path.

vacation • holiday • leisure

HANDSHAPE: Right and left OPEN hands

POSITION: In front of the shoulders

MOVEMENT: With the palms facing forward, touch the thumbtips of the right and left OPEN hands to the sides of the chest near the armpits and wiggle the fingers.

VISUALIZE: Tucking the thumbs under suspenders while relaxing on vacation.

Redefining "Disability"—Deafness on Martha's Vineyard

For over 200 years, until around 1900, there was a very high occurrence of hereditary deafness on Martha's Vineyard, an island near Massachusetts. While the number of deaf people in the United States was about one in 5,700, on Martha's Vineyard, that number was one in 155. Deafness was so common, in fact, that it was not regarded as a serious problem, and deaf islanders were included in all aspects of community life. Communication between deaf and hearing people was not an obstacle because everyone learned sign language—even hearing people who did not have deaf relatives learned it through other townspeople. In the close-knit community, *not* knowing sign language was a disability.

The high incidence of deafness on Martha's Vineyard has been traced back to a group of families from Kent, England, who settled on the island in the late 1600s or early 1700s. These immigrants carried a recessive gene for a certain form of hereditary deafness. Because Martha's Vineyard was a small community, largely isolated from the mainland, the residents intermarried and, as the population increased, the number of deaf people living on the island also increased. Indeed, the incidence of deafness did not decrease until the twentieth century, when more people from the mainland settled on the island and married into the community. The last islander with hereditary deafness died in 1952.

visit

HANDSHAPE: Right and left v hands

POSITION: In front of the chest

MOVEMENT: Hold up the right and left v hands with the palms facing in. Then move the hands alternately in forward circles.

VISUALIZE: Visiting circles of friends.

Heather Whitestone

When Miss Alabama, Heather Whitestone, was named the winner of the 1995 Miss America pageant, she couldn't hear the crowd cheering. She didn't even know she had won the crown until the other contestants extended their congratulations. But that night, twenty-one-year-old Whitestone made history as the first deaf woman—and, in fact, the first woman with a disability—to be crowned Miss America.

Heather Whitestone was born in Alabama on February 24, 1973. After a bout of influenza at just eighteen months of age, she lost all of the hearing in her right ear and became profoundly deaf in her left ear. When a doctor announced that Heather would never progress beyond third grade, her mother, Ms. Gray, decided that Heather should learn to speak. She also enrolled Heather in dance classes, hoping that learning to count to the rhythm of music would help her do the same with her voice when speaking. Because of the emphasis on learning to speak, Heather didn't learn American Sign Language until she was a senior in high school.

All through her childhood and into her adulthood, Ms. Whitestone has maintained a positive and optimistic

Heather Whitestone

attitude, despite the many challenges she faced because of her hearing loss. During her year-long reign as Miss America, she devoted much of her time to working with deaf children, as well as getting the message out to *all* children—hearing and deaf—that positive thinking is a powerful tool that can help them succeed. She has also shown a commitment to the deaf community as a whole by serving as an executive board member on the President's Committee on Employment of People With Disabilities, spearheading a multimedia public service campaign to identify early hearing loss, and acting as spokesperson for both the Helen Keller Eye Research Foundation and the Starkey Hearing Aid Foundation.

After her reign as America's beauty queen, Heather Whitestone left the public eye to marry, becoming Heather Whitestone McCallum. Together, she and her husband, John, operate Heather Whitestone, Inc. Ms. Whitestone has written two books, one of which, *Listening With My Heart,* tells the story of how she overcame obstacles through hard work, self-reliance, and faith.

V
hand

cities, states, countries & government

C onsider this chapter as your passport to explore the world! The signs presented here will help you reach your destination, whether you plan to move to a nearby *town,* visit a different *state,* drive across the *country,* hop on an *International* flight—or even travel to *Washington, D.C.* to meet the *President.*

U.S. PLACE NAMES

America • American

HANDSHAPE: Right and left CURVED hands

POSITION: In front of the chest

MOVEMENT: Lock the fingers of the right and left CURVED hands together with the palms facing in and move the hands in a counter-clockwise circle while mouthing the word "America." To sign *American,* add the *person* ending. (See page 18.)

VISUALIZE: A country made up of people from around the world all working together.

SEE HELPING HANDS ON NEXT PAGE.

275

Atlanta

HANDSHAPE: Right A hand

POSITION: Starts on the left shoulder

MOVEMENT: Place the thumb side of the right A hand on the left shoulder, and then move in an arc across the chest to the right shoulder, while mouthing the word "Atlanta."

VISUALIZE: The initial A is understood as *Atlanta* both by context and by lipreading.

Boston

HANDSHAPE: Right B hand

POSITION: In front of the right shoulder

MOVEMENT: Hold up the right B hand in front of the right shoulder with the palm facing forward. Then draw the hand down with several short movements, while mouthing the word "Boston."

VISUALIZE: The initial B is understood as *Boston* both by context and by lipreading.

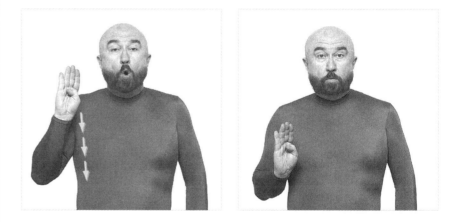

California

HANDSHAPE: Right ONE hand changing to Y hand

POSITION: Starts near the right ear

MOVEMENT: Point the index fingertip of the right ONE hand toward the right ear; then twist the hand forward and downward while changing to a Y hand and mouthing the word "California."

VISUALIZE: Suggests the elongated shape of the state of California.

A hand

B hand

One hand

Y hand

Chicago

HANDSHAPE: Right C hand

POSITION: Starts above the right shoulder

MOVEMENT: Hold up the right C hand above the right shoulder with the fingers pointing to the left. Then move the hand to the right and down a short distance, while mouthing the word "Chicago."

VISUALIZE: The initial C is understood as *Chicago* both by context and by lipreading.

Florida

HANDSHAPES: Right F hand changing to L hand

POSITION: Starts in front of the right shoulder

MOVEMENT: Hold up the right F hand in front of the right shoulder with the palm facing forward. Then move the hand to the right while changing it to the L handshape, and mouth the word "Florida."

VISUALIZE: The initial F followed by the L is understood as *Florida* both by context and by lipreading.

Hawaii

HANDSHAPE: Right H hand

POSITION: In front of the face

MOVEMENT: With the palm facing in, move the right H hand in a counterclockwise circle in front of the face while mouthing the word "Hawaii."

VISUALIZE: The initial H is understood as *Hawaii* both by context and by lipreading.

C hand

F hand

L hand

H hand

Los Angeles

HANDSHAPES: Right L hand changing to A hand

POSITION: Starts in front of the right shoulder

MOVEMENT: Hold up the right L hand in front of the right shoulder with the palm facing forward; then move the hand to the right while changing it to the A handshape, and mouth the words "Los Angeles."

VISUALIZE: The initial L followed by the A is understood as *Los Angeles* both by context and by lipreading.

New York

HANDSHAPES: Right Y hand and left OPEN hand

POSITION: In front of the chest

MOVEMENT: Slide the knuckles of the right Y hand forward and back along the upturned palm of the left OPEN hand while mouthing the words "New York."

VISUALIZE: The initial Y is understood as *New York* both by context and by lipreading.

Gestuno: The "International" Sign Language

In the 1970s, the Commission on Unification of Signs of the World Federation of the Deaf (WFD) developed an international language of signs called Gestuno to facilitate communication among deaf people from different countries. The WFD committee, which included representatives from around the globe, selected more than 1,500 signs from existing sign languages as a basic vocabulary.

Like Esperanto, an international spoken-written language developed in 1887, Gestuno has not come into widespread use. Of course, a major drawback of using the language for everyday conversation is the limited number of signs available, which restricts the range of concepts that can be expressed. Also, there are no hard-and-fast grammatical rules for Gestuno; instead, each signer uses the vocabulary according to the grammar of his or her native sign language. Finally, because the language was developed primarily for interpreting at international meetings, it's not used by the deaf communities in any country, and therefore will not be passed on from one generation to the next as a "living" language.

L hand   A hand   Y hand   Open hand

Where Are You?

Beginning signers often question whether every place has a corresponding sign. As you'll learn by leafing through this book, many states and large cities do have signs that are widely known and used. However, the signs for smaller cities and states—as well as towns—are often known only locally.

The names of most states involve the use of their initial letters. The sign for *Los Angeles,* for instance, uses the L and A hands. This makes many signs easy to remember. Not all states, however, have initialized signs. *California,* for instance, uses a ONE hand and a Y hand, as well as a movement that suggests the shape of the state. Whether initialized or not, the sign will be clearer if, in addition to the correct motion, you mouth the word.

What if you don't know the sign for a place? As explained in Chapter 1, fingerspelling is an effective means of communicating the name of a place for which there is no officially recognized sign.

Philadelphia

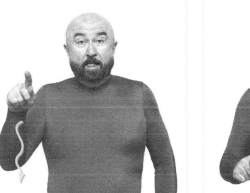

HANDSHAPE: Right P hand

POSITION: Starts in front of the right shoulder

MOVEMENT: Point the right P hand forward with the palm facing down; then move the hand down a short distance in a wavy motion, while mouthing the word "Philadelphia."

VISUALIZE: The initial P is understood as *Philadelphia* both by context and by lipreading.

Washington, D.C.

HANDSHAPE: Right D hand changing to C hand

POSITION: Starts in front of the right shoulder

MOVEMENT: Hold the D hand up in front of the right shoulder; then move the hand to the right in a small arc while changing it to the C handshape, and mouth the words "Washington, D.C."

VISUALIZE: Fingerspelling D and C is understood as *Washington, D.C.* both by context and by lipreading.

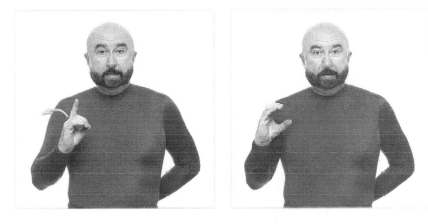

P hand   D hand   C hand

INTERNATIONAL PLACE NAMES

Africa • African

HANDSHAPE: Right A hand

POSITION: In front of the face

MOVEMENT: With the palm facing left, move the right A hand in a counterclockwise circle in front of the face while mouthing the word "Africa." To sign *African*, add the *person* ending. (See page 18.)

VISUALIZE: The initial A is understood as *Africa* both by context and by lipreading.

Asia • Asian

HANDSHAPE: Right A hand

POSITION: Near the right eye

MOVEMENT: Hold up the right A hand near the outside corner of the right eye with the palm facing forward; then twist the hand forward a few times while mouthing the word "Asia." To sign *Asian*, add the *person* ending. (See page 18.)

VISUALIZE: Suggests the almond-shaped eyes of Asian people.

Australia • Australian

HANDSHAPE: Right B hand

POSITION: On the right side of the forehead

MOVEMENT: Touch the fingertips of the right B hand to the right side of the forehead with the palm facing in. Then twist the hand so the palm faces forward and touch the fingertips again to the forehead while mouthing the word "Australia." To sign *Australian*, add the *person* ending. (See page 18.)

VISUALIZE: Suggests an informal greeting of "G'day, mate!"

A
hand

B
hand

Canada • Canadian

HANDSHAPE: Right A hand

POSITION: On the right shoulder

MOVEMENT: Grasp the right coat lapel, or shirt fabric near the lapel area, with the right A hand. Shake the hand a few times while mouthing the word "Canada." To sign *Canadian*, add the *person* ending. (See page 18.)

VISUALIZE: Shaking snow off a coat.

China • Chinese

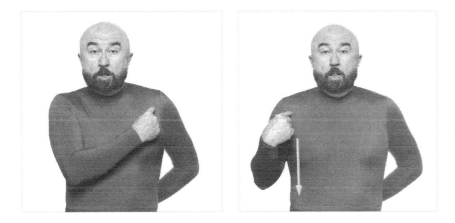

HANDSHAPE: Right ONE hand

POSITION: Starts on the left shoulder

MOVEMENT: Touch the index fingertip of the right ONE hand first to the left shoulder and then to the right shoulder; then draw the hand straight down while mouthing the word "China." To sign *Chinese*, add the *person* ending. (See page 18.)

VISUALIZE: A right angle in the Great Wall of China.

One hand

281

Body Language: A Cultural Perspective

Body language can be classified as learned, innate, or mixed. Signals such as winking or saluting are learned within a cultural context, while blinking and blushing are clearly innate. Laughing, crying, and shrugging the shoulders are said to be mixed because they're innate, but their timing and use are influenced by cultural norms.

Nonverbal communication can be very ambiguous, especially across cultures. While certain gestures are universally understood—actions such as smiling when happy and frowning when unhappy—it's clear that the significance of others is determined by culture. In fact, similar gestures that are used in different countries may actually have quite different meanings. For example, while the familiar "thumbs-up" sign has a positive meaning in America, it's viewed as an obscene gesture in some cultures.

Egypt • Egyptian

HANDSHAPE: Right X hand

POSITION: On the forehead

MOVEMENT: Touch the back of the right X hand to the forehead while mouthing the word "Egypt." To sign *Egyptian*, add the *person* ending. (See page 18.)

VISUALIZE: Suggests a cobra, which is the symbol of the royal power of the pharaohs of Egypt.

England • English

HANDSHAPE: Right and left CURVED hands

POSITION: In front of the chest

MOVEMENT: With the palms facing down, curl the fingers of the right CURVED hand over the little finger side of the left CURVED hand. Then rock both hands forward and back while mouthing the word "England." To sign *English*, add the *person* ending. (See page 18.)

VISUALIZE: An Englishman leaning on his cane.

X
hand

Curved
hand

Europe • European

HANDSHAPE: Right E hand

POSITION: In front of the right shoulder

MOVEMENT: With the palm facing forward, move the right E hand in a clockwise circle in front of the right shoulder while mouthing the word "Europe." To sign *European*, add the *person* ending. (See page 18.)

VISUALIZE: The initial E is understood as *Europe* in the appropriate context.

France • French

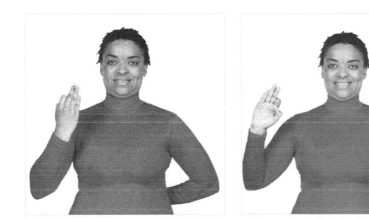

HANDSHAPE: Right F hand

POSITION: In front of the right shoulder

MOVEMENT: Hold up the right F hand with palm facing in. Then twist the hand from the wrist so the palm faces forward while mouthing the word "France." To sign *French*, add the *person* ending. (See page 18.)

VISUALIZE: Your soufflé is okay.

Germany • German

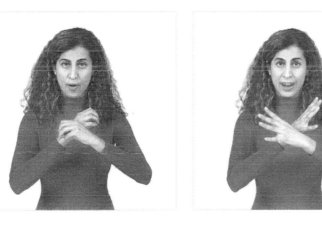

HANDSHAPES: Right and left O hands changing to OPEN hands

POSITION: In front of the chest

MOVEMENT: Cross the right and left O hands at the wrists with the palms facing in and thrust the two hands in opposite directions while changing them to OPEN hands. Then wiggle the fingers and thumbs while mouthing the word "Germany." To sign *German*, add the *person* ending. (See page 18.)

VISUALIZE: A spread-winged eagle—the symbol of Imperial Germany.

E hand

F hand

O hand

Open hand

India • Indian

HANDSHAPE: Right A hand

POSITION: On the forehead

MOVEMENT: With the palm facing left, touch the thumbtip of the right A hand to the center of the forehead and twist slightly while mouthing the word "India." To sign *Indian,* add the *person* ending. (See page 18.)

VISUALIZE: The location of the dot (called the Bindhi, Kumkum, or Tilak) worn by many Indian women.

Ireland • Irish

HANDSHAPES: Right V hand with index and middle fingers curved, and left S hand

POSITION: In front of the chest

MOVEMENT: With the palms facing down, move the right V hand in a small clockwise circle above the left S hand. Then drop the V fingertips onto the back of the left hand while mouthing the word "Ireland." To sign *Irish,* add the *person* ending. (See page 18.)

VISUALIZE: Resembles the sign for *potato,* a staple of the traditional Irish diet.

Israel • Israeli

HANDSHAPE: Right I hand

POSITION: On the chin

MOVEMENT: Draw the little fingertip of the right I hand down over the right side of the chin, then the left side of the chin, while mouthing the word "Israel." To sign *Israeli,* add the *person* ending. (See page 18.)

VISUALIZE: The initial I showing the beard traditionally worn by Hasidic Jewish men.

A
hand

V
hand

S
hand

I
hand

Italy · Italian

HANDSHAPE: Right I hand

POSITION: On the forehead

MOVEMENT: Trace the shape of a cross on the forehead with the little fingertip of the right I hand while mouthing the word "Italy." To sign *Italian*, add the *person* ending. (See page 18.)

VISUALIZE: The sign of the cross, symbolizing Catholicism, Italy's predominant religion.

Japan · Japanese

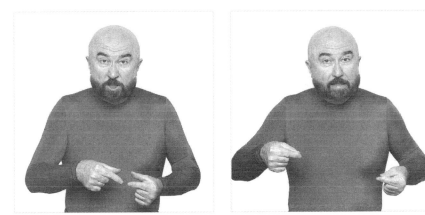

HANDSHAPE: Right and left G hands

POSITION: In front of the chest

MOVEMENT: Point the right and left G hands toward each other with the palms facing in. Then draw the hands away from each other to the sides of the body, pressing the thumbtips and index fingertips together, while mouthing the word "Japan." To sign *Japanese*, add the *person* ending. (See page 18.)

VISUALIZE: Outlining the shape of the Japanese islands.

Mexico · Mexican

HANDSHAPE: Right M hand

POSITION: On the right cheek

MOVEMENT: Slide the extended fingertips of the right M hand down over the right cheek a few times while mouthing the word "Mexico." To sign *Mexican*, add the *person* ending. (See page 18.)

VISUALIZE: The initial M suggests Mexico, while the movement suggests the facial whiskers of a traditional Mexican villager.

G hand

M hand

Russia • Russian

HANDSHAPE: Right and left OPEN hands

POSITION: On the sides of the waist

MOVEMENT: With the palms facing down, tap the thumbtips of the right and left OPEN hands against the sides of the waist a few times while mouthing the word "Russia." To sign *Russian*, add the *person* ending. (See page 18.)

VISUALIZE: Holding the hands in position for a traditional Russian dance.

GENERAL PLACE NAMES

country

HANDSHAPES: Right Y hand and left S hand

POSITION: In front of the chest

MOVEMENT: With the palm facing in, move the knuckles of the right Y hand in a counter-clockwise circle in front of the left forearm near the elbow.

VISUALIZE: Patriotically wrapping yourself in a flag.

foreign

HANDSHAPES: Right F hand and left S hand

POSITION: In front of the chest

MOVEMENT: With the palm facing in, move the thumb and index finger side of the right F hand in a counterclockwise circle in front of the left forearm near the elbow.

VISUALIZE: Using the initial F to form a sign similar to *country*.

 Open hand

Y hand

 S hand

 F hand

international

HANDSHAPE: Right and left I hands

POSITION: In front of the chest

MOVEMENT: Point the little finger of the left I hand forward with the palm facing down. Move the right I hand in a circle around the left hand.

VISUALIZE: The initial I hand going around the world.

nation • national

HANDSHAPES: Right N hand with index and middle fingers extended, and left S hand

POSITION: In front of the chest

MOVEMENT: With the palms facing down, move the right N hand in a small clockwise circle above the left S hand. Then touch the N fingertips to the back of the left hand.

VISUALIZE: Stirring the nation's "melting pot."

How Many Languages Are Spoken in the World?

It is estimated that more than 6,000 languages are spoken on our planet. This great diversity is threatened, however—linguists speculate that more than half our world's remaining languages will become extinct over the next hundred years. The languages that are most in danger of becoming extinct are those spoken by people in small communities whose way of life is being drastically changed by outside influences. Communities may be broken up or destroyed by war, famine, disease, or environmental disaster; the threat of "development"

encroaches on land and livelihoods; and economic prospects attract younger members away from their villages. Since social and economic change cannot be avoided entirely, a major cultural priority should be to videotape speakers of languages in danger of extinction, subtitle the recordings, and then preserve them in a worldwide archive.

Happily, I suspect sign languages will survive the disappearance of the dying oral languages, as they are intrinsic to the communication process of all cultures.

I hand

N hand

state

HANDSHAPES: Left FLAT hand and right S hand

POSITION: In front of the left shoulder

MOVEMENT: Hold up the left FLAT hand with the palm facing forward. Place the thumb and index finger side of the right S hand on the left hand near the fingertips; then move the right hand down in an arc to the heel of the left hand.

VISUALIZE: The initial S is understood as *state* in the appropriate context.

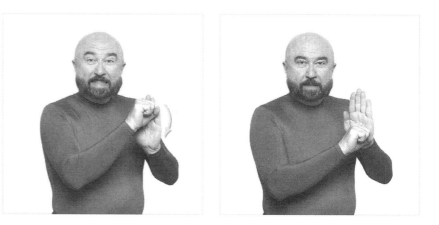

street • road • avenue • way • highway • route

HANDSHAPE: Right and left FLAT hands

POSITION: In front of the chest

MOVEMENT: Point the right and left FLAT hands forward with the palms facing each other. Then move both hands forward in a wavy motion. To sign *road*, use R hands; to sign *avenue*, use A hands; to sign *way*, use W hands; etc.

VISUALIZE: A winding road.

town • village • city • community

HANDSHAPE: Right and left FLAT hands

POSITION: In front of the chest

MOVEMENT: Touch the fingertips of the right and left FLAT hands together, palms facing each other, to form a triangle in front of the chest. Repeat several times, moving the hands to the right each time.

VISUALIZE: The rooftops of a row of houses.

 Flat hand

 S hand

GOVERNMENT

constitution

HANDSHAPES: Left FLAT hand and right C hand

POSITION: In front of the chest

MOVEMENT: Hold up the left FLAT hand with the palm facing forward. Place the thumb and index finger side of the right C hand on the left hand near the fingertips; then move the right hand down in an arc to the heel of the left hand.

VISUALIZE: Using the initial C to form a sign similar to *law*.

Democrat • Independent • Republican

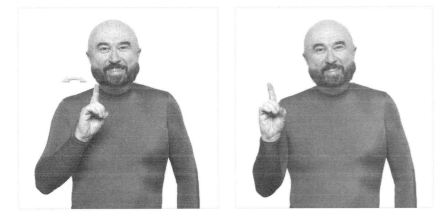

HANDSHAPE: Right D hand

POSITION: In front of the right shoulder

MOVEMENT: Point the palm of the right D hand forward and shake it from right to left a few times. To sign *Independent*, use an I hand; to sign *Republican*, use an R hand.

VISUALIZE: The movement suggests leaning to one side or the other, and the initial suggests the specific political party.

government • politics • federal • capital

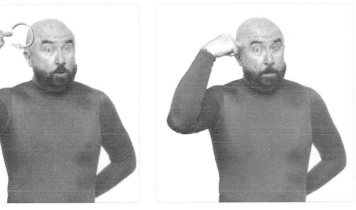

HANDSHAPE: Right ONE hand

POSITION: Near the right temple

MOVEMENT: Point the index finger of the right ONE hand toward the right temple and move the hand forward in a small circle. Then touch the index fingertip to the temple. To sign *capital*, use the C hand; for *federal*, use the F hand; and for *politics*, use the P hand.

VISUALIZE: You have to be a little "crazy" to get into politics.

C hand

D hand

One hand

judge • court • trial • judgment • justice

HANDSHAPES: 1. Right ONE hand **2.** Right and left F hands

POSITIONS: 1. On the forehead **2.** In front of the chest

MOVEMENT: 1. Touch the index fingertip of the right ONE hand to the center of the forehead. **2.** Point the right and left F hands forward with the palms facing each other, and move the hands alternately up and down a few times.

VISUALIZE: A judge considering both sides of a case before coming to a decision.

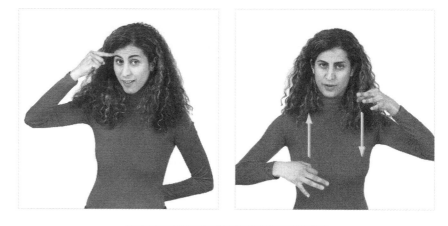

The Americans With Disabilities Act

The Americans With Disabilities Act (ADA) was signed into law by President George Bush in 1990 to protect people with disabilities from discrimination in employment, state and local government services, public accommodations, commerical facilities, and telecommunications relay services. A "person with a disability" is anyone with a physical or mental impairment that substantially limits one or more major life activities, including walking, seeing, hearing, speaking, breathing, caring for oneself, learning, and working. Also protected under the ADA are people with conditions that are not readily apparent, including psychological problems, learning disabilities, or chronic health conditions such as epilepsy, diabetes, arthritis, cancer, cardiac problems, HIV/AIDS, and others.

For people who are deaf or hard of hearing, the ADA ensures that "auxiliary aids and services" are provided so that no individual is excluded, denied services, segregated, or otherwise treated differently from other individuals. Auxiliary aids and services include: qualified interpreters, note takers, computer-aided transcription services, written materials, telephone handset amplifiers, assistive listening devices, assistive listening systems, telephones compatible with hearing aids, closed caption decoders, open and closed captioning, telecommunications devices for deaf persons (TTYs), and videotext displays. This guarantees that communication with deaf and hard-of-hearing people is as effective as communication with hearing people.

One hand

F hand

Flat hand

law

HANDSHAPES: Left FLAT hand and right L hand

POSITION: In front of the chest

MOVEMENT: Hold up the left FLAT hand with the palm facing forward. Place the thumb and index finger side of the right L hand on the left hand near the fingertips; then move the right hand down in an arc to the heel of the left hand.

VISUALIZE: The initial L showing laws printed in a book.

president

HANDSHAPES: Right and left C hands changing to S hands

POSITION: Starts on the temples

MOVEMENT: Hold the right and left C hands on the temples with the fingers pointing forward. Then move the hands out and away from the head while changing them to the S handshape.

VISUALIZE: Suggests the one who takes the bull by the horns.

vote • elect • election

HANDSHAPES: Right F hand and left O hand

POSITION: In front of the chest

MOVEMENT: Dip the thumb and index finger of the right F hand down into the opening of the left O hand.

VISUALIZE: Dropping a ballot into the ballot box.

L hand   C hand   S hand   O hand

the body & health

L et's get physical—with a chapter that focuses on the body and health! Whether you're going to wash your *face*, brush your *teeth*, get some *sleep*, refill a *prescription*, or talk to your *doctor*, these signs will ensure that you put your whole *heart* into signed conversations.

PARTS OF THE BODY

arm

HANDSHAPES: Right C hand with index, ring, and little fingers extended, and left C hand

POSITION: In front of the chest

MOVEMENT: With the palm facing down, slide the fingertips of the right modified C hand up along the left arm from the wrist to the elbow.

VISUALIZE: Showing the length of the forearm.

SEE HELPING HANDS ON NEXT PAGE.

293

birth • born

HANDSHAPE: Right and left FLAT hands

POSITION: In front of the lower chest

MOVEMENT: With the palms facing up, place the back of the right FLAT hand on the palm of the left FLAT hand. Then pivot the right hand forward while moving both hands upward simultaneously. (Common usage sign.)

VISUALIZE: Presenting a newborn to the parents.

blood • bleed • hemorrhage

HANDSHAPES: **1.** Right ONE hand **2.** Right and left OPEN hands

POSITIONS: **1.** On the lips **2.** In front of the chest

MOVEMENT: **1.** Touch the index fingertip of the right ONE hand to the lips. (This is the sign for *red*.) **2.** Hold up the right and left OPEN hands in front of the chest with the palms facing in. Wiggle the fingers of the right hand while brushing the fingertips down across the back of the left hand.

VISUALIZE: Red blood flowing from a cut in the left hand.

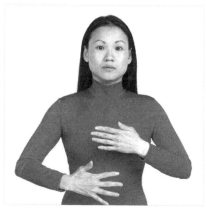

C
hand

Flat
hand

One
hand

Open
hand

body • physical

HANDSHAPE: Right and left FLAT hands

POSITION: Starts on the upper chest

MOVEMENT: Place the palms of the right and left FLAT hands on the upper part of the chest; then move both hands down and place them on the lower part of the chest.

VISUALIZE: Showing the torso of your body.

bones

HANDSHAPES: Right modified X hand and left S hand

POSITION: In front of the chest

MOVEMENT: With the palms facing down, tap the index fingertip of the right modified X hand on the knuckles of the left S hand.

VISUALIZE: Showing the bones of the hand.

brain • mind • intellect • sense

HANDSHAPE: Right ONE hand

POSITION: On the forehead

MOVEMENT: Tap the index fingertip of the right ONE hand on the center of the forehead a few times.

VISUALIZE: Showing the location of the brain.

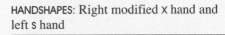

X
hand

S
hand

breasts

HANDSHAPE: Right CURVED hand

POSITION: In front of the chest

MOVEMENT: Point the fingers of the right CURVED hand first toward the right breast, then toward the left breast.

VISUALIZE: Indicating the breast area.

breathe · breath

HANDSHAPE: Right and left OPEN hands

POSITION: In front of the chest

MOVEMENT: Place the palms of the right and left OPEN hands on the chest with the right hand above the left. Move both hands forward; then place them back on the chest. Repeat.

VISUALIZE: The chest rising and falling with each breath.

ear · noise · sound · hear

HANDSHAPE: Right ONE hand

POSITION: Near the right earlobe

MOVEMENT: Point the index finger of the right ONE hand toward the right earlobe.

VISUALIZE: Indicating the ear.

 Curved hand

 Open hand   One hand

The Ear and Hearing

Looking at the ear from the outside, you might never guess at its complex—and delicate—inner workings. But there's more to the ear than meets the eye! In fact, the ear is made up of three parts, which are known simply as the outer ear, the middle ear, and the inner ear. Each of these parts serves a specific purpose in the process of detecting and interpreting sound.

The part of the outer ear that you see is called the ear flap, or *pinna*. This region serves a dual purpose, as it both collects sound and provides protection for the middle ear as a means of preventing damage to the eardrum. Just inside the pinna—but still part of the outer ear—is the *external auditory canal*, a passage along which sound travels. The eardrum, also known as the *tympanic membrane*, is a durable, tightly stretched structure located at the end of this auditory canal. The eardrum separates the outer ear from the middle ear.

The middle ear is an air-filled cavity that contains the three tiniest bones in your body, known as the *ossicles*. Each of these three interconnected bones has a name: the *malleus*, or hammer; the *incus*, or anvil; and the *stapes*, or stirrup. The ossicles stretch across the middle ear cavity, with the malleus attached to the eardrum at one end and the stapes attached to a membrane called the *oval window* at the other end. The oval window serves as a boundary to the inner ear.

The inner ear is made up of two different organs with distinct functions. The *semicircular canals* are fluid-filled chambers that actually play no role in the hearing process. Rather, they help maintain the body's balance and equilibrium. The *cochlea*, however, is the body's "microphone." Resembling a snail's shell, the cochlea is divided into three fluid-filled chambers. Within the central chamber lies the *organ of Corti*, to which 15,000 to 20,000 tiny hair-like nerve cells are attached. These nerve cells are connected to the *auditory nerve*, also called the nerve of hearing, which carries signals to the brain.

Any source of sound—whether human speech, music, the rustle of leaves, the cry of birds, or the slamming of garbage cans—sends vibrations or sound waves into the air. These sound waves are collected by the pinna, funnel through the auditory canal, and then strike the eardrum, causing it to vibrate at the exact same frequency as the sound. From the eardrum, the vibrations pass through the malleus, incus, and stapes in the middle ear—again, causing the structures to vibrate at the same frequency as the sound wave. The vibrations then move first to the oval window; next, to the fluid of the cochlea; and then, to the tiny hair-like nerve cells, each of which has a sensitivity to a particular frequency of sound. When the frequency of the sound matches the natural frequency of the cells, those cells resonate with the vibration. This induces the cells to produce an electrical impulse, which travels along the auditory nerve to the brain. Finally, in a process that is not yet perfectly understood, the brain interprets the impulses as sound.

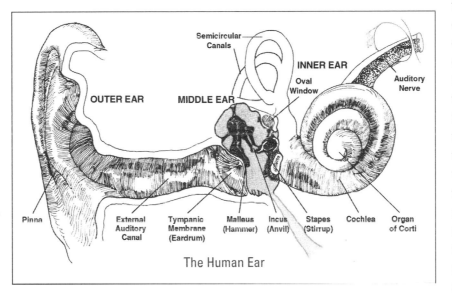

The Human Ear

Semicircular Canals

INNER EAR

Oval Window

Auditory Nerve

OUTER EAR

MIDDLE EAR

Pinna

External Auditory Canal

Tympanic Membrane (Eardrum)

Malleus (Hammer)

Incus (Anvil)

Stapes (Stirrup)

Cochlea

Organ of Corti

eye

HANDSHAPE: Right ONE hand

POSITION: Near the right eye

MOVEMENT: Point the index finger of the right ONE hand toward the outside corner of the right eye.

VISUALIZE: Indicating the eye.

face • appearance

HANDSHAPE: Right ONE hand

POSITION: In front of the face

MOVEMENT: With the palm facing in, move the index finger of the right ONE hand in a counterclockwise circle in front of the face.

VISUALIZE: Showing the shape of the face.

feet

HANDSHAPE: Right ONE hand

POSITION: In front of the chest

MOVEMENT: Point the index finger of the right ONE hand first toward the right foot, then toward the left foot.

VISUALIZE: Indicating the feet.

One
hand

hair

HANDSHAPE: Right OPEN hand

POSITION: Near the head

MOVEMENT: Grasp a lock of hair with the thumb and index finger of the right OPEN hand.

VISUALIZE: Indicating the hair—or the lack of it.

hands

HANDSHAPE: Right and left FLAT hands

POSITION: In front of the chest

MOVEMENT: With the palms facing in, draw the little finger side of the right FLAT hand across the wrist of the left hand. Then draw the little finger side of the left FLAT hand across the wrist of the right hand.

VISUALIZE: Indicating where the hands begin.

head

HANDSHAPE: Right BENT hand

POSITION: Starts on the right temple

MOVEMENT: Touch the fingertips of the right BENT hand to the right temple; then move the hand down and touch the right side of the jaw.

VISUALIZE: Indicating the top and bottom of the head.

Open hand   Flat hand   Bent hand

heart

HANDSHAPE: Right OPEN hand

POSITION: On the chest

MOVEMENT: Touch the middle fingertip of the right OPEN hand to the chest over the heart.

VISUALIZE: Feeling for a heartbeat.

mouth

HANDSHAPE: Right ONE hand

POSITION: In front of the mouth

MOVEMENT: Point the index finger of the right ONE hand toward the mouth.

VISUALIZE: Indicating the mouth.

nose

HANDSHAPE: Right ONE hand

POSITION: Near the nose

MOVEMENT: Touch the index finger of the right ONE hand to the nose.

VISUALIZE: Indicating the nose.

Open hand

One hand

teeth

HANDSHAPE: Right ONE hand

POSITION: On the teeth

MOVEMENT: Slide the index fingertip of the right ONE hand across the teeth from right to left.

VISUALIZE: Indicating the teeth.

HEALTH & MEDICINE

accident • crash • wreck • collision

HANDSHAPE: Right and left A hands

POSITION: In front of the chest

MOVEMENT: With the palms facing in, strike the knuckles of the right and left A hands together.

VISUALIZE: Two objects crashing into each other.

awake • wake up • arouse

HANDSHAPE: Right and left Q hands

POSITION: Near the outside corners of the eyes

MOVEMENT: Point the right and left Q hands forward near the outside corners of the eyes with the thumbs and index fingers pressed together. Then flick open the Q fingers.

VISUALIZE: The eyes opening suddenly.

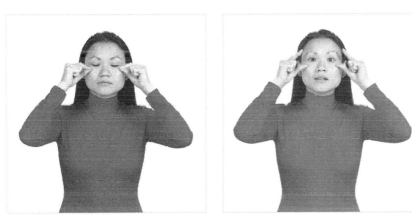

A hand

Q hand

blind

HANDSHAPE: Right v hand with index and middle fingers curved

POSITION: In front of the eyes

MOVEMENT: Point the extended fingers of the right v hand toward the eyes with the palm facing in. Then draw the hand down slightly while closing the eyes and further bending the fingers.

VISUALIZE: The closing of the eyes.

cochlear implant

HANDSHAPE: Right v hand (index and middle fingers curved)

POSITION: Near the right ear

MOVEMENT: Tap the curved fingers of the right v hand against the skull, behind the right ear.

VISUALIZE: The location of a cochlear implant.

cold • flu

HANDSHAPE: Right s hand with thumb and index finger extended

POSITION: In front of the nose

MOVEMENT: Hold the right s hand, palm facing in, in front of the nose, and place the two extended fingers on either side of the nose. Then draw the hand down a few times.

VISUALIZE: Wiping a runny nose.

v hand

s hand

Cochlear Implants

Although today's powerful behind-the-ear hearing aids can help most deaf or hard-of-hearing people understand at least some speech, conventional hearing aids offer little or no benefit for a percentage of the deaf population. People whose deafness results from inner-ear damage, and who don't benefit from hearing aids, may be considered as candidates for cochlear implants. Unlike a hearing aid, which simply makes sounds louder, the cochlear implant turns sound into an electrical current that's delivered directly to the auditory nerve, bypassing both the middle and inner ear. To date, more than 12,000 adults and children worldwide have received cochlear implants.

The cochlear implant device includes a tiny audio receiver that's implanted behind the ear; electrode wires that are inserted into the cochlea; and external components, including a microphone, a speech processor, and connecting cables. So how does it work? The external microphone picks up sounds and relays them to the speech processor, which codes the sounds into digital signals. These signals are relayed to the audio receiver, and then are routed to the electrodes in the cochlea. The electrodes stimulate the auditory nerve, which sends the signals to the brain to be interpreted as sound. Because these electrical signals are not heard exactly like normal sounds, people with cochlear implants need some training to learn to interpret and use this information.

Since cochlear implants were first approved by the FDA for testing in 1985, a storm of controversy has surrounded their use, especially in children. Implants have the potential to help profoundly deaf children develop intelligible speech, allowing them to participate more fully in the hearing world. But some members of the deaf community have condemned the surgery as a sort of "cultural genocide." People who oppose cochlear implants argue that American Sign Language is the basis for their separate culture, and that widespread use of implants will ultimately cause the death of the unique and beautiful language of signs.

cough

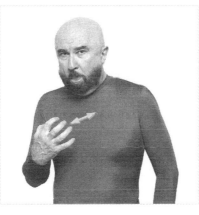

HANDSHAPE:	Right CLAWED hand
POSITION:	In front of the upper chest
MOVEMENT:	Hold the right CLAWED hand, palm facing in, in front of the upper chest, and strike the fingertips against the chest a few times. If desired, simulate the coughing action while signing.
VISUALIZE:	Feeling congestion in the chest.

Clawed hand

dead • death • die • expire

HANDSHAPE: Right and left FLAT hands

POSITION: In front of the chest

MOVEMENT: Point the right and left FLAT hands forward with the right palm facing up and the left palm facing down. Then turn both hands over simultaneously so the right palm is facing down and the left palm is facing up.

VISUALIZE: A body turning over in the grave.

deaf

HANDSHAPE: Right ONE hand

POSITION: Starts on the right earlobe, ends on the lips

MOVEMENT: Touch the index fingertip of the right ONE hand to the right earlobe, then to the lips.

VISUALIZE: Deafness affecting both hearing and speech.

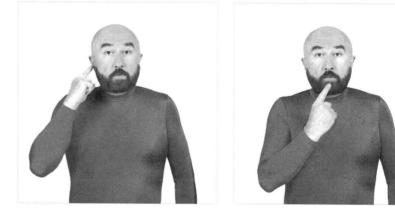

dizzy

HANDSHAPE: Right CLAWED hand

POSITION: In front of the face

MOVEMENT: Place the right CLAWED hand, palm facing in, in front of the face. Then slowly move the hand around the face in a few counterclockwise circles.

VISUALIZE: Getting dizzy as things appear to drift around in circles.

 Flat hand One hand Clawed hand

The Importance of Early Detection of Hearing Impairment

It is estimated that 33 babies are born with significant hearing impairment every day in the United States—that's 1 to 3 babies out of every thousand born. This makes hearing impairment the most common congenital disorder in newborns. For many of these children, the problem isn't detected until one to two years of age. Unfortunately, because the first few years of a child's life are critical in terms of language development, undetected hearing loss can delay speech and language acquisition, which in turn may hinder social and emotional development and future academic achievement.

In 1993, the National Institute of Health's (NIH) Consensus Development Conference on Early Identification of Hearing Loss recommended that all hospitals screen newborns for hearing impairment to catch problems early, *before* language development is affected. In response to this recommendation, Congress passed the Newborn and Infant Hearing Screening and Intervention Act of 1999, which gives Federal grants to states to implement early hearing and detection and intervention (EHDI) programs. Today, 39 states have legislation or guidelines for voluntary compliance to support EHDI programs.

Advocates for early screening are not without opposition, however. Some experts have questioned the benefit of testing hearing in newborns, citing a large number of false positive results with tests such as the auditory brain-stem response (ABR) test. ABR testing uses electrodes taped behind the infant's ears and on the forehead to measure brain activity in response to clicking sounds. According to researchers from the University of North Carolina, factors such as debris in the ear canal or noise in the room during testing may be responsible for false positives. In their article in the journal *Pediatrics,* the researchers recommended repeat testing for any infants who fail the initial screening.

doctor • physician • surgeon

HANDSHAPES: Right D hand and left A hand

POSITION: In front of the chest

MOVEMENT: Tap the thumbtip of the right D hand on the upturned wrist of the left A hand a few times.

VISUALIZE: The motion suggests checking a patient's pulse, and the initial indicates the word *doctor.*

D hand

A hand

glasses

HANDSHAPE: Right G hand

POSITION: Starts near the right eye

MOVEMENT: Point the right G hand to the left near the outside corner of the right eye. Then move the hand back toward the right ear while touching the thumbtip and index fingertip together. (The same sign can also be used in context to refer to Gallaudet University in Washington, D.C.)

VISUALIZE: Showing the lens and earpiece of a pair of glasses.

healthy • well • wholesome

HANDSHAPES: Right and left CLAWED hands changing to S hands

POSITION: In front of the chest

MOVEMENT: Touch the fingertips of the right and left CLAWED hands to the chest. Then move both hands forward while changing them to the S handshape.

VISUALIZE: A healthy body is a strong body.

hearing aid

HANDSHAPE: Right V hand with index and middle fingers curved

POSITION: Near the right ear

MOVEMENT: Hold up the right V hand next to the right ear with the palm facing forward. Twist the hand several times.

VISUALIZE: Adjusting a hearing aid.

G hand

Clawed hand

S hand

V hand

hospital

HANDSHAPE: Right H hand

POSITION: On the upper left arm

MOVEMENT: Trace the shape of a cross on the upper left arm with the fingertips of the right H hand.

VISUALIZE: Using the initial H to form the shape of the Red Cross symbol.

injection • shot • vaccination • syringe

HANDSHAPE: Right L hand

POSITION: On the upper left arm

MOVEMENT: Place the index fingertip of the right L hand on the upper left arm and bend the thumb.

VISUALIZE: Using a syringe to give an injection.

life • existence

HANDSHAPE: Right and left L hands

POSITION: Starts on the lower chest

MOVEMENT: Place the palms of the right and left L hands on the lower part of the chest; then move both hands up over chest while wiggling the fingers. To sign *existence*, use E hands.

VISUALIZE: Energy flowing through the body.

H
hand

L
hand

medicine • drug • prescription

HANDSHAPES: Right OPEN hand and left FLAT hand

POSITION: In front of the chest

MOVEMENT: Move the middle fingertip of the right OPEN hand in small circles on the upturned palm of the left FLAT hand a few times.

VISUALIZE: Grinding medicine with an old-fashioned mortar and pestle.

nurse

HANDSHAPES: Right N hand with index and middle fingers extended, and left S hand

POSITION: In front of the chest

MOVEMENT: Place the extended fingertips of the right N hand on the upturned wrist of the left S hand.

VISUALIZE: The motion suggests checking a patient's pulse, and the initial indicates the word *nurse*.

operation • surgery

HANDSHAPES: Right A hand and left OPEN hand

POSITION: In front of the chest

MOVEMENT: Slide the thumbtip of the right A hand across the upturned palm of the left OPEN hand from the fingertips to the wrist. Sometimes the incision motion is made at the site of the surgery.

VISUALIZE: Making an incision.

Open hand   Flat hand   N hand   S hand

pain • ache • hurt • injury • sore • wound

HANDSHAPE: Right and left ONE hands

POSITION: In front of the chest

MOVEMENT: With the palms facing in, jab the index fingertips of the right and left ONE hands toward each other several times. To indicate that a specific area of the body is hurting, sign *pain* near that part of the body.

VISUALIZE: A throbbing pain.

patient

HANDSHAPE: Right P hand

POSITION: On the upper left arm

MOVEMENT: Trace the shape of a cross on the upper left arm with the middle fingertip of the right P hand.

VISUALIZE: Using the initial P to form a sign similar to *hospital*.

pregnant

HANDSHAPE: Right and left CURVED hands

POSITION: In front of the abdomen

MOVEMENT: Hold the right and left CURVED hands together in front of the abdomen with the fingers interlocked and the palms facing in.

VISUALIZE: A pregnant woman's rounded belly.

 A hand

 One hand

 P hand

Curved hand

problem

HANDSHAPE: Right and left v hands with index and middle fingers curved

POSITION: In front of the chest

MOVEMENT: Touch the knuckles of the right and left v fingers together; then twist the hands in opposite directions.

VISUALIZE: Turning things over in an effort to figure them out.

What Is Tinnitus?

An estimated 50 million Americans experience tinnitus, which is the subjective sensation of hearing noise when none is externally present. People with tinnitus usually describe their symptoms as ringing, buzzing, roaring, whistling, chirping, whooshing, or hissing noises. Ninety percent of people with severe tinnitus also experience some hearing loss.

Tinnitus isn't a disease; rather, it's a symptom that can be caused by a number of medical conditions, including problems of the ear canal, middle ear, inner ear, auditory nerve, or central nervous system. Damage to the microscopic hair cells in the inner ear—one of the most common causes of the condition—is often related to age or to repeated exposure to loud noise. Other causes of tinnitus include obstruction of the external ear canal; long-term use of medications such as aspirin, quinine, antibiotics, and anti-inflammatory drugs; stiffening of the bones in the middle ear, known as otosclerosis; hypothyroidism; cardiovascular disease; high blood pressure; trauma

to or tumors of the head or neck; and temporomandibular joint dysfunction (TMJ).

At this time, there is no medical or surgical treatment specifically designed to treat tinnitus. If tinnitus is the result of an underlying condition or disease, treatment of the source of the problem may alleviate the symptoms. However, tinnitus that results from advancing age or from excessive exposure to noise cannot be handled either medically or surgically. When this is the case, people with the condition must learn to make adjustments to lessen the symptoms. For example, avoiding irritants, such as loud noises and excessive doses of aspirin, can help reduce the severity of the noise. Nicotine, caffeine, and alcohol are also known irritants that should be avoided.

Some people are able to successfully cover up or "mask" the noise from tinnitus with a fan or soft music. If tinnitus is accompanied by hearing loss, hearing aids can amplify outside sounds, which can help make the tinnitus noise less obvious.

v
hand

sick • ill • disease • nauseous

HANDSHAPE: Right and left OPEN hands

POSITIONS: Right hand on the forehead and left hand on the stomach

MOVEMENT: Touch the middle finger of the right OPEN hand to the forehead; at the same time, touch the middle finger of the left OPEN hand to the stomach.

VISUALIZE: Indicating discomfort in the head and stomach.

sleep • nap • doze • slumber

HANDSHAPES: Right OPEN hand changing to AND hand

POSITION: Starts on the forehead

MOVEMENT: With the palm facing in, touch the fingertips of the right OPEN hand to the forehead. Then draw the hand down to the chin while changing it to the AND handshape.

VISUALIZE: The hand gently closing the eyes for sleep.

temperature

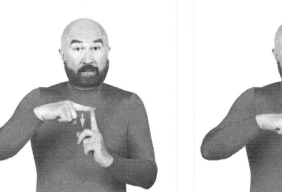

HANDSHAPE: Right and left ONE hands

POSITION: In front of the chest

MOVEMENT: Slide the index fingertip of the right ONE hand up and down the upright index finger of the left ONE hand.

VISUALIZE: The mercury in a thermometer rising and falling with the temperature.

Open hand

And hand

One hand

tired • exhausted • weary • fatigued

HANDSHAPE: Right and left CURVED hands

POSITION: On the chest

MOVEMENT: Touch the fingertips of the right and left CURVED hands to the chest. Then twist both hands downward from the wrists and touch the little finger sides of the hands to the chest, slumping the shoulders at the same time.

VISUALIZE: A tired body slumping forward.

vomit • throw up

HANDSHAPE: Right and left OPEN hands

POSITION: Starts in front of the mouth

MOVEMENT: Hold up the right and left OPEN hands in front of the mouth, palms facing in, with the left hand in front of the right. Then move both hands forward and downward.

VISUALIZE: The motion of vomiting.

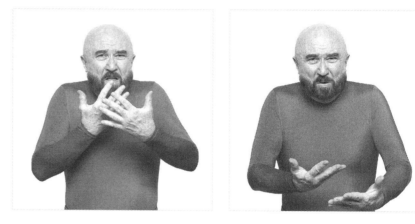

Curved hand   Open hand

religion
& holidays

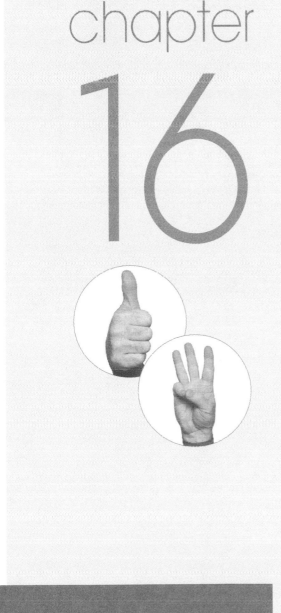

chapter 16

S pend some time learning the signs in this chapter and you'll be able to discuss ideas of a more spiritual significance. Soon you'll have enough *faith* in your signing abilities to express your views on *religion,* share your *belief* about a higher power, join with others in *prayer,* thank *heaven* for everyday blessings, or reflect on a meaningful *sermon.*

RELIGION

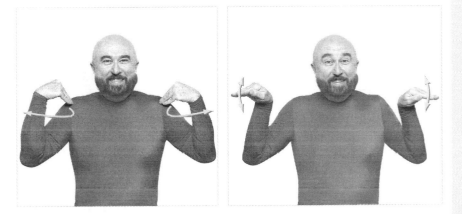

angel

HANDSHAPE: Right and left CURVED hands

POSITION: Starts on the shoulders

MOVEMENT: Touch the fingertips of the right and left CURVED hands to the shoulders. Then twist the hands from the wrists so the fingertips point out to the sides, and flap the hands up and down a few times.

VISUALIZE: The fluttering wings of the angel Gabriel.

SEE HELPING HANDS ON NEXT PAGE.

Baptist • Baptism • immersion

HANDSHAPE: Right and left A hands with thumbs extended.

POSITION: In front of the chest

MOVEMENT: Hold the right and left A hands forward with palms facing each other, and twist the hands from the wrists so the thumbtips are pointing right. Then bring the thumbs up again.

VISUALIZE: Dipping your thumbs in water and bringing them out again.

believe • belief

HANDSHAPES: **1.** Right ONE hand **2.** Right and left CURVED hands

POSITIONS: **1.** On the right side of the forehead **2.** In front of the chest

MOVEMENT: **1.** Touch the index fingertip of the right ONE hand to the forehead. (This resembles the sign for *think*.) **2.** Clasp the right and left CURVED hands together in front of the chest.

VISUALIZE: Your firm beliefs are worth holding onto.

Bible

HANDSHAPE: **1.** Right and left OPEN hands **2.** Right and left FLAT hands

POSITION: In front of the chest

MOVEMENT: **1.** Hold up both OPEN hands with palms facing each other. Touch right middle fingertip to left palm and then touch left middle fingertip to right palm. (Sign for *Jesus*.) **2.** Hold both FLAT hands together with palms touching and fingertips pointing forward. Then pull hands apart so palms face up, keeping little finger sides together. (Sign for *book*.)

VISUALIZE: Combining the signs for *Jesus* and *book* to suggest the Bible.

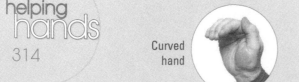

Curved hand

A hand

One hand

Open hand

bless

HANDSHAPES: Right and left A hands changing to FLAT hands

POSITION: Starts on the lips

MOVEMENT: Touch the thumbnails of the right and left A hands to the lips. Then move both hands forward and downward while changing them to FLAT hands, ending with the palms facing down.

VISUALIZE: A spoken blessing followed by the laying on of hands.

Buddhist · Buddhism

HANDSHAPE: Right FLAT hand

POSITION: In front of the stomach

MOVEMENT: Hold the right FLAT hand, palm facing in, in front of the stomach. Move the hand counterclockwise in a circular motion above the stomach.

VISUALIZE: Outlining the prominent stomach of the Buddha.

Flat hand

Catholic

HANDSHAPE: Right u hand

POSITION: In front of the forehead

MOVEMENT: Trace the shape of a cross on the forehead with the fingertips of the right u hand.

VISUALIZE: Making the sign of the cross, a principal symbol of Catholic belief.

church • chapel • synagogue • mosque

HANDSHAPES: Left s hand and right c hand

POSITION: In front of the chest

MOVEMENT: Point the left s hand to the right with the palm facing down; then tap the thumb side of the right c hand on the back of the left hand a few times. To sign *synagogue*, use the right s hand; to sign *mosque*, use the right M hand.

VISUALIZE: Using the initial letter to show that a house of worship rests upon a rock-solid belief.

devil • demon • Satan • mischief

HANDSHAPE: Right THREE hand

POSITION: On the right temple

MOVEMENT: With the palm facing forward, touch the thumbtip of the right THREE hand to the right temple; then bend and straighten the index and middle fingers a few times.

VISUALIZE: The devil's horns.

U
hand

S
hand

C
hand

Three
hand

Episcopal

HANDSHAPES: Left s hand and right ONE hand

POSITION: In front of the chest

MOVEMENT: Point the left s hand to the right with the palm facing down. Touch the index finger side of the right ONE hand first to the underside of the left wrist, then under the elbow, using an arcing motion.

VISUALIZE: The wide sleeves of a minister's robe.

faith • confidence • trust

HANDSHAPES: **1.** Right ONE hand **2.** Right and left s hands

POSITION: **1.** On the forehead **2.** In front of the chest

MOVEMENT: **1.** Touch the index fingertip of the right ONE hand to the forehead. (This resembles the sign for *think*.) **2.** Hold the right and left s hands in front of the chest, palms facing in, with the right hand on top of the left; then move both hands down simultaneously.

VISUALIZE: Holding tight to a thought or promise.

God

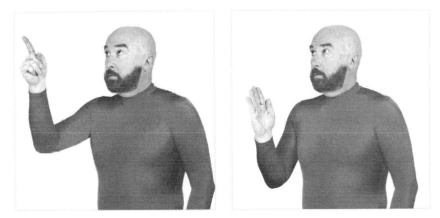

HANDSHAPES: Right G hand changing to FLAT hand

POSITION: Starts in front of the forehead

MOVEMENT: Point the right G hand up in front of the forehead with the palm facing left. Then bring the hand down and in toward the body while changing it to the FLAT handshape, ending with the fingertips pointing up.

VISUALIZE: First pointing upward to God; then moving downward to show that God is both above and with us.

One hand   G hand   Flat hand

heaven • celestial

HANDSHAPE: Right and left CURVED hands

POSITION: Starts in front of the chest

MOVEMENT: Hold up the right and left CURVED hands about a foot in front of the chest with the palms facing in. Then circle both hands upward and toward the body, crossing the right hand under the palm of the left in an upward direction at forehead level.

VISUALIZE: Rising through the clouds to heaven.

hell

HANDSHAPES: **1.** Right ONE hand **2.** Right and left OPEN hands

POSITION: In front of the chest

MOVEMENTS: **1.** Point the right ONE hand down in front of the chest. **2.** Hold up the right and left OPEN hands with the palms facing in; then move both hands alternately up and down while wiggling the fingers. (This is the sign for *fire*.)

VISUALIZE: The fires of hell below you.

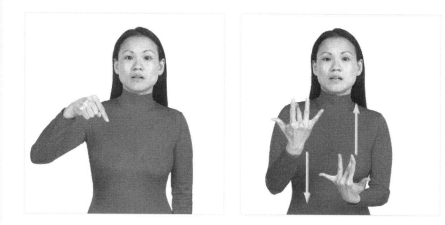

holy • divine • righteous • sanctified • hallowed

HANDSHAPES: Right H hand changing to FLAT hand and left FLAT hand

POSITION: In front of the chest

MOVEMENT: Point the right H hand to the left with the palm facing in. Then change it to the FLAT handshape and brush the palm across the upturned palm of the left FLAT hand from the heel of the hand to the fingertips. To sign *divine*, use the D handshape; for *righteous*, use the R handshape; and for *sanctified*, use the S handshape.

VISUALIZE: A place wiped clean of impurities.

Curved hand

One hand

Open hand

H hand

Jesus

HANDSHAPE: Right and left OPEN hands

POSITION: In front of the chest

MOVEMENT: Hold up the right and left OPEN hands with the palms facing each other. Touch the right middle fingertip to the left palm and then touch the left middle fingertip to the right palm.

VISUALIZE: Suggests the wounds Jesus endured at the crucifixion.

Jewish • Hebrew

HANDSHAPES: Right OPEN hand changing to AND hand

POSITION: In front of the chin

MOVEMENT: Hold up the right OPEN hand on the chin with the palm facing in. Then bring the hand straight down a short distance while changing it to the AND handshape.

VISUALIZE: The beard traditionally worn by Hasidic Jewish men.

Muslim • Islam

HANDSHAPE: Right and left M hands

POSITION: The sides of the head

MOVEMENT: Hold the right and left M hands, palms facing each other, at the sides of the forehead. Then move both hands straight down the sides of the face simultaneously.

VISUALIZE: The veil worn by Muslim women.

 Flat hand

And hand

 M hand

319

pray • prayer

HANDSHAPE: Right and left FLAT hands

POSITION: In front of the chest

MOVEMENT: Hold up the right and left FLAT hands with the palms touching; then draw the hands in toward the body while bowing the head slightly.

VISUALIZE: Folding your hands in the traditional prayer position.

preach • sermon

HANDSHAPE: Right F hand

POSITION: In front of the right shoulder

MOVEMENT: Hold up the right F hand in front of the right shoulder with the palm facing forward. Then move the hand forward and backward a few times.

VISUALIZE: A preacher showing you that everything is okay.

priest • minister • clergyman • pastor • chaplain

HANDSHAPE: Right Q hand

POSITION: On the front of the neck

MOVEMENT: Trace the fingertips of the right Q hand from the front of the neck to the right side of the neck.

VISUALIZE: The distinctive white collar worn by clergymen.

 Flat hand   F hand   Q hand

Protestant • kneel

HANDSHAPES: Right V hand with index and middle fingers curved, and left FLAT hand

POSITION: In front of the chest

MOVEMENT: Tap the knuckles of right V fingers on the upturned palm of the left FLAT hand a few times.

VISUALIZE: A person kneeling in prayer.

rabbi

HANDSHAPE: Right and left R hands

POSITION: On the chest

MOVEMENT: Touch the extended fingers of the right and left R hands to the chest with the palms facing in; then draw both hands down along the chest to the abdomen.

VISUALIZE: Tracing the shape of a rabbi's prayer shawl, called a tallis.

religion • religious

HANDSHAPE: Right R hand

POSITION: In front of the chest

MOVEMENT: Touch the extended fingertips of the right R hand to the chest over the heart; then move the hand forward while slightly twisting it, ending with the palm facing down.

VISUALIZE: Using the initial R to show that religious feelings originate in the heart.

V hand   R hand

sin • evil • wicked • crime

HANDSHAPE: Right and left ONE hands

POSITION: In front of the chest

MOVEMENT: Point the index fingers of the right and left ONE hands toward each other with the palms facing in; then move the hands in outward circles, ending in the starting position.

VISUALIZE: The opposite directions of the circles suggests the forces of good versus evil.

soul • spirit • ghost

HANDSHAPES: Left O hand and right F hand

POSITION: In front of the chest

MOVEMENT: Place the thumb and index finger of the right F hand in the opening of the left O hand; then pull the right fingers out.

VISUALIZE: The soul rising up out of the body.

temple • tabernacle

HANDSHAPES: Right T hand and left S hand

POSITION: In front of the chest

MOVEMENT: Point the left S hand to the right with the palm facing down; then tap the heel of the right T hand on the back of the left hand a few times.

VISUALIZE: Using the initial letter to show that a temple rests upon a rock-solid belief.

One hand   O hand   F hand   T hand

HOLIDAYS

Christmas

HANDSHAPE: Right C hand

POSITION: Starts in front of the left shoulder

MOVEMENT: Hold the right C hand in front of the left shoulder with the palm facing left. Then move the hand in a sideways arc until it is in front of the right shoulder.

VISUALIZE: The initial C suggests the word, while the motion suggests a bushy Christmas wreath.

Easter

HANDSHAPE: Right E hand

POSITION: In front of the right shoulder

MOVEMENT: Hold the right E hand in front of the right shoulder, with the palm facing forward. Then move the hand in a short arc to the right.

VISUALIZE: The initial E suggests the word, while the motion suggests a hopping Easter bunny.

Hanukkah

HANDSHAPE: Right and left OPEN hands with thumbs tucked under palms

POSITION: In front of the chest

MOVEMENT: Hold the right and left OPEN in front of the chest, a few inches apart, with the palms facing forward. Then move both hands simultaneously to the sides in small arcs.

VISUALIZE: The menorah that is lit during the festival of Hanukkah.

 S hand   C hand   E hand   Open hand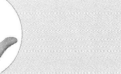

Passover

HANDSHAPES: Right P hand and left S hand

POSITION: In front of the chest

MOVEMENT: Hold the left S hand with the hand pointing right. Then tap the thumb of the right P hand against the left elbow.

VISUALIZE: The initial suggests the word, and the movement—which is similar to that of *cracker*—suggests matzoh, the hard unleavened bread eaten during the eight days of Passover.

Thanksgiving

HANDSHAPES: **1.** Right and left FLAT hands **2.** Right and left CURVED hands changing to FLAT hands

POSITIONS: **1.** Starting on the lips **2.** In front of the chest

MOVEMENT: **1.** With the fingertips pointing up and the palms facing in, touch the fingertips of the right and left FLAT hands to the lips. Then move both hands forward until the palms are facing up. (This is similar to the sign for *thanks*.) **2.** Hold the right and left CURVED hands in front of the chest with the palms facing down and the hands pointing forward. Then move both hands forward while changing them to FLAT hands and turning the palms to face upwards. (This is similar to the sign for *give*.)

VISUALIZE: Combining signs similar to those for *thanks* and *give*.

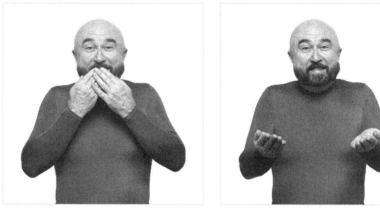

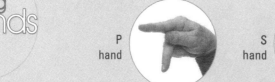

P hand

S hand

Flat hand

Curved hand

descriptions, thoughts & emotions

W ords can't describe how important this chapter will be to your signed conversations. When you want to look for a *new* job, applaud a *bright* idea, enjoy a *quiet* Sunday afternoon, order a *cold* drink, choose the *perfect* gift, or send a dozen *red* roses, you'll find that these descriptive signs will help you make yourself clear.

POSITIVE TRAITS

beautiful • pretty • attractive • handsome

HANDSHAPES: Right AND hand changing to OPEN hand and back to AND hand

POSITION: In front of the face

MOVEMENT: Point the fingers of the right AND hand toward the chin. The move the hand in a counterclockwise circle in front of the face, opening the hand and then closing it again into the AND handshape as it arrives back at the chin. To sign *handsome*, use the H hand. To sign *beautiful*, make a larger circle.

VISUALIZE: Showing off a beautiful face.

SEE HELPING HANDS ON NEXT PAGE.

325

brave • bold • courageous • fearless

HANDSHAPES: Right and left CLAWED hands changing to S hands

POSITION: Starts on the shoulders

MOVEMENT: Touch the fingertips of the right and left CLAWED hands to the shoulders; then bring both hands forward while changing them to the S handshape.

VISUALIZE: Showing that you are strong and ready to fight.

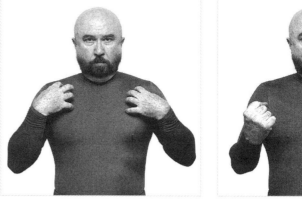

bright • light • luminous • clear • obvious

HANDSHAPES: Right and left AND hands changing to OPEN hands

POSITION: In front of the chest

MOVEMENT: Hold the right and left AND hands towards each other, with the palms facing down. Then open both hands simultaneously and move them up and out to the sides, ending with the palms facing forward.

VISUALIZE: Rays of bright sunlight bursting forth.

clean • nice • pure

HANDSHAPE: Right and left FLAT hands

POSITION: In front of the chest

MOVEMENT: Slide the palm of the right FLAT hand along the upturned palm of the left FLAT hand from the heel of the hand to the fingertips.

VISUALIZE: Washing your hands.

And hand
Open hand
Clawed hand
S hand

easy • simple

HANDSHAPE: Right and left CURVED hands

POSITION: In front of the chest

MOVEMENT: With the palms facing up, brush the little finger side of the right CURVED hand up against the fingertips of the left CURVED hand a few times.

VISUALIZE: This is easy to see when I bring it closer.

exciting • thrilling • thrill • arouse • stimulate

HANDSHAPE: Right and left OPEN hands

POSITION: On the chest

MOVEMENT: With the palms facing in, move the right and left OPEN hands forward in alternating circles, brushing the middle fingertips against the chest.

VISUALIZE: Things are really starting to roll!

favorite • prefer • rather

HANDSHAPE: Right OPEN hand

POSITION: On the chin

MOVEMENT: Tap the middle fingertip of the right OPEN hand on the chin a few times.

VISUALIZE: A cute dimple on the chin of a child.

Flat hand

Curved hand

fun • funny • amusing • humorous • comical

HANDSHAPE: Right U hand

POSITION: On the nose

MOVEMENT: Brush the fingertips of the right U hand down over the tip of the nose a few times.

VISUALIZE: The large red nose worn by a clown.

good • well

HANDSHAPE: Right and left FLAT hands

POSITION: Starts on the lips

MOVEMENT: Touch the fingertips of the right FLAT hand to the lips with the palm facing in. Then touch the back of the right hand to upturned palm of the left FLAT hand.

VISUALIZE: Sending someone a kiss to wish them well.

honest • truth • honesty

HANDSHAPES: Right H hand and left FLAT hand

POSITION: In front of the chest

MOVEMENT: Slide the middle fingertip of the right H hand along the upturned palm of the left OPEN hand from the heel of the hand to the fingertips.

VISUALIZE: Being straight and truthful with someone.

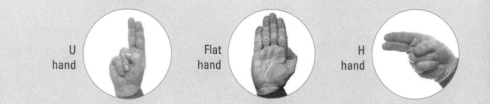

U hand   Flat hand   H hand

humble • meek • modest

HANDSHAPE: Right and left B hands

POSITION: Starts on the lips

MOVEMENT: Touch the index finger side of the right B hand to the lips with the palm facing left. Then bring the hand down and pass it under the downturned palm of the left B hand.

VISUALIZE: Holding oneself lower than others.

interesting • interested • interest

HANDSHAPE: Right and left OPEN hands

POSITION: In front of the chest

MOVEMENT: Place the thumbtips and index fingertips of the right and left OPEN hands on the chest with the right hand above the left. Bring the thumbtips and index fingertips together while simultaneously moving both hands forward.

VISUALIZE: Plucking an interest from within yourself.

kind • gracious • gentle

HANDSHAPE: Left and right FLAT hands

POSITION: In front of the chest

MOVEMENT: Place the right FLAT hand over the heart. Then circle the right hand around the left FLAT hand, which is held a short distance from the chest with the palm facing in.

VISUALIZE: Kind feelings emanating from the heart.

B hand

Open hand

patient • bear • endure

HANDSHAPE: Right A hand

POSITION: On the lips

MOVEMENT: Touch the thumbnail of the right A hand to the lips with the palm facing left; then draw the hand down.

VISUALIZE: Patiently waiting for a better time to speak.

perfect • accurate • ideal

HANDSHAPE: Right and left P hands

POSITION: In front of the chest

MOVEMENT: Touch the middle fingertips of the right and left P hands together with the right hand above the left.

VISUALIZE: An initialized sign that suggests things are coming together just right.

positive

HANDSHAPE: Right and left ONE hands

POSITION: In front of the chest

MOVEMENT: Cross the index fingers of the right and left ONE hands in front of the chest.

VISUALIZE: The plus sign.

A hand

P hand

One hand

right • correct • accurate • appropriate

HANDSHAPE: Right and left ONE hands

POSITION: In front of the chest

MOVEMENT: With the index fingers pointing forward, place the little finger side of the right ONE hand on the index finger side of the left ONE hand.

VISUALIZE: You hit the nail right on the head!

smart • intelligent • bright • brilliant • clever

HANDSHAPE: Right OPEN hand

POSITION: On the forehead

MOVEMENT: Touch the middle fingertip of the right OPEN hand to the center of the forehead. Then twist the hand from the wrist so the palm faces forward. To sign *brilliant*, use a more enthusiastic facial expression.

VISUALIZE: A clever thought taking flight.

special • unique • exceptional • except • extraordinary

HANDSHAPES: Left ONE hand and right F hand

POSITION: In front of the chest

MOVEMENT: Grasp the index fingertip of the left ONE hand with the thumb and index finger of the right F hand; then move both hands upward together.

VISUALIZE: There's no finger like this special finger.

Open hand

F hand

strong • strength • powerful • solid

HANDSHAPES: Right CURVED hand and left s hand

POSITION: Starts on the left shoulder

MOVEMENT: Touch the index finger side of the right CURVED hand to the left shoulder with the palm facing down; then move the right hand down in an arc and touch the little finger side to the inside of the left elbow.

VISUALIZE: Showing the strength of the biceps muscle.

true • truth • real • genuine • sincere • valid

HANDSHAPE: Right ONE hand

POSITION: Starts on the lips

MOVEMENT: Hold the index finger of the right ONE hand against the lips with the palm facing left; then move the hand forward in an arc.

VISUALIZE: I speak only the truth to you.

wonderful • fantastic • incredible • remarkable

HANDSHAPE: Right and left OPEN hands

POSITION: Near the sides of the head

MOVEMENT: Hold up the right and left OPEN hands near the sides of the head with the palms facing forward; then move both hands upward and forward a few times.

VISUALIZE: Expressing joy over a wonderful event. Hallelujah!

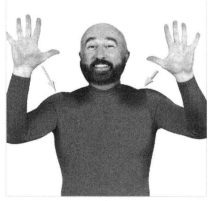

 Curved hand
 S hand
 One hand
 Open hand

NEGATIVE TRAITS

bad • disapprove • tacky • cheesy

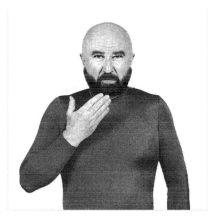 

HANDSHAPE: Right FLAT hand

POSITION: In front of the mouth

MOVEMENT: Hold up the right FLAT hand in front of the mouth with the palm facing in. Then move the hand down while twisting it from the wrist, ending with the palm facing down.

VISUALIZE: This tastes awful and I'm not going to eat it.

boring • dull • monotonous • tedious

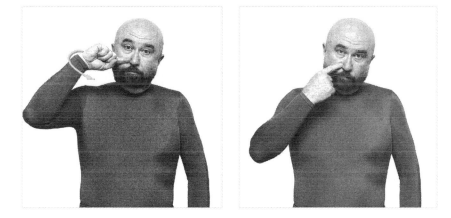

HANDSHAPE: Right ONE hand

POSITION: On the right side of the nose

MOVEMENT: Touch the index fingertip of the right ONE hand to the right side of the nose with the palm facing forward; then twist the hand so the palm faces in.

VISUALIZE: This conversation (or activity) stinks.

difficult • hard

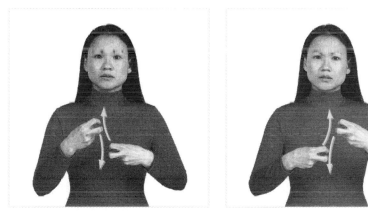

HANDSHAPE: Left and right V hands with index and middle fingers curved

POSITION: In front of the chest

MOVEMENT: Hold the left and right V hands forward with the palms facing in. Then strike the knuckles of both V hands as they are moved past each other in an up-and-down motion.

VISUALIZE: The striking motion suggests a rock hitting a hard place.

 Flat hand

 V hand

dirty • filthy • soiled • polluted • foul

HANDSHAPE: Right FLAT hand

POSITION: Under the chin

MOVEMENT: Point the right FLAT hand to the left under the chin with the palm facing down and wiggle the fingers.

VISUALIZE: Whew, you really need to take a shower.

false • fake • counterfeit • artificial • pseudo

HANDSHAPE: Right ONE hand

POSITION: Starts on the right corner of the mouth

MOVEMENT: Hold up the index finger of the right ONE hand against the right corner of the mouth with the palm facing left; then slide the hand across the lips to the left.

VISUALIZE: Talking out of the side of your mouth.

jealous

HANDSHAPE: Right J hand

POSITION: Starts on the right corner of the mouth

MOVEMENT: Touch the little fingertip of the right J hand to the right corner of the mouth and twist the hand forward.

VISUALIZE: Dr. Evil's hand gesture when he feels jealous of Austin Powers.

Flat hand   One hand   J hand

lazy

HANDSHAPE: Right L hand

POSITION: On the left shoulder

MOVEMENT: With the palm facing in, tap the right L hand against the left shoulder a few times.

VISUALIZE: Go see if that other guy will do it. I'm feeling pooped.

lousy • rotten

HANDSHAPE: Right THREE hand

POSITION: Starts on the nose

MOVEMENT: Place the thumbtip of the right THREE hand on the tip of the nose with the palm facing left; then move the hand sharply down and away from the nose.

VISUALIZE: Reacting to an awful smell, then blaming it on someone else.

mean • cruel • hurtful

HANDSHAPE: Right and left V hands with index and middle fingers curved

POSITION: In front of the chest

MOVEMENT: With the palms facing in, strike the middle finger of the right V hand down against the index finger of the left V hand.

VISUALIZE: Striking something with the intent to harm it.

L hand   Three hand   V hand

negative

HANDSHAPES: Left FLAT hand and right ONE hand

POSITION: In front of the chest

MOVEMENT: Hold up the left FLAT hand with the palm facing forward; then, with the palm facing down, tap the index finger side of the right ONE hand against the left palm.

VISUALIZE: The minus sign.

selfish · greedy

HANDSHAPE: Right and left V hands

POSITION: In front of the chest

MOVEMENT: Point the right and left V hands forward with the palms facing down. Then draw the hands in toward the chest while bending the V fingers.

VISUALIZE: Grabbing everything within reach.

strange · weird · odd

HANDSHAPE: Right W hand

POSITION: In front of the face

MOVEMENT: With the palm facing left, slide the right W hand in front of the face from right to left while bending and straightening the fingers. (Common usage sign.)

VISUALIZE: A creepy W crawling right in front of your face.

 Flat hand

One hand

 V hand

 W hand

stubborn • obstinate

HANDSHAPE: Right FLAT hand changing to A hand

POSITION: Near the right temple

MOVEMENT: Hold up the right FLAT hand near the right temple with the palm facing forward; then snap the hand into an A handshape a few times.

VISUALIZE: Represents a donkey's ear to suggest the phrase "stubborn as a mule."

stupid • dumb

HANDSHAPE: Right A hand

POSITION: On the forehead

MOVEMENT: With the palm facing in, tap the knuckles of the right A hand on the forehead a few times.

VISUALIZE: Showing that one has a thick skull.

thoughtless • careless • reckless

HANDSHAPE: Right V hand

POSITION: In front of the forehead

MOVEMENT: Hold up the right V hand in front of the forehead with the palm facing left; then move the hand from side to side a few times.

VISUALIZE: Brushing aside practical sense.

A hand

tired • exhausted • weary • fatigued

HANDSHAPE: Right and left CURVED hands

POSITION: On the chest

MOVEMENT: Touch the fingertips of the right and left CURVED hands to the chest. Then twist both hands downward from the wrists and touch the little finger sides of the hands to the chest, slumping the shoulders at the same time.

VISUALIZE: A tired body slumping forward.

ugly • homely

HANDSHAPES: Right and left ONE hands changing to X hands

POSITION: In front of the face

MOVEMENT: With the palms facing down, cross the index fingers of the right and left ONE hands in front of the face. Then pull the hands apart to the sides of the face while changing them to the X handshape.

VISUALIZE: Behind the "X" was one ugly dude.

vain • vanity

HANDSHAPE: Right and left V hands

POSITION: In front of the chest

MOVEMENT: Hold up the right and left V hands with the palms facing in; then bend and straighten the V fingers.

VISUALIZE: All eyes are on me.

Curved
hand

One
hand

X
hand

V
hand

weak • feeble • fatigue • frail

HANDSHAPES: Right OPEN hand and left FLAT hand

POSITION: In front of the chest

MOVEMENT: Touch the fingertips of the right OPEN hand to the upturned palm of the left FLAT hand; then bend and straighten the right fingers a few times.

VISUALIZE: A person's knees buckling from weakness.

wrong • error • fault • mistake

HANDSHAPE: Right Y hand

POSITION: Under the chin

MOVEMENT: Touch the knuckles of the right Y hand under the chin with the palm facing in. (This sign is often repeated a few times.)

VISUALIZE: Punching yourself on the chin for being so wrong.

Is There a Sign for Every English Word?

In my years of experience as a sign language teacher and interpreter, I have often been asked if there is a sign for every word in the English language. The answer is "no"—immediately qualified with an enormous "but." According to etymologist Stewart Flexner in his book *I Hear America Talking,* there are an estimated 600,000 words in the English language—the largest vocabulary of any language—but the average American understands only two to three percent of them and actually uses only half that amount.

"Just ten basic words account for over twenty-five percent of all speech and fifty simple words for almost sixty percent," says Flexner, "with between 1,500 and 2,000 words accounting for ninety-nine percent of everything we say." (Our written language is only slightly more varied than our spoken language with about seventy words making up fifty percent.) A skilled sign language interpreter can communicate any idea using the existing vocabulary of more than 6,000 signs that will be clearly understood by any deaf audience. And, of course, words for which there are no signs can easily be fingerspelled.

 Open hand

 Flat hand

 Y hand

GENERAL DESCRIPTIONS

accustomed • habit • custom • practice

HANDSHAPES: 1. Right ONE hand **2.** Right and left S hands

POSITIONS: 1. On the forehead **2.** In front of the chest

MOVEMENT: 1. Touch the index fingertip of the right ONE hand to the forehead. (This resembles the sign for *think*.) **2.** With the palms facing down, cross the right and left S hands at the wrists in front of the chest; then move both hands down a short distance simultaneously.

VISUALIZE: Thinking you are bound to the same thought or action again and again.

awake • wake up • arouse

HANDSHAPE: Right and left Q hands

POSITION: Near the outside corners of the eyes

MOVEMENT: Point the right and left Q hands forward near the outside corners of the eyes with the thumbs and index fingers pressed together. Then flick open the Q fingers.

VISUALIZE: Now you're sleeping; now you're awake.

busy

HANDSHAPES: Left and right B hands

POSITION: In front of the chest

MOVEMENT: Point the left B hand to the right with the palm facing down. Then, with the palm of the right B hand facing forward, move the wrist of the right hand alternately right and left, striking the left wrist with each movement.

VISUALIZE: Using the initial B to form a sign similar to *work*.

One hand   S hand   Q hand   B hand

cold • chilly • frigid • shiver

HANDSHAPE: Right and left s hands

POSITION: In front of the shoulders

MOVEMENT: Hold up the right and left s hands with the palms facing each other and shake them.

VISUALIZE: Shivering from the cold.

curious • inquisitive

HANDSHAPE: Right OPEN hand

POSITION: On the front of the neck

MOVEMENT: Make a pinching motion at the front of the neck between the thumb and index finger of the right OPEN hand; then wiggle the hand slightly from side to side.

VISUALIZE: The Adam's apple, which is a reminder of the apple in the Garden of Eden that was eaten as the result of curiosity.

dark • dim • dusk

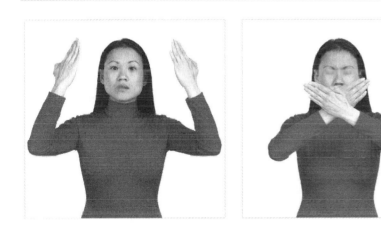

HANDSHAPE: Right and left FLAT hands

POSITION: In front of the face

MOVEMENT: Cross the right and left FLAT hands in front of the face with the palms facing in.

VISUALIZE: Closing the drapes to darken a room.

Open hand

Flat hand

different • diverse • varied • unlike

HANDSHAPE: Right and left ONE hands

POSITION: In front of the chest

MOVEMENT: With the palms facing forward, cross the index fingers of the right and left ONE hands in front of the chest; then move the hands apart and out past the shoulders.

VISUALIZE: Pulling two different things apart.

empty • bare • vacant • naked • bald

HANDSHAPE: Right OPEN hand with middle finger pointing down, and left FLAT hand

POSITION: In front of the chest

MOVEMENT: Hold the left FLAT hand with the palm facing down and the fingers pointing to the right. Then slide the middle finger of the right OPEN hand along the back of the left hand from the wrist to the fingertips.

VISUALIZE: Showing that the back of your hand is bare of hair.

fast • quick • rapid • suddenly • right away

HANDSHAPE: Right A hand with thumb under index finger

POSITION: In front of the chest

MOVEMENT: Hold the right A hand forward with the palm to the left; then flick the thumb out from under the index finger.

VISUALIZE: The quick action of shooting marbles.

One hand Open hand Flat hand A hand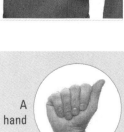

fat • plump • chubby • obese

HANDSHAPE: Right and left CLAWED hands

POSITION: Starts on the cheeks

MOVEMENT: Place the fingertips of the right and left CLAWED hands on the cheeks; then draw the hands away from the face.

VISUALIZE: Showing chubby cheeks.

full • fill

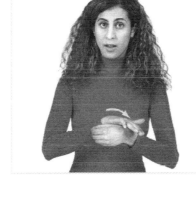

HANDSHAPES: Right FLAT hand and left S hand

POSITION: In front of the chest

MOVEMENT: Hold the left S hand forward, with the hand pointing to the right and the palm facing in. Then move the right FLAT hand to the left over the thumb side of the left hand.

VISUALIZE: Levelling off an overflowing measuring cup.

hot • heat

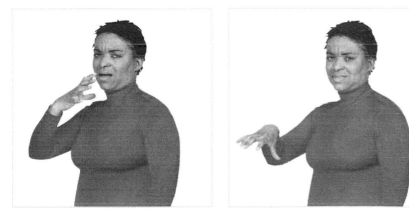

HANDSHAPE: Right CLAWED hand

POSITION: Starts on the corners of the mouth

MOVEMENT: Hold the thumbtip and fingertips of the right CLAWED hand on the corners of the mouth. Then twist the hand forward quickly, ending with the palm facing down.

VISUALIZE: Pulling hot food from your mouth and throwing it away.

Clawed hand

S hand

large • big • enormous • huge • great

HANDSHAPE: Right and left L hands with index fingers crooked

POSITION: Starts in front of the chest

MOVEMENT: Hold up the right and left L hands in front of the chest with the palms facing each other; then draw the hands apart and out past the shoulders.

VISUALIZE: Something starting small and growing larger.

new • modern

HANDSHAPES: Right CURVED hand and left FLAT hand

POSITION: In front of the chest

MOVEMENT: Brush the back of the right CURVED hand across the upturned palm of the left FLAT hand from the fingertips to the heel of the hand. Continue to move the right hand up and off the left hand.

VISUALIZE: The birth of a baby.

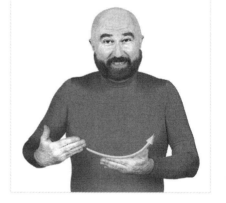 

noisy • loud

HANDSHAPES: Right and left ONE hands changing to OPEN hands

POSITIONS: Starts on the earlobes

MOVEMENT: Touch the index fingertips of the right and left ONE hands to the earlobes with the palms facing down. Then move both hands down to the shoulders while opening them and shake the hands up and down a few times.

VISUALIZE: Trying to block out noise.

 L hand   Curved hand   Flat hand   One hand

old • ancient • antique • age

HANDSHAPES: Right c hand changing to s hand

POSITION: Starts under the chin

MOVEMENT: Touch the thumb and index finger side of the right c hand under the chin; then draw the hand down while changing it to the s handshape.

VISUALIZE: The long beard of old Father Time.

opposite • contrast • contrary

HANDSHAPE: Right and left ONE hands

POSITION: In front of the chest

MOVEMENT: Hold the right and left ONE hands with the palms facing in and the index fingertips pointing toward each other. Then draw the hands to the sides and apart.

VISUALIZE: Two objects that were once together but are now separate and opposite.

poor • poverty

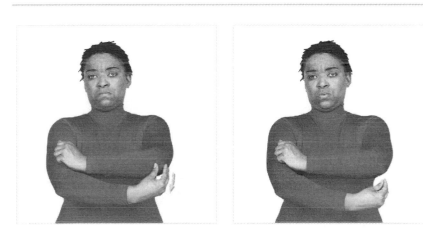

HANDSHAPES: Right CURVED hand changing to AND hand

POSITION: In front of the chest

MOVEMENT: Touch the fingertips of the right CURVED hand to the bent left elbow; then pull the right hand down while changing it to the AND handshape.

VISUALIZE: A panhandler pulling at your sleeve for some spare change.

Open hand

C hand

S hand

And hand

quiet • calm • peaceful • silent • serene

HANDSHAPES: **1.** Right ONE hand **2.** Right and left OPEN hands

POSITIONS: **1.** On the lips **2.** In front of the chest

MOVEMENT: **1.** Touch the index finger of the right ONE hand to the lips with the palm facing left. **2.** Point the right and left OPEN hands forward with the palms angled toward each other; then drop both hands down and out to the sides, ending with the palms facing down.

VISUALIZE: Urging someone to be quiet and settle down.

rich • wealthy

HANDSHAPES: Right AND hand changing to OPEN hand and left FLAT hand

POSITION: In front of the chest

MOVEMENT: Place the back of the right AND hand on the upturned palm of the left FLAT hand; then open the right hand while raising it up off the left hand and turning the palm side down.

VISUALIZE: Showing the money, and that you have a huge pile of it.

rough • coarse • scratch

HANDSHAPES: Right CLAWED hand and left FLAT hand

POSITION: In front of the chest

MOVEMENT: Slide the fingertips of the right CLAWED hand in a wavy motion along the upturned palm of the left FLAT hand from the heel of the hand to the fingertips.

VISUALIZE: Scratching an itchy palm.

One hand Open hand  And hand Flat hand

same • similar • alike

HANDSHAPE: Right and left ONE hands

POSITION: In front of the chest

MOVEMENT: Point the right and left ONE hands forward with the palms facing down, and bring the hands together.

VISUALIZE: Holding two things together to show that they're exactly alike.

secret • private • confidential • classified

HANDSHAPE: Right A hand

POSITION: On the lips

MOVEMENT: Tap the thumbnail of the right A hand against the lips a few times.

VISUALIZE: Sealing your lips to keep a secret from leaking out.

separate • apart

HANDSHAPE: Right and left BENT hands

POSITION: In front of the chest

MOVEMENT: Hold the right and left BENT hands in front of the chest, with the palms facing in and the knuckles touching. Then simultaneously pull the hands apart by moving them towards the sides.

VISUALIZE: The act of separating two things by pulling them apart.

Clawed hand

A hand

Bent hand

short • small

HANDSHAPE: Right BENT hand

POSITION: In front of the right shoulder

MOVEMENT: Hold up the right BENT hand in front of the right shoulder with the palm facing left. Then move the hand down a short distance, repeating a few times.

VISUALIZE: The typical gesture for someone of short stature.

shy • bashful • embarrass

HANDSHAPE: Right and left OPEN hands

POSITION: Starts below the face

MOVEMENT: Hold up the right and left OPEN hands below the face with the palms facing in and raise the hands alternately in front of the face.

VISUALIZE: Trying to hide the face behind the hands.

slow

HANDSHAPE: Right and left FLAT hands

POSITION: In front of the chest

MOVEMENT: With the palms facing down, slide the palm of the right FLAT hand slowly over the back of the left FLAT hand from the fingertips to the wrist.

VISUALIZE: Slowly stroking an obedient pet.

Bent
hand

Open
hand

Flat
hand

small • little • tiny

HANDSHAPE: Right and left FLAT hands

POSITION: In front of the chest

MOVEMENT: Point the right and left FLAT hands upwards a short distance apart with the palms facing each other; then bring the hands toward each other with several short movements.

VISUALIZE: The space between the hands getting smaller.

smooth

HANDSHAPE: Right and left FLAT hands

POSITION: In front of the chest

MOVEMENT: With the palms facing down, slide the fingertips of the right FLAT hand slowly over the back of the left FLAT hand from the wrist to the fingertips.

VISUALIZE: Showing off your silky smooth hands.

soft • tender • ripe

HANDSHAPES: Right and left CLAWED hands changing to AND hands

POSITION: In front of the chest

MOVEMENT: Point the right and left CLAWED hands forward with the palms facing up; then draw both hands downward while changing them to the AND handshape. Repeat.

VISUALIZE: Plucking soft, ripe fruit from a tree branch.

 Clawed hand

 And hand

349

straight

HANDSHAPE: Right B hand

POSITION: In front of the face

MOVEMENT: Hold the right B hand in front of the face with the palm facing left and the fingers pointing up. Then swing the hand forward and downward.

VISUALIZE: Straight from the horse's mouth.

tall

HANDSHAPES: Right ONE hand and left FLAT hand

POSITION: In front of the chest

MOVEMENT: With both hands pointing up, slide the index finger side of the right ONE hand up along the palm of the left FLAT hand from the heel of the hand to the fingertips.

VISUALIZE: Someone who's growing taller and taller.

thin • slim • lean • skinny

HANDSHAPE: Right G hand

POSITION: In front of the face

MOVEMENT: Point the thumbtip and index fingertip of the right G hand toward the cheeks; then draw the hand down a short distance.

VISUALIZE: The gaunt cheeks of a very thin person.

B hand   One hand   Flat hand   G hand

together • accompany

HANDSHAPE: Right and left A hands

POSITION: In front of the chest

MOVEMENT: Hold the right and left A hands together, in front of the chest, with the palms facing each other. Then, still holding the hands together, move them away from the body in a counterclockwise circle until they are once again in front of the chest.

VISUALIZE: Sticking together to find your way around.

COLORS

black

HANDSHAPE: Right ONE hand

POSITION: In front of the right eyebrow

MOVEMENT: Point the index finger of the right ONE hand toward the inside of the right eyebrow; then move the hand to the right.

VISUALIZE: Showing off your black eye.

blue

HANDSHAPE: Right B hand

POSITION: Starts in front of the right shoulder

MOVEMENT: Hold up the right B hand in front of the right shoulder with the palm facing left; then move the hand to the right while shaking it from the wrist.

VISUALIZE: Blue ocean waves.

A
hand

brown

HANDSHAPE: Right B hand

POSITION: On the right cheek

MOVEMENT: With the palm facing left, stroke the index finger side of the right B hand down along the right cheek a few times.

VISUALIZE: Pointing out a brown smear of dirt.

color

HANDSHAPE: Right OPEN hand

POSITION: In front of the mouth

MOVEMENT: Hold up the right OPEN hand in front of the mouth with the palm facing in, and wiggle the fingers.

VISUALIZE: A peacock's tail of many colors.

gray

HANDSHAPE: Right and left OPEN hands

POSITION: In front of the chest

MOVEMENT: With the palms facing in, pass the fingers of the right and left OPEN hands back and forth through the open spaces between the fingers.

VISUALIZE: Not all things are black and white; you have to read between the lines.

B hand

Open hand

green

HANDSHAPE: Right G hand

POSITION: Starts in front of the chest

MOVEMENT: Point the G hand to the left; then move the hand to the right while shaking it from the wrist.

VISUALIZE: Shaking the initial G suggest fields of green grass blowing in the wind.

orange

HANDSHAPES: Right C hand changing to S hand

POSITION: In front of the mouth

MOVEMENT: Hold the right C hand in front of the mouth with the fingers pointing to the left; then squeeze the hand closed into the S handshape a few times. (Used for both the color and the fruit.)

VISUALIZE: Squeezing the juice from an orange into your mouth.

red

HANDSHAPE: Right ONE hand

POSITION: On the lips

MOVEMENT: Brush the index fingertip of the right ONE hand down over the lips. This can also be signed with the R hand.

VISUALIZE: Showing the redness of your lips.

| G hand | C hand | S hand | One hand |

white

HANDSHAPES: Right OPEN hand changing to AND hand

POSITION: Starts on the chest

MOVEMENT: Touch the thumbtip and fingertips of the right OPEN hand to the chest; then bring the hand forward a few inches while changing it to the AND handshape.

VISUALIZE: The white breast feathers of a snowy owl.

yellow

HANDSHAPE: Right Y hand

POSITION: In front of the right shoulder

MOVEMENT: Hold the right Y hand in front of the right shoulder with the palm facing forward; then move the hand to the right while shaking it from the wrist.

VISUALIZE: The initial Y hand shaking in fear because it's yellow.

THOUGHTS & EMOTIONS

afraid · frightened · terrified · scared

HANDSHAPES: Right and left AND hands changing to OPEN hands

POSITION: Starts in front of the shoulders

MOVEMENT: Hold the right and left AND hands in front of the shoulders with the fingers pointing toward each other. Then move the hands across the chest in opposite directions while opening them.

VISUALIZE: Two mice just scurried by—Eeeek!

Open hand

And hand

Y hand

anger • rage • wrath

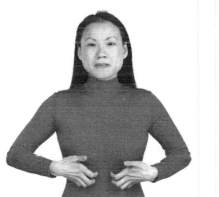 

HANDSHAPE: Right and left CLAWED hands

POSITION: Starts on the waist

MOVEMENT: Starting at the waist, draw the fingertips of the right and left CLAWED hands up over the chest toward the shoulders.

VISUALIZE: Anger boiling up inside the body.

ashamed • shame

HANDSHAPE: Right CURVED hand

POSITION: On the right cheek

MOVEMENT: Touch the back of the right CURVED hand to the right cheek with the fingers pointing down. Then twist the hand from the wrist so the fingers point back.

VISUALIZE: A blush of shame rising in your face.

brain • mind • intellect • sense

HANDSHAPE: Right ONE hand

POSITION: On the forehead

MOVEMENT: Tap the index fingertip of the right ONE hand on the center of the forehead a few times.

VISUALIZE: Showing the location of the brain.

Clawed hand   Curved hand   One hand

confidence • trust

HANDSHAPES: Right and left **C** hands changing to **S** hands

POSITION: Starts in front of the left shoulder

MOVEMENT: Hold the right and left **C** hands in front of the left shoulder, palms facing in, with the left hand above the right. Then pull both hands down while changing them to **S** hands.

VISUALIZE: Holding tight to something sturdy and trustworthy.

depressed • discouraged • despair

HANDSHAPE: Right and left **OPEN** hands

POSITION: On the chest

MOVEMENT: Touch the middle fingertips of the right and left **OPEN** hands to the chest; then draw both hands straight down.

VISUALIZE: Hopes sinking as depression sets in.

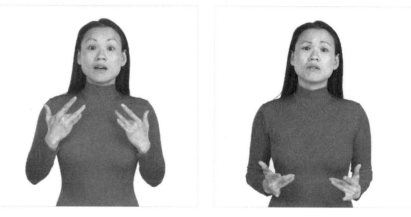

Dream a Little Dream

Over the years of teaching sign language classes, I thought I'd entertained every known question in the field until a student in one of my classes posed a most intriguing question: "When deaf people dream, do they use sign language to communicate with each other?" Her inquiry prompted me to conduct a limited, unscientific survey to find the answer. As I couldn't remember seeing anything in the literature or finding any study related to the matter, I queried a number of deaf people I have known in New York, Philadelphia, and Washington, D.C. To my surprise, the vast majority said they "just know" what the other person in the dream is thinking, even though their companion is not signing, as if their deafness made them extremely sensitive to the elusive phenomenon of what many believe to be mental telepathy.

C
hand

S
hand

Open
hand

dream • daydream

HANDSHAPE:	Right ONE hand
POSITION:	Starts on the forehead

MOVEMENT: Touch the index fingertip of the right ONE hand to the forehead. (This resembles the sign for *think*.) Then move the hand up and away from the forehead while bending and straightening the index finger.

VISUALIZE: Thoughts drifting away from your mind.

emotion

HANDSHAPE:	Right and left E hands
POSITION:	On the chest

MOVEMENT: Stroke the palm sides of the right and left E hands alternately over the chest a few times with an upward circular motion.

VISUALIZE: Emotions being stirred up.

experience

HANDSHAPES:	Right C hand changing to AND hand
POSITION:	Starts on the right temple

MOVEMENT: Touch the thumbtip and fingertips of the right C hand to the right temple; then pull the hand to the right while changing it to the AND handshape. Repeat the movement.

VISUALIZE: Pulling a past experience from your mind.

 One hand

 E hand

 And hand

feeling • sensation • motive

HANDSHAPE: Right OPEN hand

POSITION: On the chest

MOVEMENT: With the palm facing in, draw the middle fingertip of the right OPEN hand up over the chest.

VISUALIZE: Feelings welling up inside.

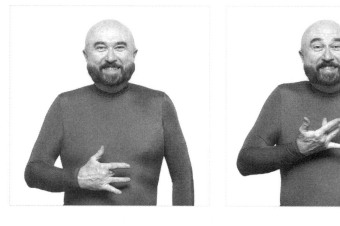

happy • joy • merry • glad • delight

HANDSHAPE: Right and left FLAT hands

POSITION: On the chest

MOVEMENT: With the palms facing in, point the right and left FLAT hands toward each other in front of the chest. Move the hands alternately in forward circles.

VISUALIZE: Being delighted with what's going on around you.

hate • hatred

HANDSHAPE: Right and left OPEN hands

POSITION: In front of the chest

MOVEMENT: Point the right and left OPEN hands forward with the palms facing down. Then flick the middle fingertips of each hand against the thumbtips.

VISUALIZE: Flicking away something that's detested.

Open hand

Flat hand

idea • concept • opinion

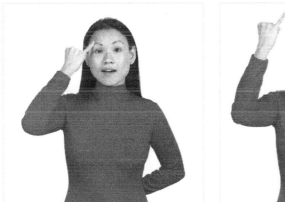

HANDSHAPE: Right I hand

POSITION: Starts on the forehead

MOVEMENT: Touch the fingertip of the right I hand to the forehead with the palm facing in. Then move the hand forward and upward. To sign *concept*, use the C hand; for *opinion*, use the O hand.

VISUALIZE: I have an I-dea.

imagination • fiction • fantasy • theory

HANDSHAPE: Right I hand

POSITION: Starts in front of the forehead

MOVEMENT: Hold up the right I hand in front of the forehead with the palm facing in. Then move the hand forward and upward in a few small circles. To sign *fiction* or *fantasy*, use the F hand; for *theory*, use the T hand. (This sign can also be made with both hands moving simultaneously.)

VISUALIZE: I have a "crazy" but wonderful I-dea.

lonely • lonesome

HANDSHAPE: Right ONE hand

POSITION: Starts in front of the mouth

MOVEMENT: Hold up the right ONE hand in front of the mouth with the palm facing left. Then draw the right hand down slightly. Repeat the movement.

VISUALIZE: One is definitely the loneliest number.

I hand

One hand

love • loving • lovingly

HANDSHAPE: Right and left A hands

POSITION: On the chest

MOVEMENT: With the palms facing in, cross the right and left A hands at the wrists and press them to the chest over the heart.

VISUALIZE: Hugging something dear to the heart.

sad • despondent • sorrowful • gloomy

HANDSHAPE: Right and left OPEN hands

POSITION: In front of the face

MOVEMENT: Hold up the right and left OPEN hands in front of the face with the palms facing in. Then draw the hands down and tilt the head forward slightly.

VISUALIZE: Tears of sorrow falling down your face.

sorry • regret • repent • apology • penitent

HANDSHAPE: Right S hand

POSITION: In front of the chest

MOVEMENT: With the palm facing in, rub the right S hand in a few circles on the chest over the heart.

VISUALIZE: Feeling a regretful ache in your heart.

A
hand

Open
hand

S
hand

index

Every word that appears in this typeface indicates that a sign is found on that page. For ease of use, every word that appears in blue type is a sign that means the opposite of the concept listed directly above it. For instance, BELOW (found on page 38) is the opposite of Above (found on page 37). This will allow you to quickly find the opposite of common signs.